D0961015

dr. caroline leaf

WHO SWITCHED OFF
YOUR
BRAIN?

solving the mystery of **he** said/**she** said

Dr. Leaf has an amazing way of explaining the complexity of the human brain and the uniqueness found between males and females. Reading *Who Switched Off Your Brain? Solving the Mystery of He Said/She Said* is like turning on a light bulb and seeing the truth. Although God created the male and female to be different, He also created them to compliment each other. As you read Dr. Leaf's book, anticipate the Aha! moment.

Dr. Marilyn Hickey
Marilyn Hickey Ministries Founder

Betty and I have been married almost 50 years, and we can honestly say that as wonderful as it is to fall in love, it is even more exciting to learn to live in love. Clear communication is key. This book can serve as a tool to help couples, families and friends learn how to better communicate and enjoy each other—even though you may be wired very differently. Dr. Leaf has been a guest on the *LIFE TODAY* show, and her insights have been a tremendous encouragement to our audience.

James Robison
LIFE Outreach International Founder

Dr. Leaf is a tremendous motivator and has amazing insights on how our brains function! You absolutely MUST buy *Who Switched Off Your Brain? Solving the Mystery of He Said/She Said* to help you in your daily living. This book will help you to not only understand and improve yourself, but it will dramatically help you to more effectively communicate with the opposite gender—buy the book today!

Reece and Sarah Bowling
Orchard Road Christian Center Senior Pastors

What a powerful resource! For years I have understood that you must equip and empower people in the kingdom of God in order for their gifts to shine through. Dr. Leaf's book, *Who Switched Off Your Brain? Solving the Mystery of He Said/She Said,* is a tool for just that. This book clearly and logically explains the differences in male/female communication and brain function in any type of relationship—whether it be with your family, friends or work colleagues. Nick and I are so excited to start implementing this knowledge into our everyday relationships. Now it's your turn—equip yourself today!

Nick and Christine Caine
Equip & Empower Ministries

As a worship leader, my goal in life is to communicate God's love to the hurting. While music is often universal, sometimes one-on-one communication is a little bit tricky, especially between men and women. I love Dr. Leaf's practical and often humorous look at communication and the differences between the male and female brain functions. Whether I'm on the road ministering in churches or even just interacting with my family and friends—this book is such a valuable tool to help understand where others are coming from while being able to communicate in a clear and effective way. Thank you, Dr. Leaf!

Kari Jobe
Gateway Church Worship Pastor, 2-time Dove
Award winner and EMI Recording Artist

For further information, please contact Dr. Caroline Leaf
by visiting www.drleaf.com or write to the office of Dr. Leaf.

2140 E Southlake Blvd. · Suite L #809 · Southlake, TX 76092

Distributed by Thomas Nelson Publishers,
Printed in the United States of America.

DEDICATION

This book is dedicated to:

Jesus Christ, my Lord and Savior . . .
the ultimate and perfect expert in relationships . . .
thank you for creating us in Your Image . . .
Male and Female.

Mac, my special, beloved husband, my best friend . . .
we have grown and are growing together emotionally,
spiritually and in every possible way . . .
you make me feel the depths of love . . .
you make me feel special.

Jessica, Dominique, Jeffrey and Alexandria,
my precious children . . .
you bring me joy and love unfathomable . . .
you each seal and perfect and complete . . .
our family relationship in your special and unique ways.

My mom, Ann and my late dad, Bennie . . .
for showing me that love truly conquers all.

TABLE OF CONTENTS

Introduction

"What are you talking about?"

"I didn't say that . . . now you're putting words in my mouth!"

"Are you even listening to what I'm saying?!?"

"Can we talk about this later?"

Does any of this sound familiar?

As a culture we've come up with all kinds of metaphors and explanations to describe the differences between men and women—one is from Mars, the other is from Venus; one doesn't listen, the other can't read maps; one doesn't have a clue and the other always wants more shoes.

You don't need a PhD to understand that men and women are not the same.

We don't think the same, we don't talk the same, we don't listen the same, we don't look the same, we don't play the same and we don't relax the same. And I'm just scratching the surface.

But as crazy as it may sound, over the last forty years, if you had a PhD, you had to insist that we are *the same!*

As a culture we've spent the last several decades arguing about gender roles, equality and environmental conditioning. Through the process it became unpopular and professionally dangerous to imply that men and women had fundamentally unique characteristics.

While some of this discussion was necessary, suggesting that two subjects are "different" is not the same as declaring one "superior" and one "inferior." Different isn't better or worse—it's just different.

And if we're honest, the truth is, we've always known we're different. Boys and girls aren't socially conditioned to gradually become different—they come out of the womb that way. It's hard-wired into them. From our earliest days these unique expressions emerge that only become stronger and clearer as we grow into maturity.

Through my experience as a scientist, a counselor, a therapist, a mother, a wife and a daughter, I've discovered many fascinating insights that have helped me navigate these differences. I'm not perfect—like you, I'm still growing and learning all the time to improve my understanding and my ability to put what I've learned into practice.

But science and Scripture both have so much to say to us on this critical subject that affects every one of us. Males and females are different from the moment of conception, and these differences show up in every system of the body and brain.

It's become safe and even acceptable, to once again talk about these gender differences, and it may be more urgent than ever as conflict over our inability to understand and work together continues to rise.

If love is the most powerful force in the world, then why does communication between men and women often feel more like war than love? Nowhere is this more painfully evident than in the relationship designed to be filled with love—the bond between a husband and a wife.

Divorce, separation and ugly breakups leave lasting wounds that take time to heal—wounds that go beyond the man and woman and impact the entire family as a whole. And because God created families as the foundation of society, it's not an overstatement to say the future of the world depends on our ability to love and understand one another.

But this isn't a marriage book. My hope is that through this process you'll grow in your compassion, understanding and practical insights that will help every relationship in your life. That's God's desire for all of us—He wants our relationships to be healthy and life-giving.

This book will take you on a journey to finally find some solutions by exploring the differences between the male and female brains and how they affect our ability to understand and love one another.

Throughout this book I often use the word "different." Different is not a value judgement; it does not mean better or worse. To acknowledge difference is not to expose weakness, but rather to celebrate uniqueness. Unique differences are the building blocks of philosophy and dreams, great art, poetry and science: they are the essence of our God-created humanity.

As we embark on this great journey, we will stop at various brain structures along the way, seeing how the gender differences in our genetic structure and physiological makeup influence the very essence of maleness and femaleness. But don't be scared by the science. You don't need a PhD to be able to understand and appreciate these principles. There are five images of the brain in the appendix I use for my lecture series. Reference these when I refer to different parts of the brain.

Our culture often pits science and faith against each other as if somehow the two are incompatible. I believe God created science like He created everything else—not to frustrate us or diminish His importance, but in order for us to love and appreciate Him more. Science gives us tangible, practical ways of measuring and understanding the greatness of God and the artistry and brilliance He demonstrated throughout creation. Because of this I believe there's great value in using the scientific method to leverage the valuable insights that He's provided for us in this field.

As both a scientist and a follower of Christ, my starting point is always the Bible, and Scripture tells us, God made humans in His image . . . over and above the animals. Therefore, humans are not a higher form of animal (Genesis 1:27-28); humans are unique (Psalm 139) and have a *divinely implanted sense of purpose* (Ecclesiastes 3:11 AMP).

Unlike any other part of creation, humans are gifted with what I call the "I-Factor" *the ability to think and choose for oneself.*[1] God made human beings uniquely . . . in all of creation there is nothing else like us.

We have been given what theologians and philosophers describe as "free will"—the ability to think, choose, believe and wrestle with our consciences. We're not robots—we're surprising, capricious, constantly changing beings who are capable of a seemingly endless spectrum of choices.

Choice isn't just a gift—it's a responsibility. Choices have consequences. What we choose to think about and how we act on those thoughts and feelings has a massive impact on the quality of our lives (Deuteronomy 30:19). Have you ever looked back on some bad choices you made and thought, "What in the world was I thinking?"

Sometimes it's because we're tired and unfocused. Other times it's because we're discouraged and distracted by difficult circumstances. In those moments, it's like our brains have been "switched off." In my first book, *Who Switched Off My Brain? Controlling toxic thoughts and emotions*, I discussed in detail the good news from neuroscience and Scripture that clearly showed we don't have to lose hope. Our minds can be renewed. If we have toxic, unhealthy thoughts and emotions, they can be controlled and replaced with healthy, life-giving mindsets that allow us to enjoy our lives to the fullest.

But life is all about relationships. Even when our brains are "switched on," we're still surrounded by people whose attitudes and actions are puzzling. Their behaviors seem crazy. If you're a parent, I'm sure you've had moments when you looked at your child and thought, "What were YOU thinking?"

It's one thing when you realize that your own brain has been "switched off"—but when it's someone else, it's so much more frustrating. If you just come right out and say, "Who switched off your brain?" it could start an argument that leads to a fight. But if you do nothing, your relationships will never get better.

Healthy relationships are built on communication, forgiveness, understanding, mutual respect and love.

I've written this book out of my great desire to help men and women understand, appreciate and love one another—whether they're husband and wife, brothers and sisters, fathers and daughters, mothers and sons, co-workers, neighbors and any other combination between.

There are fabulous implications in the mysterious complementary differences of the male and female brains. Anytime we discuss these differences, we have to realize that while there are scientific findings that are statistically true there are also many anecdotal generalizations that feel like they're true. For example, "men speak in headlines and women speak in details," or "men don't share their feelings and women won't stop talking." Depending on your life experience this may seem more or less true—but it's certainly not true of ALL men and women.

However, I try to avoid oversimplification as much as I can because, while these notions may have an element of truth to them, they miss something essential that applies to everyone.

Basic human qualities that God has placed within us should not be labeled as "male" or "female." Love, empathy, compassion, development, discipline, passion, systematic analysis, strategy, sympathy, kindness, communication, etc.—the list goes on—are basic human qualities that can and should be shared by both men AND women. How this takes shape and the way it's expressed in the lives of individuals is always filtered through each person's unique "I-Factor."

For example, consider two prominent characters in the Bible, one male and one female: King David and Rahab. Both were emotional, yet at times both were analytical and brilliant strategists. But how they applied these skills/character traits was very different.

We would be oversimplifying their reality to simply say that David was an emotionless, analytical military leader and Rahab was an emotional, undisciplined, free-thinking woman. David's psalms are characterized by some of the most incredibly intense emotions in the entire Bible. Rahab's brilliant, unconventional leadership decision didn't just save her own life, but also her family and the future plans of Israel. Her contribution was so extraordinary that God ensured that she would be included in the physical ancestry of the Messiah.

We don't build principles and laws on isolated, anecdotal facts, but we can discover patterns that emerge through many different situations. For example, females *on average* tend to favor the use of unique landmarks to help them with directions; men *on average* tend to favor compass directions and geometry. This isn't a matter of personality preference—it comes from the hard-wiring of the brain.

These types of breakthroughs in neuroscience provide a wonderful way for us to understand the differences in how men and women process, view and interact with the world.

And the overwhelming result of this research confirms what we've already said: men and women are different. Not superior and inferior, but unique, and these differences can be observed all the way down to the hard-wiring in our brains.

But the good news is, different doesn't have to mean misunderstood. We don't have to live life frustrated, upset and discouraged by strained relationships. Just as you can renew your mind and create healthy thought patterns, you can grow and develop insight and understanding that will lead to peace, respect and love in all of your relationships.

God's plan for our relationships is so much higher than the goals we've given ourselves. We tend to define success by the absence of conflict or arguments—a peaceful co-existence between the two parties. But God's intention is much higher. He's hard-wired different perspectives, gifts and characteristics into men and women so that our partnerships will be exponentially greater than anything we could do on our own.

In other words, we need each other. We complement each other in every setting—the office, the community, the classroom, the courtroom, the church, the town hall, the park and the home.

Men and women were designed to benefit from each other—and not just in marriage. You can't be the real "you" all by yourself. That's why relationships define every aspect of our lives, and that's why it's critical we do everything we can to make them as healthy as we possibly can.

It can be done. You don't have to be a neuroscientist to understand it all. That's what I'm here for—to help you on this journey to wonderful, healthy relationships with those who frustrate, confuse and baffle you. Brothers and sisters, co-workers, neighbors, friends, parents and children, and husbands and wives—we can improve our relationships if we'll be intentional.

That's my prayer for you as we take this journey together.

CHAPTER 1

Solving the Mystery of He Said/She Said

I've often thought that trying to understand what men are up to is a bit of a mystery. I'm certain that men feel the same way about women.

In so many ways, much of our interaction gets lost in translation and we're left to piece together what just happened. In those moments, misunderstandings, unmet expectations and unresolved issues come together to create toxic thoughts which over time poison relationships. With only a series of clues and undesirable outcomes we're left to try to figure out what actually happened.

Whether you're a man or a woman, you'll be able to relate to this brief tale, but how you relate to it will depend upon which group you belong to.

If you're a woman you can relate to this situation.

"She said . . ."
THE STORY FROM HER PERSPECTIVE

It's the end of a particularly long day and you and your husband are in the kitchen cooking dinner together. While he prepares some food, you move behind him—cleaning up the mess and trying to talk about your day. He's not listening, however, and he soon moves to pick up his phone that's just buzzed on the table. He's not trying to hurt you—he's still preoccupied with mentally finishing up his to-do list of projects from work.

Frustrated, you give up and continue cooking while helping two of your children with their homework. Somehow, you also manage to listen to your other two teenagers as they talk about their days at the same time. Your older son leaves after a few words while your older daughter passionately asks you for hairstyle advice for this Friday's party. At your feet, the dog barks for supper and attention and your cell phone rings: it's your mom wanting to chat.

You can cope with all of this, no problem, but your emotions are really starting to boil over more than the potatoes on the stove. You need to sort out the day's events, and your man is the only one you want to talk to because you instinctively know he will be able to sort out the mess of ideas and events and emotions racing through your mind.

But you bite your tongue at this point as you realize that your husband needs to retreat into his own space to sort out the day's events and process them in his mind. If you give him his space now, then he'll be able to engage with you later. You need to satisfy the empathetic part of who you are and you can do this by helping your family—making dinner, helping the children, bonding and sharing.

You will be able to better explain the racing thoughts and emotions from this crazy day with your husband a little later in the evening when your busy mind has calmed down just a little. You trust he will be able to helpfully process and listen to what you have to say once he has processed his own thoughts.

By waiting until he is ready to listen, you will prevent him from resorting to an aggressive retort. If you speak when you're not yet ready to express yourself, you will only confuse your husband and yourself, leading to an unnecessary and undesired argument.

If you're a man you may process through this situation like this.

"He said . . ."
THE STORY FROM HIS PERSPECTIVE

Work was crazy today as you tried to manage several impending deadlines that all needed to be taken care of on a project you'd been working on for weeks. There were still a few loose ends that you needed to tie up but you're home now, and when you're home, it's important for you to pitch in.

You don't wait for your wife to ask; you just jump right in, pick up the potato peeler, roll up your sleeves and get to work. She smiles, gives you a kiss on the cheek and starts to fill you in on all the events of her busy day. Out of the corner of your eye you see your phone light up—a text message or an email just came in. Maybe the last piece of the puzzle fell into place at work or maybe there's still something you need to do.

Meanwhile your wife is fully engaged in the story of the latest happenings in her office that have made her both excited and frustrated, hopeful yet discouraged. You want to be there for her, you really do, but it's hard for you to concentrate while you're wondering what's happening with the project at work.

You recognize that two of your four children are at the table doing their homework, so you say hello and ask them about their day on your way over to check your phone. Just as you go to pick up your phone the dog barks and the phone rings—you're trying to concentrate on this critical update from work and it's impossible with all the commotion that's taking place in the kitchen.

Because you want to take care of things quickly and you know how much your wife is counting on you, you step into the family room and check your phone. You were right—they needed your approval on one more document. You open it, dive right in, fully confident you can knock it out in a minute or two.

By the time you make it back to the kitchen you realize it's been ten minutes, the potatoes are boiling over and spilling onto the stove, the kids gave up on their homework and your wife is mad. Things just got worse—you're either headed for a fight or the doghouse.

If you don't choose your words and your actions carefully in the next few moments, you could spend the night on the couch.

Most of us can relate to this scene—and many of us have lived through it many times. The facts of the story are exactly the same in both versions—but how we process them, and how we emotionally react to what takes place largely depends on our perspectives.

We're different. We don't process things the same. If we view and interpret our spouse's actions on the basis of our own motivations and intentions, then we'll misunderstand, end up hurt and likely lash out.

But if we take a moment and reflect that what she said wasn't what you heard and what he thought wasn't what you assumed, then grace, forgiveness and love can prevail.

You can be on the same page even when it feels like you're reading from a different book. With a few clues, a change in perspective and a willingness to grow and learn, things can begin to make sense. These situations aren't unsolvable—they're like a well-told mystery that over time produces clues that explain actions and intent that fills in our gaps.

We can solve the mystery of he said/she said. It's not too difficult for us. But it's going to take effort, humility and grace.

By following scientific brain advice, you can make the right choices that will allow you to avoid the argument (which could make life miserable for the next few days), and instead increase healthy communication and intimacy with each other. Instead of fighting and attacking each other, you can grow in your love and respect. And in the process, you'll also give your children a great example of excellent relational skills.

Whether you're a man or a woman I believe you will find that applying simple brain science to your marriage is absolutely worth it. God has wired you for love, not conflict. By listening to what brain science has to say and applying God's Word, you can reach soaring heights as you learn to understand your spouse, colleague, son, daughter or friend and yourself.

CHAPTER 2

Embrace the Mystery

Science is filled with all kinds of wonderful, complex, descriptive terms that can be confusing. You don't have to understand and remember all of the terminology in order to benefit from the research and the studies that these words represent. However, there are some words and phrases that I want you to grasp so that you can be equipped to receive as many insights as possible.

"Neuroscience" is the term used to describe the field of study devoted to understanding the nervous system and its relationship to human behavior.[1] The nervous system contains the brain and spinal cord, and at its most basic level it functions as the communication hub for your entire body. So when I'm talking about the field of neuroscience and neuroscientists, I'm describing trained professionals who've made studying and teaching the mysteries of the brain and the nervous system their lives' work.

In recent years, neuroscientists have been making great strides in discovering scientifically-proven anatomical and functional differences between the brains of males and females.[2] No single reason accounts for all of the differences, but slowly, one step at a time, scientists are unraveling this great mystery.

BRAINY TIP

Scientists are slowly unraveling the mystery of the differences between the male and female brain, one step at a time. Therefore you need to realize this process isn't a quick fix; it's a lifelong commitment to grow and learn.

One of the big questions neuroscientists are asking is, "Are there more differences between male and female brains than similarities?" At this point in the research the results are not conclusive—in other words, we're not sure yet. Surprisingly, some researchers have actually found more differences between members of the same sex than between members of opposite genders!

Discovering what this research means and how it all fits together is a very complex puzzle, with all kinds of moving parts and clues—there are no simple, easy answers. I like to think of scientists as detectives—relentlessly following a series of clues and evidence until the moment of discovery.

Mysteries can be thrilling, exciting and wonderfully adventurous. But when you're stuck in the middle of them and nothing makes sense, they can be so discouraging. In that moment you have a choice—give up or embrace the mystery and follow it wherever it leads.

And much like science, you can't manage relationships strictly with rules—they're living and breathing; they require effort and a commitment to embrace the mystery. Understanding and improving our relationships are some of the most important parts of life.

BRAINY TIP

And much like science, you can't manage relationships strictly with rules—they're living and breathing; they require effort and a commitment to embrace the mystery.

Don't let the often puzzling and confusing tendencies of the other gender frustrate you. It's a mystery—but don't see it as a helplessly complicated, unsolvable puzzle. Instead treat it as an invitation to an exciting adventure—a journey of discovery that will lead you to a new place and change you along the way.

We serve a magnificent Creator who loves us so much that He makes each of us unique. And while that makes understanding all of us nearly impossible, it proves that regardless of gender, every individual is a masterpiece crafted by the Maker's hands like the Bible says in Ephesians 2:10.

Yet our uniqueness shouldn't keep us from searching for answers. I'm convinced that there are many valuable and fascinating insights that we can gain through discovering the distinct differences in the brains between men and women and their impact on our daily lives.

As science progresses, we need to progress with it, searching constantly for answers and never assuming we know it all. Because of this I will refer to scientific discoveries (for example, certain parts of the brain are bigger in females than males) with the understanding that these discoveries are fluid in nature and could change as brain science advances.

BRAINY TIP

As science progresses, we need to progress with it, searching constantly for answers and never assuming we know it all.

The brilliant quality and accuracy of imaging techniques currently available to study the brain are outstanding, and as a scientist, the subsequent findings that they've provided are incredibly exciting. However, we need to remember that even our most advanced techniques are rather limited—because the average brain contains millions of nerve cells (thought networks) that can fire up to a hundred impulses a second, our most precise functional imaging technology can only capture large-scale activity.[3]

This is a bit like standing at the top of a twenty–story building and trying to discern the conversation of the people walking on the sidewalk below!

All scientific process involves some personal interpretation—we need help to make sense of the data and our findings. If you've ever sat in class frustrated or confused as you struggled to grasp the material, you know what I mean. In this situation, most people throw their hands in the air and wonder when they'll ever need to know this information in "real life."

That's where I come in. I've developed set, practical, easy-to-apply principles that combine the research of science and the truth of Scripture. I call them "Brainy Tips," and this book is filled with them. I have no doubt that I will have to revise some of my interpretations over time as science progresses, but I am confident that we can apply and run with certain generalizations that we know to be true. Your job is to simply read what I have to say and use your own judgment as you apply it to your life.

Originally brain research was done on dead bodies (cadavers) or by observing individuals with brain damage. Now due to current non-invasive brain technology, some of which include positron emission tomography (PET) and functional magnetic resonance imaging scans (fMRI) and diffusion tensor imaging (DTI), the brain can be observed solving problems, speaking, remembering and thinking in real time. DTI specifically provides a sharper view of the complex network of nerve fibers—the literal wiring of the brain as we think.[4]

This gives us great new insight and new knowledge providing a way of not only helping scientists to discover different ways to explore these brain differences in terms of the treatment of diseases, but also another efficient and exciting way of understanding each other.

Researchers have been able to identify and document extremely insightful structural, chemical, genetic, hormonal and functional brain differences between the male and female brains that can successfully guide us in the direction of deeper understanding. Some of the latest research derived from these techniques indicates that male-female brain differences are genetically hard-wired in place right from the beginning—at conception, even before the influence of hormones.[5]

This means there appears to be an order influencing the male-female brain differences: first genetic, then hormonal, then structural, then functional. In other words, the differences emerge at each step of the developmental process and continue on through life.

Those of us who are familiar with Scripture aren't surprised. *So God created man in His own image, in the image and likeness of God He created him; male and female He created them* (Genesis 1:27 AMP) and *I knew you before I formed you in your mother's womb* (Jeremiah 1:5 NLT).

As you can see, gender differences are not entirely rooted in society or family history. From that understanding, we can increase in acceptance, in patience and in respect for each other.

On the surface, the male and the female brains look the same, but internally, there are differences wonderfully complex and widespread. We see differences in spatial skills favoring men; we see differences in verbal skills favoring women; we see differences in hormones; differences in how males and females think about empathy, morality, stress, aggression, memory, resting and we even see equal but different processes for formulating and communicating ideas between men and women.

Neuroscience is just beginning to understand the great mystery of gender differences in the brain. We can say, though, that these differences are not just compatible; they're *complementary*. To be compatible means that you fit together, but to be complementary means that each unique person contributes to and improves the other.

And I want to stress that they are *complementary*. They don't have to be in constant competition; they don't have to create unhealthy conflict. Instead, when these differences take advantage of each other's inherent strengths, the result becomes far greater than what either could accomplish on his/her own.

We need each other.

The male and female brains are both compatible and complementary. They don't have to lead to toxic arguments and constant fighting. If we understand the differences, it can lead to better relationships between husbands and wives, mothers and sons, fathers and daughters.

A true harmony between the two is absolutely possible.

CHAPTER 3

The "I-Factor"

When it comes to the differences between males and females there are so many stereotypes. Some of them are funny and some might be true, but most of them are just labels, which don't help us understand or appreciate anyone.

You are so much more than just a label. And so is everyone else in your life—unique, wonderful individuals created by God to be loved and appreciated.

BRAINY TIP

Stereotypes and labels don't help us understand

or appreciate anyone.

Labels limit people. You can probably list quite a few familiar labels and stereotypes used to simplify the differences between men and women. Do these sound familiar?

- Women are emotional, men don't have feelings.
- Women won't stop talking, men don't listen.
- Women love shopping, men hate it.
- Women cover every last detail, men speak in headlines.

I could name many more, and they would all have the same thing in common: partial truths that end up limiting people and ignoring the wonderful individuality that God has placed in each of us.

Your "I-Factor" is your gift—not your talents or skills—but the unique and special way that you think. It's more than just your personality—it's the unique design God hard-wired into you that forms and influences every thought you think, every choice you make, every word you speak and every action you make.

BRAINY TIP

Your "I-Factor" is your gift, the unique way you think. Therefore you need to remember that it's going to take others time to understand the best way to relate to you.

I know many men who talk more than women—and I'm sure you do too! I know women who hate to shop and men who are great at remembering details. It would be unfair to these people to judge them based on general stereotypes. So even as we study fundamental differences between men and women, we must be careful not to limit people by pre-conceived labels and generalizations.

You see, it's far more accurate to say that we *all* experience emotion . . . men and women just experience it differently. We *all* talk and communicate, but in different ways. Even within the same gender, people react, think and respond in different ways.

I cannot stress how interconnected the human brain is. No thought or trait stands on its own. Every thought and feeling is the result of extensive crosstalk or interneuron "chat" spread across the network of connectivity in the brain—and no two people, male or female, have the same network.

BRAINY TIP

There isn't one kind of male and one kind of female.

So you see, there isn't one kind of male and one kind of female. If you carefully observe the people in your life, you'll experience this profound and obvious truth on a daily basis. An individual's "I-Factor" will always set him/her apart more than his/her maleness or femaleness—some men really are better at expressing their feelings than their wives and some women really can fix a leaking pipe. Generalizations or labels may end up being true if you're examining a huge group of men and women—but that information won't help you to relate to the man or the woman sitting next to you right now.

BRAINY TIP

No one will perfectly fit into a label, and everyone is unique.

So the first step in understanding the differences between maleness and femaleness is to understand you: the "I-Factor," the unique gift that God's hard-wired into you.[1] This gift has a specific structure and once you have found the structure, you will understand your "I-Factor" more clearly. When you understand how God has designed you and who you are in Christ, you'll be empowered to love yourself and to extend grace, forgiveness and love to others.

Without God's wisdom and guidance, we're all left to love and understand the people in our lives from the reservoir of our own kindness and compassion. And for most of us, that "well" will never be deep enough. We can't love others the way God's called us to through our own strength and willpower.

Helping people discover the unique structure of their gifts is a big part of mine. It fills me with passion and joy. It motivates me to get up in the morning and to apply myself diligently to research the science of thought—a task I've given many years to.

Drawing on my experience through years of scientific research, clinical experience working with clients and leading practical leadership seminars and training, I developed an extensive questionnaire designed to teach you about your gift.

You can find the gift profile along with a description of the science behind the process and practical tips to apply the knowledge of your gift in your daily life in my book *The Gift in You: Discover new life through gifts hidden in your mind.*

Understanding the characteristics and structure of your "1-Factor" is an important place to start. The better you grasp the nuances and intricacies of your own "1-Factor," the more generous, patient and understanding you will be towards others, especially those of the opposite sex.

However, you don't need that book to keep reading this one.

My goal is to show you how understanding the differences in the male and female brains can make communication and relationships easier—a process which is impacted greatly by the role of the "1-Factor." If you've already read that book and taken the gift-profile, I encourage you to refer to your test as a refresher so that you can maximize the impact of what you're going to discover.

Discovering the specifics of your own "1-Factor" will be a great developmental blessing to you and I encourage you to pursue it, but don't stop reading this book now. You don't need those specifics to learn how to improve the quality of your relationships. We all have to start somewhere. Whether you've done personality tests, leadership profiles or gift assessments before or this is the first time that you've ever heard of such a thing, I believe this process is going to be incredibly valuable for you.

After all, life is all about relationships. This isn't just a marriage book designed to help couples. While there's no doubt that the wisdom here will help any couple willing to apply it, the potential is so much greater. Every one of us has a wide variety of relationships and all of these relationships require growth in order to be healthy. We're brothers, sisters, mothers, daughters, fathers, sons, co-workers, friends, neighbors, business partners, coaches and athletes, and on and on and on.

As we invest, grow, strengthen and develop those relationships the quality of our lives are transformed.

CHAPTER 4

More Than Your Genes

Every single person is born already wired as either a male or a female. This is both a Godly truth and a scientific fact:

So God created man in His own image, in the image and likeness of God He created him; male and female He created them (Genesis 1:27 AMP).

Scientifically, God designed us as either male or female in our *genes*—He is our genetic programmer.

BRAINY TIP

God is our genetic programmer.

Genes are the foundational instructions that determine how a human being is created. Imagine that each gene has different combinations of letters. 3.2 billion of these letters (base pairs) join together to form what's known as "the human genome"—this magnificent document contains all the instructions necessary to make a living thing, controlling its development from a single cell to a complex adult body.[1]

The human genome consists of somewhere between 30,000 to 70,000 genes, carried on the double set of 46 chromosomes (23 x 2—one chromosome from the mother and one from the father) found in nearly every kind of body cell.[2]

A gene is a piece of DNA needed to construct one protein. It consists of all the sections of DNA that have the genetic code (the combination of letters) for the amino acids that make up that particular protein.

Proteins are made up of amino acids. Some proteins are the body's major structural molecules, others make enzymes, which control chemical reactions in the body, and so on.[3]

The DNA is found inside the nucleus of the cell coiled into 46 X-shaped chromosomes. Only 3 percent of the DNA contains the genetic codes, the other 97 percent has a regulatory function, but the full understanding of this 97 percent is not yet understood.

The 46 chromosomes are labeled in pairs from 1-22 and the 23rd pair of chromosomes is the sex chromosomes XX and XY. So, the only difference between the genders is the sex chromosomes, which are labeled as XX and XY. Out of the approximately 30,000 or more genes that make up the human genome, the X and Y-chromosomes only account for two percent of the body's genes. So, 98 percent of genes are the same in the male and the female.[4]

BRAINY TIP

Ninety-eight percent of genes are the same in the male and the female.

This two percent difference influences everything: the physical structure of the brain, the way we experience emotions and feelings and the manner with which we behave, communicate and think. These massive differences between men and women can be traced all the way back to a slight 2 percent genetic difference.[5]

I want to give you a little more insight into how this process works—it starts with one pair of sex chromosomes (one from each parent) being replicated into each cell of our body: the male-making Y-chromosome carrying 300 genes; the female X-chromosome carrying 1,000 to 1,500 genes.[6]

And the process is not random or arbitrary—it follows a clearly defined pattern of instructions set in motion by our Creator God. A specific gene instructs early gonadal tissue to become testes, which in turn secretes the hormone, testosterone. Testosterone masculinizes, influencing the size of specific structures and the wiring of nerve cells in the brain. The X-chromosome instructs fetal tissue to become ovaries, which secrete estrogen feminizing the brain structures and wiring.[7]

BRAINY TIP

The sex genes continue to play ongoing roles in developing the unique properties of the brain and its behavior on the basis of its male or female predisposition.

While Mom and Dad wait to find out whether their new bundle of joy will be a boy or a girl to start picking out the baby's wardrobe and designing the nursery, at the genetic level, clear distinctions are also taking place in the development process depending upon whether the child is male or female. These distinctions are quantifiable—genes have been found to actually behave differently in the same organs of males and females.[8]

BRAINY TIP

Genes have been found to actually behave differently in the same organs of males and females.

Researchers saw striking and measurable differences in more than half of the genes' expression patterns between males and females.

So essentially males and females share the same genetic code, but it is gender that regulates how quickly the body can convert DNA to proteins which is gene expression.[9]

Research has even shown that female brain tissue is intrinsically different from male brain tissue. Just by analyzing the expression of two different genes in brain tissue, researchers can correctly identify whether the brain is male or female.[10]

The Y-chromosome in men is directly responsible for differences in the brain. And I stress the word: *different,* not one better than the other.

BRAINY TIP

Just by analyzing the expression of two different genes in brain tissue, researchers can correctly identify whether the brain is male or female.

Important traits and gender differences are determined by our genes. For years, this fact has been used to support a dangerous notion: that our genes control us—these microscopic, fundamental instructions determine who we are at a physical and even emotional level.[11]

If this were true, then we'd all be the victims of a biological roll of the dice.

Fortunately, science is proving otherwise. The truth is that genes do not *cause* behavior; yes, they might give us certain tendencies to behave one way or another, but they do not have the final say. In many ways, we have the opportunity to choose who we're going to be. It's not completely out of our control.[12]

In fact, scientific research is now suggesting that many genes can "switch" on or off depending on our thinking, our behavior and our environment.[13]

BRAINY TIP

Genes do not cause behavior; they give us certain tendencies to behave in certain ways, but your genes do not have the final say . . . you do.

I cannot stress this enough. Don't miss the significance of this truth—it's life-changing.

This view, that genes control our destiny and that we cannot change anything in our relationships or in ourselves, is not just damaging . . . it's not true.[14]

Embracing this misguided and popular view will create major problems in all of your relationships, especially those between males and females. For example, you can choose to believe that you're constantly unhappy in your marriage because you and your spouse are "genetically incompatible." But you're not limited by your current genetic code. You're not helpless . . . none of us are.

BRAINY TIP

You are not limited by your current genetic code.

We are not being victimized by missing or mutant happiness genes. Instead, we are responding to thoughts and choices and belief systems wired into our brains

We have to move away from the excuse that our genes control our emotions and behavior. We have to take responsibility for who we are and how we are reacting in our relationships.

You are more than your genes. You're not trapped by the code that you've been given—you can grow, change and develop.

BRAINY TIP

We need to take responsibility for two big reasons:

1. Genes do not control us.
2. While we cannot control the events and circumstances in our lives, we can control our reactions to those events and circumstances.

This is so important: *we can control how we react to our circumstances.* This might seem difficult or impossible, but because of my knowledge of neuroscience, I can tell you without a doubt that you can influence your genes. Being able to influence your genes is called the science of epigenetics.[15]

This growing field of epigenetics studies the things outside of the cell that influence genetic expression. We have all heard and read that genes are influenced by diet and environment. Research is now proving that thoughts, feelings and the resultant belief systems exert the same, if not stronger epigenetic effect. The chemicals catalyzed by our mental activity, our thought patterns, can switch genes "on" or "off."

Furthermore, what we think changes the architecture of our brains; we can quite literally rewire our brains in a positive or negative direction. You can alter damaging thought patterns and habits and establish strong, healthy vibrant ones in their place because of this neuroplasticity (the ability to change the networks of the brain).

In the next chapter I'm going to tell you how.

CHAPTER 5

Genes, Epigenomes, Trees & The Power to Choose

God blessed us with the ability to think and choose. That statement may seem obvious and mundane to you. It's so easy to take for granted, but you need to know that your thoughts are very, very powerful. The way we think influences the way we talk and behave—every action or word first begins as a thought. Thoughts grow into words and actions that affect all of our relationships and can physically change the structure of our brains.

Your thoughts are the result of the information you receive from your environment. Your five senses interact with everything you experience externally (people, situations, etc.), transmitting all of this to the internal world of your brain.

Imagine that your thoughts are like trees. When your senses transmit information to your subconscious mind, you think thoughts, which grow like trees. Over time, you grow more and more trees until you practically have entire forests living in your brain.

God designed us to build big, strong, healthy trees. I call this being "wired for love." Because God gave us free will, we play a vital role in choosing the kinds of trees we cultivate in our brains. We can choose to have negative thoughts, which unfortunately grow into unhealthy, toxic trees.

BRAINY TIP

Because God gave us free will, we play a vital role in choosing the kinds of trees we cultivate in our brains.

This power to choose makes all the difference. God said in the Bible, *I call heaven and earth to witness this day against you that I have set before you life and death, the blessings and the curses; therefore choose life, that you and your descendants may live* (Deuteronomy 30:19 AMP).

BRAINY TIP

What we need to do is to learn how to grow healthy trees in our brains so that we can continually "choose life."

Your subconscious mind processes 20 million environmental stimuli per second and performs 400 billion actions per second. The conscious mind, on the other hand, processes only 40 environmental stimuli per second, performing 2000 actions as it becomes aware of the relevant thoughts moving into consciousness and relates these to the incoming environmental stimuli.[1]

All of this is happening in your brain right now as you read these words. Your brain is an incredible organ that no supercomputer could ever hope to match, processing stimuli as you read this book, or when you interact with a spouse, son, daughter, friend, mother or father. Your brain processes stimuli that affect and grow your thought trees, which in turn affect how you relate to people. Your relationships themselves become stimuli, further supporting and growing the thought trees that have already been planted in your mind. This is a constant, ongoing cycle.[2]

Here's a practical example of how this cycle shows up in our lives: As children we watch our parents and download what they say and do and store it in our subconscious minds. So the words, behaviors, beliefs and attitudes we observe in our parents grow into strong thought trees.

The words, behaviors, beliefs and attitudes we observe in our parents grow into strong thought trees in our own brains.

These observed lifestyle patterns we take in as children create an epigenetic imprint—thought networks in the brain of the watching child—a bit like a template for behavior. When that child is grown up, this often shows up when spouses notice that their partners sit, talk with their hands, walk or pronounce words in a similar manner as one of their parents. Even deeper, we react from these templates and the reactions may not necessarily be good ones. They're not trying to do it—they don't have to. It's been hard-wired into their brains.[3]

However, the presence of these "thought networks" is not a guarantee that the child will emulate all of the observed patterns. When they recognize these behaviors they can exercise their free will and choose to change.[4]

We can exercise our free will and choose to change.

But these thought networks in the brain are a physical reality. If people choose not to react in the way their parents did but the thought pattern is never dealt with, it will pass through to the next four generations or more until it is dealt with. Scientifically this has been proven through the science of epigenetics.[5]

Clearly then, once wired in, these words and actions become "characterizations of the self:" truths that can unconsciously shape our behavior and personalities, our brains and body health—our lives! This is the epigenetic factor I introduced you to in the previous chapter: our thought-patterns switch genes "on" or "off." What we think changes the wiring of our brains and influences new thoughts, and our words and actions.

BRAINY TIP

Wired in thoughts can unconsciously shape our new thoughts, choices, words and behaviors.

As you can imagine, this is great if "wired-in" actions and words are healthy, but if they're toxic, that toxicity runs through your brain and taints everything you do—especially your relationship with your spouse.

BRAINY TIP

Toxicity can run through your brain and taint everything you do—especially your relationship with your spouse.

These toxic patterns can have significant, long-term influence. Scientifically, thought patterns become epigenomes that are physically rooted in the brain. This means that the decisions we make today are based on thoughts we have created in our brains. These become epigenomes that can remain strong for four generations or more if they are not dealt with.[6]

BRAINY TIP

Decisions we make today are based on thoughts we have created in our brains.

Once again, this research discovery falls right in line with what the Bible teaches.

The Lord is long-suffering and slow to anger, and abundant in mercy and loving-kindness, forgiving iniquity and transgression; but He will by no means clear the guilty, visiting the iniquity of the fathers upon the children, upon the third and fourth generation (Numbers 14:18 AMP).

This is why we see negative behavior patterns repeating in families and marriages, causing terrible damage.

BRAINY TIP

No thought is harmless because thoughts create networks in our brains which influence both our attitudes and our actions.

"Neuroplasticity" is simply the ability to rewire one's brain. God has designed you to rewire so that when you build toxic trees in your brain, you can remove them and build strong healthy trees in their place.

BRAINY TIP

God has designed you with the ability to rewire so that when you build toxic trees in your brain, you can remove them and build strong healthy trees in their place.

It all boils down to what I call the "I-Factor"—your built-in capacity to become the unique masterpiece God created you to be. We think, we make choices, and they get wired into our brains.

BRAINY TIP

Through the signals of our thoughts and choices, which become epigenomes, we can literally override toxic thinking—our own and those that have come down through the generations.

Epigenetics is in essence the process by which environmental and internal thought signals become thought impulses and how these thought impulses select, modify and regulate gene activity.

Epigenetics essentially relates to a higher level of control than the genes, and it is what I call: the "I-Factor." It trumps both nature and nurture. The "I-Factor" creates change. You can change your own brain through the way you think. In my book *Who Switched Off My Brain? Controlling toxic thoughts and emotions. The Revised Edition,* I go into this in depth.

This thinking and choosing activates reactions, which in turn activates genetic expression, meaning proteins are made. These proteins are used to grow another thought (more branches on your trees) because they are building blocks. So, there is an actual physical change in brain structure as we think.

BRAINY TIP

We can use our thoughts to create signals in our brains that change other negative toxic thoughts for the better.

Therefore our thoughts and choices shape our biology and not the other way around. Understanding scientifically how cells respond to our thoughts and actions empowers us to take responsibility for what we think, say and do as well as the impact that this has on others. This is a huge factor in male/female relationships because the "1-Factor" interacts with the male/female factor.

BRAINY TIP

Understanding scientifically how cells respond to our thoughts and actions empowers us to take responsibility for what we think, say and do as well as the impact that this has on others.

So, whatever a child or adult is thinking about influences genetic expression that leads to the formation of thoughts. The stimulation for thinking and the subsequent development of thoughts comes from the existing thoughts/memories inside our heads and through the five senses from the external environment—this includes mom and dad, who are literally epigenetic influencers. Children need a safe nurturing environment to activate the genes that develop healthy minds and bodies and relationships. A child's social world and environment supply the most important experiences influencing the expression of genes. These factors create the thought networks which give rise to mental activity.[7]

BRAINY TIP

Mom and Dad are epigenetic influencers and children need safe loving environments to activate the genes that develop healthy

---

minds, bodies and relationships.

This epigenetic and neuroplastic (the brain's ability to change its structure) influence on genetic expression in the brain at both the pre-natal (in the womb) and birth through childhood levels, can go both ways: life-enhancing optimization or life-draining distortion affecting our lives, relationships, lifestyle choices, health—everything.

BRAINY TIP

So, the patterns for adulthood are laid down in childhood, not genetically alone, but epigenetically because genes wait for epig-enomes to "switch" them on.

Now, you may be feeling that you might as well give up . . . that you've already carried so much toxic stuff into your relationship that it cannot be saved. I believe there is still hope because of the miracu-lous, transforming power of epigenetics and neuroplasticity, which are absolute gifts from God.

Let me explain the most exciting fact about epigenetic neuroplas-ticity, first from a spiritual view and then from a scientific one.

Spiritually, God tells us that it is important to renew our minds:

Don't copy the behavior and customs of this world but let God trans-form you into a new person by changing the way you think. Then you will learn to know God's will for you, which is good and pleasing and perfect (Romans 12:2 NLT).

Why would God tell us to do something if it weren't physically pos-sible? He wouldn't. Because He's told us to do it we can be sure that He's also given us the power not only to obey in one moment but to consistently live this way over time.

BRAINY TIP

Renewing your mind is part of your natural design—it's how you were created to function.

Scientists tell us that our bodies come genetically and epigenetically equipped to deal with the mental and physical challenges of life. Your response to the ongoing events and circumstances in your life (your literal mental equilibrium) have a tangible, physical impact on your brain and body. Your reactions create thought networks—whether they're toxic and damaging or healthy and life-giving is up to you.

BRAINY TIP

Scientists tell us that our bodies come genetically and epigenetically equipped to deal with the mental and physical challenges of life.

Scientifically, it is very clear that he has equipped us to renew our minds and to be our own neuroplasticians. He designed us with epigenetic neuroplasticity which essentially means that whatever toxic thought you unintentionally or intentionally wire in to your brain, you can also wire out. That's the beauty of the "1-Factor." Not only did He design you with a unique set of gifts, He also gave you the ability to make good choices that will develop and protect those gifts.

BRAINY TIP

Not only did God design you with a unique set of gifts, He also gave you the ability to make good choices that will develop and protect those gifts.

You are not a victim of your genes or any epigenomes that you picked up from someone else. *You are a neuroplastician* and can therefore perform mental brain surgery on yourself and get rid of the bad thought trees and grow new ones. Because God's given you the power to choose, you've been given the ability to choose life which transcends the formative power of your genetic coding. You don't have to conform to your genes—you can make your genes fit you!

BRAINY TIP

You are a neuroplastician—you can perform simple brain surgery on yourself by getting rid of toxic thought trees and planting healthy ones in their place.

You see most toxic thought patterns operate out of selfishness. When you and your spouse are experiencing relational problems, chances are, you are thinking with a "me-first mentality."

While this mentality expresses itself differently, "He never listens to me" or "She's always yapping at me," the root is the same—selfishness.

Selfishness isn't atypical for our fallen nature, male or female. It's our negative default mode, it's our toxic instincts and our culture which constantly reinforces that behavior.

BRAINY TIP

The real key to cleaning out toxic thoughts, operating in your true gifting and having a successful relationship with your spouse is to rewire your brain to follow the message of Jesus. You will function best when you love God and you love people.

I want to encourage you to find your true "gifting" as I mentioned in Chapter Three. When you know who you are, who God has made you to be in Christ, you don't have to walk around feeling threatened. You don't need to fight and argue with your spouse because of your own self-esteem issues. You can set aside your own issues and make your spouse's needs your priority.

Too many couples seek to meet only their own selfish needs, and the results are always chaotic, confusing and frustrating. But God has made a better way. We don't have to settle for this.

BRAINY TIP

When we make loving and helping our spouses the most important goal in our relationships, it will help them to walk in their true gifting giving them the security they need to help you with your needs.

This is the Jesus model of communication and it will work in every relationship, not just between spouses. When you love and serve others generously, not for what you'll get out of it, it's transforming.

If we can begin by understanding ourselves better and realizing how we've been designed with the capacity to change through healthy choices, we're on the road to healthier relationships. And that's before we even begin to figure out how the other gender lives.

As we begin part two, we'll look at how men and women experience things differently through their senses. You may be surprised by what you discover.

CHAPTER 6

Vision: He Sees Tan, She Sees Relaxed Khaki

Back in South Africa when my husband Mac and I were building our dream home I was deeply involved in every detail of the plans. Like many of you ladies, I love picking out colors, textures and designs for everything from the tile backsplash in the kitchen to the stylish throw pillows for the couch.

As I was meticulously deliberating between the fifteen different shades of beige for the carpet and the twenty different swatches of taupe for the walls, I asked Mac, my husband, to help me choose the best combination.

He glanced up from his phone for a moment and replied: "They all look the same!"

Thanks for the input dear.

When it comes to vision we really do see through different lenses— a man and a woman don't see the same thing whether shopping for clothes or flipping through paint swatches. While a man calls it all "tan," a woman will contemplate long and hard for the subtle nuances between "Sand Dollar" and "Relaxed Khaki." It's not just a matter of personality or conditioning either. These distinctions are hard-wired into our anatomies.

Without these insights it would be so easy to get discouraged. I could assume that Mac switched off his brain because he doesn't care—not about the color, not about our house, and therefore . . . not about me!

Males see multiple distinct colors, while females see multiple colors *and* multiple shades of color. Females, on average prefer colors like red, purple, orange, and beige. Males tend to prefer colors like black, gray, silver, green and blue.[1]

Also, for women, color discrimination varies during their menstrual cycles with the most accurate color discrimination occurring at ovulation.[2]

One of the reasons for these differences lies in the anatomy of the eye, which is different in males and females.

The X-chromosome provides the cone-shaped cells that handle color.[3] Women have two X-chromosomes and men have one, so women have more cells that allow them to see subtle changes in shades of color.[4]

Females also have more P-cells—special cells in the retina that help the brain interpret texture and color. These P-cells allow women to be more detail-oriented than men.[5] Males, on the other hand, have more M-cells, other specialized cells in the retina that help the brain analyze motion, action and direction. M-cells help men see how things move and work.[6]

BRAINY TIP

Ladies, you should help your man coordinate his color combinations—you can see what he can't!

Gents, we didn't mean to dent the bumper or scrape the door, but you see parking spaces, angles and spaces better than we do!

When it comes to driving, a man uses his superb long-distance tunnel vision—binocular eyes with greater concentration on depth and a better perspective than women.[7] Combined with great spatial ability (more on this later) this helps his ability to drive at night because he's keenly able to distinguish and separate the movement of other cars on the road.

Men also see better than women in bright light; women see better in the dark.

A woman, on the other hand, can see more details in the dark, but only for short distances. She also has great peripheral vision—this can make her an excellent daytime driver, but men are better night-time drivers.[8]

The differences between M and P-cells also mean that females are wired to be interested in faces and boys are wired to be more interested in moving objects. This is true from infancy—many studies show that girl babies' track faces and boy babies track moving objects.[9]

That's why women are naturally better at reading faces and expressions and it's also why women can communicate and express themselves merely through changing the angles of their eyes and lips. Most men have a really difficult time picking up on these subtleties, but once they do, they are better than women at doing something about them.

My mother has what I call a "Queen Victoria look" that can instantly freeze any of her grown-up children to this day. Even though I'm now 47, that look hasn't lost a thing—it works as well as it did when I was 7.

My three daughters say that I give them the same look, although they don't call it the "Queen Victoria." Interestingly, my son doesn't notice expression and will innocently hang around while the girls hide in their rooms. There's a whole line of communicating going on in our home that he's not picking up on. I don't blame him because I understand he's wired differently.

As a woman, it would be easy to assume that the men in our lives are ignoring us when they don't respond to what we would immediately identify. But that's not the case—they're just not getting it. "Subtle facial mannerisms" is a language most men don't speak.

BRAINY TIP

The next time your wife seems to be staring rather intently at you, I suggest you look closely and ask a few questions about what she is trying to communicate to you. You may not like it if she has to yell at you with her eyes!

The difference in the hard-wiring in the brain that leads women to study faces intently while men focus on motion will manifest itself in the other senses as well as we'll see in subsequent chapters.

For example, baby girls are born interested in emotional expression. They look for it and are drawn to it. Their meaning about themselves is derived from the nurturing around them: every touch, every smile, every hug; every kiss and every communication converges in their brains that are genetically and hormonally primed in the female to receive information through the rose-colored lens of emotion.[10]

Baby boys, on the other hand, are born interested in the way things in the world work around them—the opposite of the baby girl. The boy's lens is clinical, practical and focused. Females watch faces; males investigate.[11]

BRAINY TIP

Ladies, he tracks you when you move, like the famous Beatles song, "Something," says: "Something in the way she moves attracts me like no other lover . . ."

Gents, she wants to look into your eyes. Barbara Streisand and Celine Dion aren't your favorite, but they might be hers. That's why in their duet, "Tell Him," they sing: ". . . tell him that the sun and the moon rise in his eyes."

Women in general have higher visual perceptiveness when it comes to social perception. This is the perception of reading other people's non-verbal cues and behaviors especially while communicating.[12]

Men have a different type of social perceptiveness in the sense of *doing* something about the problem or issue—once they are fully aware of it—often faster and more effectively than women.

For example, a mother is able to read her husband or child's state of mind from facial and body expressions without any verbal expression. A man has the complementary ability to see what to do to solve the problem. So it's almost as though God has made the women able to sense if a problem exists and the man, once he is aware of the problem, to take the appropriate action.

I see this all the time with Mac. One of my daughters will say something and I can see from their eyes and body movement that something is wrong even if she can't articulate it. So I (the nurturer) will react to this by pursuing the matter and trying to help fix whatever is worrying her.

Mac—the problem-solver—on the other hand will give her a kiss and say "Okay, love you"—and then tell me to leave her alone, when of course this would be the worst thing to do. He completely missed the eye and body signals.

This kind of interchange has led to some hilarious situations where daughter and mom turn the counselling session onto Dad. Mac gets lost in translation—it happens so fast it practically knocks him off his feet. One minute he thinks he's solving the misunderstanding between his girls and then all of a sudden he's the one with the issue!

Mac's biggest challenge is my biggest strength—I can quickly figure out what's going on. But once Mac knows what the problem is, there's no one better in our family at taking the appropriate action to fix things. He's a wonderful problem-solver and will go out of his way to ensure he has helped in every way he can.

In the example above, this is exactly what he did. Dominique, our daughter had been concerned about getting her SAT prep and college applications done in time and was stressing over all the details. I picked up the stress in her voice and body language even though she was saying, "Nothing is wrong" with her words.

I knew to keep pressing so I asked her again and we talked it through until she communicated what was really going on. She wasn't being deceptive with me—she just needed a gentle nudge to help her talk it out. And she was doing the "female indirect and opposite thing:" we say something but mean the opposite.

After we had all the details, Mac promptly got onto the internet and phone and found all the necessary information we needed to book appointments, purchase the required resources and take care of every detail.

I sensed and saw the problem and helped our daughter articulate it and then Mac took the necessary action to solve it. Our differences created a great team dynamic that allowed us to do far more together than either of us could have done on our own.

BRAINY TIP

Ladies, if he fails to notice your cues, don't immediately jump to conclusions and get irritated. Remember, he can't pick up everything you would and he'll respond negatively to your indirectness. But once he has the information, he is amazing at making things happen. We see emotional nuance; he sees how to fix things.

Even when a man fails to notice the relational, unspoken details his ability to identify strategic patterns once he has the appropriate information gives him the ability to develop and execute a plan. This could explain why men on average seem to be naturals at strategic games like chess and careers like politics.

An interesting feature of the function of a man's brain is his superior hand-eye coordination—typically we think of this as an advantage in sports and recreation but it also has intellectual influence. This ability allows a man to more easily rotate, imagine and alter an object in his mind's eye. It's as if he can take a problem and view it from multiple angles in his mind more quickly than a woman.[13] Add this to the woman's ability to see the detail, and you have a winning formula.

Women on the other hand see intimate detail and their eyes and brains can discern these details very quickly and make rapid comparisons. This enables a woman to see the crumbs on the kitchen table and the messy books opened on the couch which have knocked over the cushions; walk into a room and within seconds, figure out what's going on. Her eyes will see who's wearing what, what everyone's expression is, how the room is decorated, how the food looks, etc. All the while, her brain is interpreting this information, allowing her to discern the state of everyone's emotions, who's fighting with whom . . . even whether or not the evening's going to be boring or enjoyable. This is a great quality but can become a negative in that women can get so caught in the details, that they miss the big picture.

Men on the other hand, see details differently: they like informative factual details for decision-making, the kind of details that are practical, logical, cohesive and lead to action.

That's why when I'm studying and evaluating the subtle differences between Relaxed Khaki and Sand Dollar, Mac's looking for the sales guy, figuring out where we need to go and developing a plan to get us what we need and on our way as quickly as possible. When these two approaches are complementing each other instead of competing, you gain the benefit of both the magnifying glass and the bird's eye view. It's the best of both worlds.

BRAINY TIP

Gents, when she tugs your arm and wants to discuss someone's emotional state, pay close attention. She's already given you clues that you've missed—you can be sure she's passionate about what she's saying!

Ladies, be patient with him and start with things you agree on before you start unloading big new ideas and conclusions on him. He'll have a much easier time seeing what you are saying if you do.

Men and women "see" equally well, but differently. It doesn't have to be a mystery or a competition. It's designed to be a beautifully, complementary partnership. We can enrich each other's views.

CHAPTER 7

Hearing:
He Hears the Boom,
She Hears the Footsteps

He wants to turn up the volume, she's asking him to turn it down.

There's a reason men like loud music in the car, surround sound at the movies and the latest innovations in audio technology. It's the same reason so many women are looking for a moment of quiet.

You guessed it—*it's hard-wired in our brains.*

According to the most recent scientific studies it appears that when it comes to our hearing, girls are born with a superior ability to decipher minor alterations in human vocal tones.[1]

Hearing sensitivity is measured by determining at how low a volume a person can hear a "pure" tone. This pure tone threshold is lower in women than in men, which means women's hearing is more sensitive throughout the range of sounds that humans can hear.[2]

It helps to explain how a mother's sense of hearing is almost supernatural—she can hear the pitter patter of her children's footsteps two floors up, even half-asleep in the middle of the night. The unusual sound has the woman on high alert before the man has even awakened.

And while a loud bang is painful to a woman's ears, a man can register the sound and react very quickly because his ears aren't as sensitive.

Girls can hear a broader range of sound frequency and tones in the human voice than boys.[3] A girl just needs to hear a slight change in her mother's voice and she will know she is doing something wrong; a boy will normally have to be physically restrained to keep him from destroying what he is not supposed to be touching, even after Mom's given every verbal warning at her disposal.

And it's not that he is ignoring the warning—he's simply not as good at deciphering the tone in her voice.

When it comes to husbands and wives, the tone of our voices communicates before we understand the words we're delivering.

BRAINY TIP

Ladies and gents, the tone of our voices communicates powerfully before the other person hears or understands a single word we say.

My husband Mac and I have had this exchange more times than I could count. I ask him, "What's wrong?" and eventually he'll answer, "Nothing."

Or we'll be in a serious conversation and I'll appeal to him, "Why are you using that tone?" By now I realize that when he responds with a simple, "What tone?" he's not disagreeing with me, tuning me out or switching off his brain. In the early days of our relationship that's what I assumed was happening, but it wasn't the case.

The fact is that the two of us hear and process things through the unique attributes of two different brains. That's why we get lost in translation when we miss the clues that reveal the mystery between he said/she said.

The clues are there—we just need some help making sense of them.

When I continue by explaining to him, "That tone tells me . . ." and I give him a thesis on the nuances of communication he's floored. Even though we've had this exchange many times before he's amazed by my conclusions, which seem so obvious to me.

"Where did you get that from," "You're imagining things," or "Stop putting words in my mouth" are his next steps in our little dance.

I'm guessing you can relate. The truth is we're both right—we're hearing things through a filter that changes the intended communication. Once you realize this, it's so much easier to understand the other perspective and take a deep breath.

BRAINY TIP

From the look in a man's eyes and the tone of a man's voice, women can tell if something is wrong. But sometimes we read what's not there and when we do, we create a fight or offense that he never intended. With a little practice, his focused hearing can balance her hyper-sensitive ears.

The female brain is also highly capable of determining whether she is being listened to or not as this is also a part of the development of her self-esteem. Her brain is keenly astute at picking up a wandering mind.[4]

A father may find it quite a challenge to keep up with the relationship with his daughter because a male needs to consciously focus on being attentive. But the rewards are huge as he sees the confidence of his daughter developing because she knows she has his full and undivided attention. This may seem like a small thing to him, but to her, it communicates that she's valued, she's loved and her voice is being heard.

A husband may find it a challenge to keep up with his wife as she zig-zags her way through all the various adventures of her day, constantly inserting random factoids and minutiae. There's a reason she knows where she's going even when he's completely lost and beginning to lose interest. Her girlfriends love all the extra details she gives when she's telling a story—her husband's wondering, "What does *this* have to do with *that*?"

The female brain is innately attentive; it has the ability to group sounds and analyze them. The male brain listens for a specific focused purpose and can tell the direction that the sound came from.[5]

BRAINY TIP

Gents we know when you're not listening—you're not fooling us! So stick with us because there is a point and we know where we're going. Keep eye-contact.

Feel free to jump in and ask, "How did that make you feel?" or "Wait a minute. Did you just say . . ."—this shows you are listening.

Ladies, don't expect him to listen like your girlfriends or sisters. His listening is compartmentalized and focused and he likes relevance, so give the big picture and as you move into the details remember he's trying to follow you.

And watch your hand and body movements, the more you move around the more distracted he will become.

Men have a greater tolerance of loud sound, so women will find noise unpleasantly loud at lower levels of stimulation than men.[6] This helps to explain why men keep turning up the action movie—they're not trying to hurt you, they just want to feel the explosions AND the dialogue.

BRAINY TIP

Gents if you find your lady is asking you to turn the TV or sound system down, it's not because she is irritated with you but because she is more sensitive to loud sounds.

Ladies, he's not always turning it up because he loves his speakers—his hearing isn't as sensitive as yours!

Men's brains are not equipped to see and hear the details to the same extent as women's.[7] Men's processing of what they see and hear has a big picture to detail emphasis and magnitude through increased coherence and logic.

Women are the opposite in a beautiful complementary way. Men hear the boom and are able to respond, while women can hear the faint footsteps of a child two floors up.

Life is filled with both loud "booms" and delicate "footsteps." When we can learn to respect and appreciate each other, we're both stronger.

CHAPTER 8

Touch:
Hugs and Handshakes

Touch is vital. Touch communicates, often in ways our words cannot.

The mother who holds her daughter's hand as they walk to her first day of kindergarten.

The father who picks up his son and holds him tight while he sobs after he scrapes his knee falling off his bicycle.

The loving, tender backrub a wife gives her husband after a long day at work.

The comforting embrace from a good friend the moment you get terrible news.

The kiss on your wedding day.

Lack of touch (scientifically referred to as "cutaneous deprivation") damages us.[1] It's been shown to contribute to emotional problems, stunted intellectual and physical growth and a weakened immune system.

When you stop and think about it, this makes sense. Your entire body is covered with an organ specifically designed to receive touch—the skin. The skin is the largest organ in the body and houses a myriad of receptors for touch, pressure, pain, cold and heat.

Women are at least ten times more sensitive to touch than men and as a result they respond to touch much more quickly. However, the differences between the two are far more complicated than one simple statistic could ever show.[2]

Gender differences in touch sensitivity are wired in from birth, influencing the early neuro-cognitive development of infants. Because females are born more sensitive to touch, their reactions to minor touch are definitely stronger than boys.[3]

The impact and significance of our touch receptors are also greatly affected by the hormone oxytocin. Oxytocin stimulates the desire for more touch. While it is released in large quantities in the mother during both childbirth and nursing, it's released in both parents over the course of childrearing.[4]

BRAINY TIP

From infancy females show an overwhelmingly greater sensitivity to touch than males.

A gentle loving touch goes a long way towards increasing bonding. Be generous with your children because those thoughtful, loving expressions are vital for their development and they strengthen your bond.

Oxytocin is also released in both men and women when they fall in love and when they have sex. It is often called the bonding or commitment chemical because one of its primary roles is to increase trust, decrease fear and strengthen relational bonds.[5]

Oxytocin is a neuromodulator, meaning it enhances or diminishes the overall effectiveness of memories. It also helps change memories from bad ones into good ones. So it quite literally helps to change brains.[6]

Not only do men and women *feel* touch differently, but their brains also *interpret* it differently. Some research shows that men are more likely to initiate touch during courtship and women are more likely to initiate touch after marriage.[7]

BRAINY TIP

Gents, women hug each other and get touchy in groups because it's how they're wired! Don't worry, it's perfectly normal.

For men, touching occurs primarily through the hands—think handshakes and high-fives. Women on the other hand tend to be more expressive and are more inclined to engage in other methods of expression that require more than the hand like hugs and kisses.

I'm sure you won't be surprised to realize that research has shown when a conversation includes a female, more touching occurs than if the conversation involves only men.[8]

BRAINY TIP

Ladies and gents, touch is something you can both engage in to help mental processes flow in a positive direction but don't be surprised if your comfort level and expressions are different. And that's okay!

According to research, women react faster to pain and show greater sensitivity to pressure on their skin than males on every part of the body. It does appear that the threshold to detect vibrations on the palm is the same for men and women.[9] And not surprisingly, women seem to have the greatest sensitivity to touch during the middle of her cycle.[10]

If you're a parent you know how much children love to cuddle. Research has shown that not only is this hard-wired into them, it's beneficial. The more children are cuddled and touched the better for their emotional, self-esteem and intellectual development. Females have a greater natural tendency to be "touchy-feely" but males also respond well to intentional, healthy touch.[11]

Both males and females have some amazing neurons on the top and sides of our brains that are called mirror neurons. Neuroscientists have discovered that these mirror neurons play a very interesting role in "mirroring" the actions and emotions of others.[12] *Mirroring* is a powerful mechanism for understanding the emotional states of other people, which increases our ability to empathize, sympathize and express compassion.

For example when you choose to hug someone, these neurons get all excited and start firing in the same part of the brain in both the person initiating the hug and the person receiving the hug.[13]

Although both males and females need touch, it may not surprise you to learn that the desire to touch and hug is six times more likely to be initiated by a female than a male.[14]

Men respond more to the visual and women more to touch—that's why when a man sees someone crying or visibly moved they'll be motivated to embrace. Women on the other hand often embrace first and then cry, laugh, smile and express themselves.

BRAINY TIP

Gents, hold your wife's hand when you're out at the movies. When she's upset, touch is a wonderful way of calming her down. She will mirror your concern or your irritation, which ever you are thinking. So a decision to lovingly touch will release endorphins and oxytocin (good bonding chemicals) and activate mirror neurons.

Once you do this, you will mirror her response and the net effect is a positive reaction between the two of you. Of course this process works in reverse in the negative direction as well.

Ladies, touching doesn't mean the same to him as it does to you. He enjoys it from a physical point of view, but you experience touch in a very emotional way. Just because he may not be as expressive as your female friends, does not mean he doesn't care.

CHAPTER 9

Non-Verbal Communication: More Than Words

We don't just speak with our words. Our eyes, eyebrows, shoulders, back, arms, hands, legs and feet can all talk. They can whisper and shout too.

Half of all communication is non-verbal. That means how we say what we say is as important as what we actually say—maybe even more so.[1]

And like the careless words we can speak if we fail to consider their impact, our non-verbal communication will tell the truth of what we believe deep down in our subconscious. That's why it's so important to get congruency between what we are thinking and what we are saying because in the long run the truth will come out.

No matter how sneaky you think you are, you can't hide your attitudes. No thought is harmless. Even when we're able to disguise what we really mean with our words, our eye-talk, body language and gestures will tell the truth.

When we are attentive, supportive, gentle and encouraging with our body language we can provide peace, understanding and love without saying a single word. At the same time our posture and facial expressions can also be confrontational, aggressive, demeaning or rude.

Many times our body language betrays our words—our mouths may be saying "I'm sorry, I didn't mean to upset you," while our bodies are saying, "What are you crying about? It's not that big of a deal."

If we fail to understand the basics of non-verbal language we'll continue to send mixed messages which will damage our relationships or at least keep them from getting stronger.

Sometimes, ignorance isn't the issue. We know exactly what we're doing. We're trying to be sneaky and say one thing when deep down, our hearts not in it. But most of us haven't been trained by the CIA. We can't beat a lie-detector. We can't even fool our friends or family. We might be able to disguise our true feelings for a moment or two, but sooner or later, our body language will give us away because it physically reflects our thoughts.

Women and men are both good at reading non-verbal communication, but women are better at naming and describing what is really meant.[2] Maybe this explains why we always win at *Charades*.

BRAINY TIP

Gents, you're not as sneaky as you think you are. Your body language gives you away. Save yourself the time and the trouble and carefully tell us what you really think.

Ladies and gents, remember more than half of all communication is non-verbal. And your body has a harder time hiding the truth than your words do. When you're not telling the truth your heart rate will speed up and your adrenaline will start pumping due to stress. I believe God created us with these warning signs to show us when our minds are not right. I call them "discomfort zones."

As the brain processes non-verbal cues which include eye, hand, body and mouth movements as well as combined facial expression and deliberate gestures, these are registered in the superior temporal sulcus (on the sides of the brain), a brain area concerned with how we relate to others. The amygdala (two almond-shaped structures deep inside the middle of the brain) notes the emotional content and the orbito-frontal cortex (front of the brain) analyzes it. (Please see the appendix in the back of the book for image illustration.)

Interestingly, these two areas mentioned above (superior tempo-ral sulcus and the orbitofrontal cortex) are bigger in women. The right amygdala is bigger in the male. So the female has more active circuits in terms of analyzing and relating self to others through non-verbal communication. The men's circuits are picking up the emotional, which they tend to experience rather than express.

This is why women naturally evaluate how others respond to them, even before they speak a single word. It would be easy for a man to mis-take this behavior as being over-sensitive but it's very real for the woman.

Men have more active circuits in terms of noting the emotional content of the non-verbal communication and *doing* something about it, specifically whether it is safe to approach or avoid things.

This is why men (especially young men) size each other up when they enter a new environment. You see this at any sporting event, whether its kids or professional athletes. They're checking out the other team to see how they match up.

Because non-verbal communication is such a big part of relation-ships and communication in general, the truth is carefully observing body language is a form of listening. And listening is always a founda-tional part of healthy relationships.

BRAINY TIP

Gents, lean on your lady to understand non-verbal cues. She's always watching, observing and interpreting what's going on around her. She can't help it—it's how God made her.

This is very useful information in any relationship, whether it is with your lady or in a business meeting or friendship. She knows whether you are relaxed or happy or tense or stressed just by looking at you. She can also read whether you are being honest in what you are saying to her by looking at your eyes and body movements.

You can do this too—but you sense it and move to action rather than analyze and express. That is why very often the woman is the peacemaker in relationships.

Ladies, trust your gent if he's seen something that's triggered his protective instincts. He's reading non-verbal cues that you have a harder time spotting and he's forming a plan to protect you and your loved ones.

Researchers have discovered that, not only do men and women listen differently—women listen as a means of support; men listen to get the information—but the facial expressions in men and women differ while they are listening.[3]

Women want to participate while they're listening to you—sometimes it feels like they're pulling the words right out of your mouth. Men want to get to the point—they want to know what the bottom line is so they can begin to formulate the response.

A woman can use up to six listening expressions on her face in any one ten-second time frame and men listen with almost no facial expression. In fact it's pretty difficult to decipher who is sharing and who is responding between two women because women express so much feeling on their faces.[4]

BRAINY TIP

Gents, don't be daunted by the multiplicity of facial expressions your lady or daughter or work colleague is using—that's how they participate with you. And don't stare off while you're listening—try to mix in a few different expressions so they know you're engaged.

CHAPTER 10

He Speaks in Headlines, She Tells Every Detail

There are no empty words.

When a word makes its way off your tongue and out of your mouth it's no small feat or random event—it's a complex process that begins as a thought.

The phenomenal process of thinking, choosing and building a single thought is incredibly complex. Before a thought is formed, many structures are working together—chemicals are flowing, epigenetics is dictating the expression of unique genes and all of this is simultaneously taking place with unbelievable accuracy, precision and speed.[1]

It's almost impossible to understand this fact, but the subconscious mind is operating at around 400 billion actions per second!

Sorting out the differences between male and female responses involves filtering through multiple interactive factors and many circuitous loops happening in the brain at any one time.[2]

Our memories (thoughts) in our subconscious mind have substance and structure. We are thinking beings, and all day long we think, make choices and build thoughts. At night our minds shift from building thoughts to sorting and reflecting on them, but this is another expression of our ability to think. This is the natural result from one of God's greatest gifts to man . . . *free will*. Our minds have incredible power.

BRAINY TIP

Ladies and gents, we both need to be very aware of what we choose to think about. Sooner or later the thoughts we build in our minds become words and actions.

Healthy, life-giving thoughts will lead to healing words and loving actions. The same holds true for toxic thoughts and emotions—they may seem normal or unthreatening as internal thoughts, but if they're not dealt with, eventually their influence begins to show up in every part of our lives.

The good news is that God's given you the ability to change your way of thinking. I discuss and explain this process in detail in *Who Switched Off My Brain? Controlling toxic thoughts and emotions. The Revised Edition* and show you a helpful program that will allow you to literally rewire your thoughts.

The Complexity of Communication

We all know that communication is one of the most important factors in any relationship. And we all do it every day—some of us better than others. But we can all improve and that's what this chapter is all about.

Communication can feel like verbal gymnastics—to be effective it requires serious effort, sometimes you "fall down" and get hurt, the process stretches you and in the end you wind up exhausted. Every once in a while you stick the landing and get a "perfect 10."

In terms of brain function, conversation is one of the most complicated activities we regularly engage in. It highlights God's beautiful artistry and design genius. Large and widespread areas of the brain are involved with many different levels of cognition. The unique individual aspects of the "I-Factor" and maleness and femaleness further complicate this. Brain function is so complex during conversation it's a wonder that we can even articulate our own thoughts, let alone understand each other.[3]

Because we're all unique and interact with the world through our special "I-Factor," same-sex communication creates enough complexity on its own. But when you move to communicating with the opposite sex and add all of the physical and functional differences between the male and female brains, you're operating at the highest degree of difficulty.[4]

As daunting as all of this may sound, my goal is to encourage you. Healthy male-female conversations are truly a miracle of science. I'm not encouraging you to quit because it's hard—I'm trying to inspire you to keep at it because while it's difficult . . . it can be done well.

The process of listening is multi-tiered—after words are spoken the initial raw sound has to be registered; then the emotional tone is registered producing an emotional reaction; next the structure of the word stream is analyzed and meaning of words is extracted; and finally the meaning is comprehended by linking to previous memories and context.

And remember, all of this information is added to the non-verbal communication we've already described. The entire process takes about half a second. Isn't it amazing what can go wrong in that short time span?

The speech process starts about a quarter of a second before the words are actually spoken because the brain begins selecting words to deliver the intended message. But the process of how you say what you say was developed in your thoughts (memories) minutes, hours, days, months even years before. No matter how well you know someone, words must become sounds in order to be spoken and understood.

Science shows that the art of conversation is a little more natural for a woman, which may be a big reason why so many of us love it—both the desire and the capacity are hard-wired into our minds.

Research shows that the circuits in a woman's brain between the emotional processing and memory centers are large, very active and closely connected to the language centers in the brain. In general, men speak the language of facts, actions and results; women speak the language of feelings and emotions.[5]

Where a man feels comfortable speaking in headlines, women have an innate desire to tell every detail. While men primarily stick to the basics (who, what, when, where and how), women make sure every base is covered, how it makes them feel, how it made their friends feel, and what they heard someone else felt.

These approaches are certainly different, but that doesn't have to create conflict. Instead they can beautifully compliment and strengthen one another.

BRAINY TIP

Gents, she is designed to link words, emotions, and memories. Ladies, he is designed to separate words, emotions and memories.

So women bond as they are having a conversation and give support by listening. Men have a conversation as a way of getting facts in order to solve problems and accomplish tasks which produces a greater bond in their relationships.

Riding Down a River vs. Playing Tennis

Women do not use language as literally or directly as men. In an average lengthy conversation, a woman will use as many words as she needs, exaggerate, empathize, emote, and speculate on how the events must have made the other person think or feel. The conversation begins with a general direction in mind but it can flow and shift wherever the moment leads. As the words, metaphors, tangents and directions flow freely, the conversation branches off in new directions, circling back again before taking off on another new path.

This kind of conversation is like riding down a river on a beautiful day—it's all about the experience—there's so much to look at and enjoy, you're not rushing anything and you're willing to go wherever it takes you.

Men on the other hand will be literal, direct, speak with brevity and tend to frame the discussion around objective facts instead of subjective or emotional responses. This kind of conversation is like a game of tennis—words bounce back and forth until someone scores a point. After one point is made the other party returns serve and responds as the conversation lobbies back and forth to its clear conclusion.

BRAINY TIP

Typical words that ladies use are "sort of, sometimes, kind of, almost, maybe, whatever, etc." These are process words that sound indirect or vague and can cause problems with men when trying to have a conversation. Men use more direct words like "will you; when will you, none, always, never, absolutely."[6]

His brain is built to see conversation as a means to an end; her brain is built to see talking as an end in itself.

This isn't a function of personality or social conditioning—it's anatomical. The male brain has less circuit connections between the verbal, emotional and conversational centers—but they have more circuits in the problem-solving and action areas. The main hubs of language are larger and work differently in women. Therefore women tend to "external talk" more and men "internal talk" more.[7]

Born to Communicate

BRAINY TIP

Don't be surprised at the differences in development. On average, girls are more verbally fluid than boys; they tend to speak earlier, talk faster, use more words and generate longer sentences. By age two girls have about 100 more words in their vocabulary. At this time the boys are more focused on developing their fluidity in spatial skills versus language skills. These scientific signs are part of God's intelligent design of healthy difference.

After a baby girl is born, her communication skills develop over the next three months 400 percent more quickly than a baby boy. Girls are practically born needing to communicate, and words simply aren't enough. That's why a woman is bothered when she sees her man's expressionless face. She will strive to get a visual response out of him.[8]

If we look at research examining children ages two months through sixteen years, definite conclusions can be drawn that the brain areas responsible for language, spatial memory, motor coordination and communication are different in terms of order, rate and time between boys and girls.[9]

Adding to this is scientific research that girls learn to speak earlier, know more words, recall them better, pause less and glide with ease through tongue twisters.[10]

This female edge in verbal fluency is consistent over time and cultures.[11] In the womb and through life many factors work together to enhance the linked thought and verbal circuits in the female to make them more robust and more sophisticated in their communication, ability to read emotions, social nuances, and to nurture others.

In the male these same circuits are trimmed and refined by the Y-chromosome and the hormone testosterone to become more sophisticated in the complementary areas of visualizing objects, independence, leadership, protection and guidance.[12]

Don't Fix Me . . . Just Listen

A man will feel, express and verbalize his emotions independently while a woman will feel, express and verbalize her emotions at the same time. This makes a man's conversation on average more filled with facts and a woman's conversation on average is more filled with emotion. Men are built to do something about problems. Women are built to listen to problems.

BRAINY TIP

When a lady talks about a list of problems she has, a man automatically reacts by thinking, "I need to solve these problems," or
"She's blaming this on me." However, sometimes we ladies don't
want you to fix us, just to listen!

Overall two main sections of the brain involved in language run
through a section of the frontal (front of the brain) and temporal (side
of the brain) lobes across the left and right sides. These are like the two
main hubs of language.

Although these two main hubs are involved in speaking, comprehension and communication, the complexity of communication
involves a lot of integration between many circuits in many areas of
the brain in both men and women. Most women use circuits actively
in and across both sides of the brain; most men use mainly left hemisphere circuits for language.[13]

In terms of thinking, choosing and building thoughts the bigger
frontal and temporal lobes in the female means men are not as verbally
"gymnastic" as women—they use fewer words to say what they need to say.

BRAINY TIP

Gents, you talk in facts and action statements—a little goes a
long way in building relationships. Ladies talk to express themselves and build relationships through the shared experience of
conversation.

Men focus on facts, actions and results while women savor the
whole process.

The main hubs of language, parts of the frontal and temporal lobes
have been found to be larger and more active in women than in men.
In the female there are about 12–13 percent more neurons than in the
male brain and these are mostly clustered in the second and fourth layer

of the temporal lobe (on the side of the brain called the superior temporal lobe)—the region associated with language (and also perception and memory and integration of thoughts). Signals are also processed through the temporal lobe.[14]

There is also a 23 percent difference in the third, fifth and sixth layers of the front part of the brain (prefrontal cortex)—a region responsible for carrying outgoing signals. This allows the language skills of women to be better integrated and more networked with other cognitive abilities such as memory, emotion and empathy.[15]

So, men have about 23 percent less volume in the front of the brain (prefrontal cortex) and about 13 percent less volume in the side of the brain (superior temporal lobe). Men's brains are simply less versatile than women's brains when it comes to flexibility and processing speed in language functions lateralized in the left hemisphere.[16]

A quick note to the men here: Your smaller frontal and temporal lobes are balanced by your much bigger spatial lobe. This means there are things specifically related to language and communication that you don't do as well as us; but at the same time there are things related to spatial and logical thinking that you do far better than we do.

It's a complementary difference that develops an intimate dependency between us. I think God was drawing on his sense of humor when he designed the male/female differences, because not only can they be a lot of fun, but they teach us to be more giving and less selfish . . . and the bonus of increasing our intelligence when we target our struggle.

Intensive neuro-anatomical studies have produced discernable patterns that only gender appears to explain. In other words, basic mental differences between males and females are in part the result of physical differences in the brain.

Women tend to score higher on tests that involve language and communication, and research shows that these differences are present from birth.[17] Generally speaking, the physical advantage of these nerve-rich layers in the perception, speech and language areas account for the higher results among females.

On average women have more diverse interests, better social and communication skills, and are more attuned to determine the impact of their words and behavior on others. Girls get this head start in interpersonal and communication skills early in life.[18]

BRAINY TIP

So gents, when your wife or girlfriend or teenage daughter or secretary edits your email to make it more friendly or palatable, don't be offended or think you are being corrected; they are seeing things about the communication event that you are not. It may save you a friendship or even a business deal!

FAST FACT

When signing greeting cards, women are much more likely to write lengthy and emotional messages. The greeting in the card is a launching pad for them to express their hearts.

Men tend to choose cards with more words so they write less. As they choose the cards they read through them carefully finding the closest wording that expresses their internal feelings so they don't have to. They pick the greeting carefully.

So, although both sides of the brain are used in language and communication in both men and women, men's language circuits appear to process predominantly big picture to detail direction, and the detail is more focused internal talk. This means their brains are hard-wired to eliminate talking or writing about any detail that doesn't directly contribute to the end result.

Women's circuits on the other hand seem to be equally balanced between detail to big picture (left brain processing) and big picture to detail (right brain processing). Both the details and the big picture matter which explains why women will include an abundance of details that seem superfluous to a man. A woman also has more white matter, which are the long tree trunk-like parts of the nerve cells. This facilitates the swing back and forth and the need she has to think out loud through all the details. She doesn't want to leave anything out because it all contributes to her understanding.

He Thinks They've Settled it, She Thinks They Haven't Even Started

Nearly any long-standing relationship between a man and a woman (co-workers, siblings, friends, spouses, etc.) has had a conversation that ends with the man saying, "Why didn't you just say that?"

Remember . . . he started with the big picture and "internal talked" most of the details.

And on different occasions the same relationship has included a brief conversation that often leaves the man with the impression that the subject has been dealt with while the woman feels like they haven't begun to discuss it. In fact, you would be surprised at how often a woman feels this way. Statistics show that 98 percent of women want the men in their lives to talk to them more about personal thoughts, emotions, feelings and plans; 74 percent are disappointed that their husbands don't want to talk much at the end of the day (I will tell you why in a later chapter) and 81 percent of woman have to initiate conversation.[19]

These differences appear in all kinds of communication. It's common for a woman to discuss something that happens with loads of detail arriving at conclusions, and then she takes her conclusion and reanalyzes it back down to the tiniest detail. The man will assume they're done; they've chosen a course of action and will begin to take the steps to complete the intended result.

While the process seems indecisive to a man, it's fundamentally in keeping with the way the female brain is designed to function. The back-and-forth (detail to big picture and big picture to detail) helps create confidence and peace in a woman but typically leads to unease and confusion for a man.

BRAINY TIP

Think about what happens when you go shopping. Gents will be focused on the result—"I need to buy a shirt." Details are only necessary to complete the action.

Ladies focus on the shirt, but also see the big picture, "What does it go with...you need pants and a jacket...and...Oh so do I...and what about a belt and...oh we need to make sure you have the right shoes...so let's go here and we need to check there...let's get...and, etc."

Gents, she's not trying to frustrate you. Her left/right, detail/big picture mentality is keeping her busy sorting through a whole list of mental exercises. She's not trying to complicate things...she's trying to help you.

Male brains on the other hand, feature circuitry oriented to solving problems. They work from detail to conclusion to pull together a solution. Once they've considered the details and drawn the conclusion, the process is over.

This can drive a female into a frenzy if she hasn't finished processing through her circuits. She feels like they haven't properly discussed it—he feels like they're going round and round and talking the subject to death.

In these circumstances we both need to look at how we can help each other. This means compromise. It doesn't mean the female way is the correct way and the male should adapt. It doesn't mean the opposite either. It means each of us has something valuable to contribute and we should be tuning into each other.

Ladies may get stuck going backwards and forwards in the process and fail to make a decision. The man who uses approximately the same amount of words can help her get closure and bring the thinking through to a focused closure of sorts.

Gents may miss or overlook some excellent options in their race to a solution and their desire to move on to the next thing.

If we're wise, we'll learn to make the most of both approaches and allow the strengths of each perspective to shine through. Lean on the female attention to details and gather as much information from as many perspectives as possible. Then embrace the male approach of confident analysis that leads to a resolute decision. Each tendency improves and benefits the other.

Embrace Your Differences

Men mentally index their thoughts; women externally pour out their thoughts. This gives the impression women talk more, but it's not really word amount that counts but rather how the thoughts process into words differently in men and women.

BRAINY TIP

Men and women have different expectations and experiences in communication—and that's okay!

Ladies, sometimes your gent will let a conversation die out, but he is not being rude or standoffish. Rather he enjoys and interprets periods of silence as quality companionship. He also uses these periods of silence to continue to process the communication inside his richly packed parietal lobe (the top of the brain moving towards the back).

By the same token, gents, your lady is hard-wired to love to talk and she views conversation as quality time. After all she has more nerve cells in this area with very active XX-chromosomes making the language centers in her brain very busy.

Women are hard-wired to love to talk. Connecting through conversation activates the reward circuits in a female's brain—and we're not talking about a small amount of pleasure. There is a huge dopamine and oxytocin rush which is a wonderful neurological reward women receive in the process. Men on the other hand don't receive the same stimulant from the process and therefore use words more deliberately to express what they have already worked out in their minds.[20]

The brain circuitry of males and females causes them to talk about the same thing differently and these common distinctions can be observed in different cultures and countries around the world. Women tend to talk about people, relationships and personal issues and men talk about work, recent accomplishments or experiences, current events, sports and technology. While women communicate around subjective experiences and emotions, men are more likely to focus on objective, results-oriented subject matter.[21]

Healthy Expectations
Lead to Healthy Relationships

BRAINY TIP

Gents, ladies get an enormous rush of pleasure out of talking: it makes them feel good, helps relieve tension, makes them feel happy and decreases stress. So just be a bucket, and let her pour it all out. She's not racing to a conclusion—she's enjoying the process. Don't be quick to correct her or solve her problems.

You may feel it's over . . . but it's not over for her! This is especially true when the issue or circumstance is highly emotional—in those cases, it's never over quickly.

Her emotional area is so strongly connected to her verbal thinking and the expressive areas in her brain while also having those busy XX genes it is no wonder she has all those female hormones flowing. There are a lot of things working together on the inside of her but that's where all that passion you love about her comes from! It's how God designed her.

85

Ladies, when a man speaks out clearly on a matter you can be sure that he's gone over it repeatedly in his mind. So if he looks away, or starts working on the computer, or moves off to another part of the room, he is not trying to ignore you, disregard your opinion or shut you out of his process.

Patiently tell him you would like to talk some more as you haven't quite dealt with whatever it is and ask him when it would suit him to finish listening to your part of the conversation, because you understand his part is over.

And it's not so much about number count, which is how many words we each speak, but more about how males and females process and use words differently. There does not seem to be any solid scientific research backing up the claim that women speak two-to-three times more words, something that is commonly quoted.[22] In fact a review of research from the 1960s to 2007 found that men may even be slightly more talkative than women depending on the situation. Women talk more in emotional situations—their feelings, their families, or working with children. Men talk more during decision-making tasks.

Some research discovered that on average women were only 0.11 percent more talkative than men, which is minimal statistically.[23]

Recent studies show that men and women both speak on average 16,000 words per day. James Pennebaker using his device called the EAR (electronically activated recorder) which samples thirty seconds of ambient noise including conversations every 12.5 minutes, found that the chatter patterns between men and women to be roughly the same: 16,215 words per day for women and 15,669 for men. His subjects were 396 university students (210 women and 186 men) at colleges in Texas, Arizona and Mexico.[24]

Another study conducted among a wide variety of ages, regions and backgrounds revealed that speaking rates of 5,202 transcribed and time-aligned telephone conversations showed the average speech rate for males was 174.3 wpm, and the average speech rate for females 172.6 wpm.[25]

FAST FACT

There's no conclusive research that proves women talk more than men—it only appears so because women are more likely to speak emotionally, using words as tools.

The bottom line is the biggest deciding factor of how fast or how many words you speak is not whether you're male or female. There are stronger determining factors at work here—your unique "1-Factor," the context of the conversation, your familiarity with the subject matter, your emotional investment—end up influencing the speed and volume of the conversation to a much greater degree than your gender.

What appears to be central in all of this is not *how many* words but *how* words are used. Women use words flavored by emotion. They color words, they work things out by talking through their mental processes using words as their tools. Words are used for support, for comfort, for consolation, for nurturing, for clarification and for tension release. It's a collaborative, exploratory process that uses extended reasoning.

Men use words to contribute information and opinions. Their words carry information and facts, referencing other positions while establishing their own to generate and exercise influence.

Because of this, men on average talk more than women in formal public contexts. Women on average talk more than men in private informal relational contexts.

This difference in how words are used could in part be due to the genetically active second X-chromosome that scientists thought used to be inactive. So, women have more gene activity than men. In addition, on an anatomical level, the areas involved in these processes are bigger in the female.

BRAINY TIP

Gents, she colors her speech with emotional details, not just be-cause she's in the mood—it's how she's been designed. So when you're listening and it feels like she's adding all kinds of superfluous details, listen for that bottom line. It's in there somewhere. This will help you get in her head.

Ladies, bottom-line speak does not mean he is cross or irritated with you. He's not leaving out details because he doesn't feel like you're worth it or because he's not willing to make the effort that would require. It's how he's wired.

Think of his words as headlines, not whole stories.

I believe healthy communication in any relationship includes right expectations. Managing expectations doesn't mean that you settle for less or that you compromise your communication to the lowest common denominator so that no one is ever honest in fear of hurting the other person.

Right expectations and a healthy understanding of the other person will help your relationships—it will put you in a great position to grow and develop them.

If a woman expects a man to catch the hints that her girlfriends immediately pick up on, she's going to be frustrated. It doesn't mean that he's not paying attention or he doesn't care. Men aren't as skilled as women at reading subtle emotional cues. Parts of the limbic cortex, which is involved in the subtle nuances of emotional responses, are smaller in men than in women. As mentioned earlier, researchers have found that men have a smaller density of neurons in areas of the temporal and frontal lobes that deal with language processing and talking.

That's why it's probably a good idea to tell him directly how you're feeling. Expecting him to infer from your hints could leave both of you scratching your heads. At the same time, men should know that the direct approach can have a much greater emotional impact on a woman than it would on one of your friends. If you think what you're going to say may hurt her, chances are good that it will.

BRAINY TIP

Here are some hints for dealing with these polar opposite ways of using language: gents, you don't always have to respond to a lady's need to talk, sometimes you can just listen. So use your directness and ask her: "Do you need me to help you solve something or do you just want me to listen?"

Ladies, be direct in your communication and use you verbal fluency to make yourself clear, speaking about one thing at a time. Give him a time, a place and an indication of what you need to discuss and whether you need to just be listened to or whether you want help.

CHAPTER 11

The "Gear-Shifter"

Have you ever felt "stuck" in a negative thought pattern? Do you know people who are constantly angry or depressed or worried? Something happens and they find themselves in a mental and emotional rut that they can't seem to pull out of.

These lifestyles of toxic thoughts can happen when the "gear-shifter" of the brain gets stuck.

Here's what I mean: Each part of your brain has a significant role to play in who you are and how you function. The whole frontal part of the brain is critical, as it helps us make decisions. But there's one part of that area that I would like to point out. It's called the anterior central gyrus (ACG), and could be called the "gear-shifter" of the human brain.

Imagine the gear-shifter of a car. In the same way that shifter helps move the car through different speeds, the ACG helps "shift" the brain through different thoughts and emotions. While this simple image helps describe the overall role that the ACG plays, it doesn't even begin to describe all of the ACG various complex jobs. The ACG accomplishes so much that we aren't even aware of:

- It links emotions to actions. It helps you predict the consequences of certain actions.
- It connects with the outer part of the brain, called the cortex, specifically in the frontal and temporal lobes (these areas of the brain deal a lot with language, memory and emotion).
- It helps you weigh options and make decisions.
- It's key to building emotions and thoughts.

· It oversees intimacy and bonding.
· It feels emotional and physical pain.

Essentially, the ACG is the part of your brain that enables you to "shift" between thoughts and behaviors.[1] However, on occasion, in both males and females, the "gear-shifter" can get stuck. This tends to happen when someone keeps dwelling on a toxic thought. Rehearsing and rehashing the toxic thought and intertwined emotions over and over makes it harder for the ACG to "shift gears" to other emotions.

Have you ever been hurt and found yourself thinking over and over *and over* about the event or circumstance in the car, at work, watching TV . . . wherever. Well whatever you think about the most grows and will dominate your thinking. Once toxic thoughts begin to dominate your thinking your clarity of thought and ability to make wise choices is greatly reduced and so more bad choices tend to follow.

Because all thoughts are intertwined with emotions, physical *and emotional* pain are both felt in the ACG, in these dark moments it can function as a toxic pathway. A literal "superhighway" gets built between the toxic thought and the ACG keeping us fixated in a downward spiral of negative thinking.[2]

Unfortunately we all tend to develop these negative toxic reactions to events and circumstances, which seem to fire off automatically when we perceive a certain look, mannerism, attitude or damaging word. The good news is—you don't have to stay trapped in this toxic spiral. Your brain can be rewired! (Please see my book *Who Switched Off My Brain? Controlling toxic thoughts and emotions. The Revised Edition.* for a complete explanation and guide to a healthier way of life.)

As the ACG's shifting efficiency decreases, serotonin levels, which influence mood, start to drop. In addition, dopamine levels, which contribute to pleasure, focus, and attention, start to drop.[3] All of this causes slight inflammation in the middle part of the brain, as well as in the area where the toxic thoughts are located.

A toxic thought might start with something small like worry, but when the "gear-shifter" gets stuck, that worry can lead to anxiety, which leads to full-blown fear. In extreme cases, this can progress into depression, phobias, obsessive-compulsive behaviors and other mental and physical disorders.

Now here's where the ACG really contributes to the differences between males and females: A woman's ACG is larger than a man's, and it also has many more connections to the cortex, which means it has a greater effect on emotions, memory and reasoning.

Because the ACG is bigger in a female than a male, the chances of it getting stuck are stronger if her thinking becomes toxic. It will impact more of her brain more quickly than a man's would.

BRAINY TIP

Gents, your lady's ACG is also connected to the part of her brain that deals with language and speaking. That's why women need to talk through their emotions! Don't think that all her talking leads nowhere. Be a good listener and realize that this process really helps her work through problems.

Any type of negative thinking causes electrical chemical chaos and inflammation in the brain, which will reflect in the body because of the connection between our minds and our bodies. Current research tells that 87-95 percent of current mental and physical illness comes from our thought life.[4] Toxic thoughts are real physical wiring changes in our brains that don't just stay in our minds—they have serious physical consequences throughout our bodies.

You may have noticed that I've highlighted some of the unique contributions that come through the female brain, but I'm not playing favorites! God designed the male brain with many complementary and wonderful features too. God designed men and women as equals, capable of balancing out each other's flaws with unique strengths.

Men, you're the pros when it comes to "gear-shifting" the brain! Your slightly smaller prefrontal cortex (PFC) allows you to shift through emotions and get to the heart and focus of an issue quickly. This helps you to see reason and logic, something we ladies desperately need when we have trouble shifting gears. When our "gear-shifter" breaks down and we end up in a mental "ditch," you're excellent at coming alongside and pulling us out of it!

Gents, you can really help us out by listening and helping a woman talk through her thoughts.

These differences in how men and women process through emotions and logic in our minds can benefit each other in all relationships, but it's especially helpful with significant relationships like spouses.

Ladies, a husband can be the best counselor in the world, simply because men are great at the shifting that happens in the ACG and possess a terrific ability to focus. If you're feeling a bit confused and worried, go talk to your husband. His insight and talent at identifying a great plan of action could be the perfect antidote needed to diffuse the situation. I know from my own experience that Mac is invaluable when it comes to helping me sort through toxic thoughts and stressful situations.

However, ladies, this does not mean you can't talk to a brother or male friend if you are married or single.

BRAINY TIP

Ladies, we sometimes give the men a hard time for not being as emotional as we would like them to be, but think of this as a blessing when you're too confused to sort through your emotions. His ability to set aside his emotions and fix a problem could be just the thing you need!

And gents, be sure to listen to your lady when she needs to talk. Her larger language area and acg work together to sort through things. If she can't talk through her thoughts, it will cause

blockages in her ACG. Simply listening to her is an excellent way
to help.

At the same time, don't be afraid to speak your mind and offer advice. I can speak for most women and say that sometimes, if left uninterrupted, we can talk ourselves into a hole. Your perspective and bottom-line approach can be really helpful when it employs the appropriate respect and care. Don't let us get stuck!

CHAPTER 12

The Sixth Sense: She Reads the People, He Reads the Room

A married couple walks into a room full of people. In just a few moments the woman has a clear sense of who's fighting, who's in love, who's happy, who's angry, and who's self-conscious.

Did anyone actually tell her any of this? Nope. She's worked out all of this information by simply watching and observing.

The man on the other hand, sees none of this. He doesn't have a clue about any of the emotions or the relationships in the room. Everything his wife learned in no time at all has flown right over his head.

When people talk about women having a "sixth sense," this is usually what they are referring to: the ability to read emotions and intuitively understand what's really going on.

Women are naturally gifted at assessing and reacting to completely different emotions—love and hate, gratitude and resentment, self-confidence and embarrassment, trust and distrust, empathy and contempt, approval and disdain, pride and humiliation, truthfulness and deception, atonement and guilt . . . the list goes on and on.

Men have this sixth sense too, but it's not nearly as strong as it is in women and they don't tend to spend as much time developing this ability.

All of this stems from a part of the brain called the insula, which enables men and women to integrate rational thinking and emotions.

The brain's two insula (one on each side) are prune-sized pieces of brain tissue between the frontal and temporal lobes. (Please see the appendix in the back of the book for image illustration.) They are uniquely involved in nearly every human behavior and emotion. They give rise to moral intuition, empathy, the capacity to respond emotionally to music, and the ability to read body states (like hunger). They also create what we would call "gut-feelings" or "instinct."[1]

When he or she says, "I'm gonna go with my gut on this . . . " he or she is responding to his or her insula.

> **FAST FACT**
> Research into the anatomy of the insula is helping scientists further understand the differences between humans and animals. Animals are not nearly as emotionally integrated as humans—this is a key difference.[2]

Because of its functions, the insula is absolutely critical. In fact, current research suggests the insula is a central structure to both the body and the mind.[3] As a result, when thoughts become toxic, the consequences can be drastic—the insula cannot successfully combine rational thought and emotion. This contributes to plenty of emotion-related syndromes that I'm sure you've heard of . . . things like addiction, anxiety, depression, and in extreme cases schizophrenia.

The two insula work closely with the amygdala, frontal lobe and the hypothalamus, and function as parts of multiple circuits.[4] However, when the insula are working properly you don't notice them—their contributions feels so natural and effortless . . . like a sixth sense. They quietly make sure that your rational mind and your emotions function together seamlessly.

FAST FACT
The insula helps translate physical sensations into emotions, turning a touch from a loved one into delight, or a bad taste or smell into disgust.

Your insula, working with the rest of the brain, anticipates what something will feel like before it happens. For example on a cold day, your insula gets your body ready by pumping blood to where it will be needed and adjusting your metabolism. This happens on a psychological level as well, so you anticipate the emotional content of how you feel now and how you may feel in a particular situation.

It's your insula that almost acts like a translator between the existing memory (thought) of a circumstance or event and what's about to happen. So it predicts and anticipates.

This can be a good and a bad thing: its good if the thought network the anticipation is based on is healthy, but not so good if it's toxic. In the latter case, the "toxic anticipation and prediction" can get in the way of some decent communication and even cause us to fear confrontation in anticipating things will turn out poorly.

This often happens in a relationship when two people have reacted in certain ways and have built the toxic thoughts and then all new communication is viewed through the filter of the previous painful interactions. Every future conversation is shaped by the experience of the previous encounter. That's why we need to deal with these toxic patterns so our relationships can grow and become healthy.

The insula helps to do that.

Ladies, you are naturally better at picking up on, analyzing, and understanding emotions because the female insula is larger and more active. Gut feelings are not just floating esoteric emotional states, but actual physical sensations that deliver meaning to certain parts of the brain. A womans larger insula can track bodily sensations very well. This allows a woman to have a stronger sixth sense or a stronger "gut feeling" than a man.

Estrogen and oxytocin further enhance a woman's insula to help her look at physical, external signs and understand the emotion involved.[5]

BRAINY TIP

Ladies and gents, both of you can sense them but she is an expert at picking up and sensing the subtle differences in emotional spectrums like love and hate, like and dislike, gratitude and resentment, self-confidence and embarrassment, trust and distrust, empathy and contempt, approval and disdain, pride and humiliation, truthfulness and deception, and atonement and guilt.

Now let's go back to the couple who entered the room at the beginning of the chapter.

The woman understands the emotions and relationships because her larger insula has helped her to read facial expressions and body language. Her emotional sixth sense has kicked in, processing her observations and translating that information into "gut feelings."

The man isn't processing this information and developing those feelings to the same extent, because his sixth sense isn't as developed as his wife's to read and react to the emotions of other people. That doesn't mean that his insula isn't functioning—he's applying it to process different information and develop strong "gut feelings" of his own.

He knows where the best places to sit or stand are, he knows who is there and who isn't, he knows where the entrances and exits are, etc. While his wife has been reading the people and their emotions, he's strategically been reading the environment.

Both are important, innate abilities—sixth senses that allow us to enjoy the party. When you put them together, you get two different but complementary perspectives.

True wisdom is not overly emotional but it's not unfeeling and overly practical either. Without each other, our perspectives are unbalanced, skewing towards one end of a broad spectrum.

But when we work together as God intended, we gain the benefit of the full range of His wisdom and insight, which allows us to enjoy the party, and life in general, to the fullest.

CHAPTER 13

Pain in Your Brain

Not every old saying can be trusted.

"Sticks and stones may break my bones but words can never hurt me."

You and I both know this is not true. In many cases the painful impact of a word cuts deeper and lasts longer than the blow of a stick or a stone. Research has demonstrated this.

I'm sure you've experienced emotional pain—it's just as real as physical pain. But while most people realize the reality of emotional pain, most people don't understand how closely connected physical and emotional pain actually are.

The physical and emotional experience of pain is processed through the whole brain, but it's specifically controlled by the insula (the "sixth sense" from chapter 12), the anterior central gyrus (ACG, the "gear-shifter" from chapter 11) and the somatosensory cortex in the frontal lobe.[1] These areas light up with both physical and emotional pain.

These areas are all bigger in the female brain and because of this women experience pain more intensely than men.[2] Another area of the brain that is activated during pain is the amygdala. Interestingly researchers have discovered that in men pain triggers the right amygdala while women experience increased activity in the left amygdala.

The right amygdala has more connections with the areas of the brain that control external functions while the left amygdala has more connections with internal functions. This difference is another reason why women perceive pain more intensely than men.[3]

The ACG is particularly concerned with the emotional significance of pain and in determining how much attention physical or emotional pain should get. The ACG actually lights up in the same place for physical and emotional pain. The brain is actually able to modify pain.[4]

The ACG (the "gear-shifter") plays a very significant part in how emotional pain is experienced in the brain and then the body. Remember, when the brain's "gear-shifter" gets stuck on something negative, it reinforces that thought, rehearsing it over and over, turning it into a toxic thought. Over time these toxic thoughts become a painful toxic block that will only get worse as the source of this unhealed pain is constantly reinforced and acted upon.[5]

Most toxic thoughts stem from some kind of emotional pain. When the "gear-shifter" gets stuck on this emotional pain, the insula eventually turns these thoughts into physical pain.

In simple terms toxic thoughts cause the ACG to get stuck which causes the insula to anticipate and prepare for emotional and physical pain.[6] We can feel this pain on such a deep emotional level that the nervous system of the body translates this into a stress response experienced as an actual physical pain. The neurochemical and electromagnetic chaos from this stress can over time develop into mental and physical illness.

It may sound far-fetched, but the science proves that you can actually think yourself sick—not just mentally ill but physically too.

Some of you may have experienced this: those IBS (irritable bowel syndrome) symptoms when you are under pressure; those excruciating headaches when you are in a constant conflict situation; those nagging aches in your shoulders or back when you anticipate something going wrong; those whooshes of adrenaline that make you bend over in agony when a situation arises that you can't control . . . and so on.

Women tend to experience this type of thing more intensely. Men tend to compartmentalize and internalize which puts them in the danger zone of heart attacks because the internal peace of the body is strained until the tension becomes so great it finally snaps.

I don't know about you, but I think this mind-body connection is pretty amazing. God truly made our emotions and body to work together. We are wired for love, so when we live the way He lovingly made us to live, the human system works splendidly.

But when we find ourselves outside God's design for us, every part of us experiences the negative results.

God didn't just integrate your individual components (spirit, soul, and body) to work together as a whole, but He also designed you to live and work with other people as part of a larger, unified whole. You were designed to live in community, in healthy relationship with others.

This becomes very clear when studying how the brain processes empathy. Research shows that watching a loved one feel pain and actually feeling pain yourself activates some of the same neural circuits.[7] God literally designed you to tune into and feel the pain of others.

However, if you let toxic thoughts build up towards loved ones, it can deaden your ability to feel their pain. It can also keep you from realizing or caring when you're the one who is the source of that pain. It will destroy your empathy, deaden your feeling, and cause your heart to become "hardened" (John 12:40).

So you see, when it comes to pain, we not only need to make sure that our emotions and bodies are working together in a healthy way, but we also need to make sure that we are interacting empathetically with those around us.

BRAINY TIP

Negative or unhealthy communication patterns lead to toxic thoughts. And over time toxic thoughts lead to emotional and eventually physical pain.

Think carefully—your thoughts have consequences. How you communicate matters. Words can hurt far more than sticks and stones.

Women experience this more intensely and therefore react more quickly through maybe tears, emotional outbursts, yelling and screaming or withdrawing. This will become a painful toxic block that just gets worse because unresolved issues lead to consistent behaviors that become harder and harder to break out of.

These negative patterns cause the physical experience of pain and over time they have the ability to make us physically and mentally sick.

In studies, women require more morphine than men to reach the same level of pain reduction. Women feel pain quicker but can endure it longer. Men don't feel pain as intensely or quickly but can't endure as long as women. Women are also more likely to vocalize their pain and to seek treatment for their pain than are men.[8]

The body has natural pain relief which are chemicals called endorphins and enkephalins that are produced by the thalamus and pituitary gland in the brain during stress and pain.[9] These substances also get produced in exercise, sexual activity and even in arguing or talking through problems. They act like opiates in the brain and help us control pain. However, their effectiveness is reduced the more toxic or traumatised we become.

There are nerve endings throughout the brain and body that have receptors (doorways) that receive these natural opiates. These opiates dampen the emotional and physical pain and allow us to get through difficult moments and situations filled with extreme physical or emotional pain.

BRAINY TIP

Ladies and gents, both emotional and physical pain are felt in the same region of the brain. Talking through conflict in a loving way helps reduce pain and minimize damage. Don't turn your words into weapons—they can be much more destructive than sticks or stones.

God has designed you with special abilities to cope with extreme circumstances, but you weren't created to live in a state of constant trauma and crisis. You were wired for love.

CHAPTER 14

Here Come the Hormones!

"Wow . . . you're just a ball of raging hormones!"

At certain moments in life, this statement would seem to equally describe both men and women.

And once again, the differences between the influence and regulation of hormones between men and women stems from the unique characteristics of their brains.

If you understand how these hormones work they can be a powerful force that deepen connections and create wonderful balance in a relationship. But when you don't realize how they work their damaging, toxic impact can be destructive.

Your endocrine system controls the flow of hormones into your bloodstream. These hormones influence all kinds of things in your body including mood, metabolism and tissue function.

The hypothalamus is the part of the brain responsible for controlling and directing the endocrine system.[1]

It sends out various types of chemical messengers to the endocrine system in response to stimulation. Stimulation can come either from a thought or a memory or it can be from an external source experienced through your five senses.

In this way, the hypothalamus regulates and responds to both the environment of your thought life and your body through your five senses.

The hypothalamus is a regulator of major things like attitude, appetite and sex—and while physically it's bigger in a male, it develops earlier in the female. This is one of the reasons girls mature more quickly than boys and it could also be one of the reasons why men on average tend to be more emotionally calm than women.[2]

According to a McGill University study, the male brain produces 52 percent more serotonin than the female brain.[3] Serotonin is a mood-influencing chemical, and its strong presence in men may explain why fewer men than women suffer from depression and why men often seem to be more easygoing and laid back than women.

FAST FACT

Gents, your regulator is bigger and you have 52 percent more serotonin than women. This is one of the reasons you are, on average, more easygoing and calmer than women and can calm down quicker than a lady.

Gents, you can also be good at calming your lady down once you are calm. Believe it or not, men tend to get a better attitude quicker than women—while the intensity of their emotions may be as strong or stronger, men tend to be able to calm down more quickly than women.

This may not have been what you have heard or read before, but this is the case when they are operating in a positive love state because it's in their design.

Men can use this physical design distinctive to their advantage through helping their loved ones work through their feelings clearly to regulate their emotions. While they are not as fluent as females in describing emotion, their analytical approach helps to quickly sort through the issue to a bottom line result.

Females have approximately 11-13 percent more linguistic neurons, bigger interpersonal and intrapersonal areas and two very active

X-chromosomes in each cell, which in general give them an increased ability to describe in detail the nature and impact of their emotions.[4] This design allows them to help lead the males in their lives to process and articulate emotions they may have passed over.

Both designs can provide tremendous benefit to the other in a healthy environment, but when things get toxic and hurtful these distinctives can also create the feeling that the two parties are so different that they're ultimately incompatible.

The hypothalamus also secretes two important hormones—vasopressin and the great pleasurable bonding chemical oxytocin that creates powerful and lasting attachment.[5]

Vasopressin is found in larger quantities in the male hypothalamus because of the Y-chromosome, which increases the density of vasopressin-producing fibres in the males. Vasopressin keeps males very focused, almost aggressively so, and fixes that laser-like focus on the one they love and on solving problems.[6]

Oxytocin and vasopressin work together in the processing of social cues involved in recognizing friends and loved ones and forming shared memories through communication and experience. It's likely that oxytocin has an almost addictive effect, like "dopamine" another neurotransmitter which helps with focus, attention and alertness.[7]

These chemical combinations may explain why people feel a deep anguish when they're separated from loved ones. The science demonstrates that this is not just sentimental, but a chemical reality. God created us with a strong biological and chemical reward system that we experience in healthy, dynamic relationships.

BRAINY TIP

I believe one of the main reasons God gave man a bigger hypothalamus was to create a strong dependency between a man and a woman. Don't be threatened by the different expressions of emotions in your relationships—these hard-wired differences create a healthy balance.

When men get toxic they begin to over-regulate and exert un-healthy control. When females get toxic they get lost in their emotions and can't find the way to sort through the vast sea of feelings to make sound, quality decisions.

Men need help to avoid dominating the relationship and to consider a broader perspective. Women need help processing through the wide range of emotions to form wise choices and decisions based on that information.

While both can manage on their own they're greatly improved by the influence of the other.

Another important difference between how the hypothalamus functions in men and women relates to its cooperation with the amygdala. (Please see the appendix in the back of the book for image illustration.) The amygdala is like a library holding perceptions of memories.

Let's say one of the kids misbehaves at school and the principal calls the father, can't reach him and leaves a message. The principal then calls the mother and notifies her of the issue.

The woman needs to talk it through a few times because she gets so involved in all the emotions, the nuances and the extraneous issues. The husband on the other hand sees the basic facts from the voicemail. He identifies the problem, thinks of a solution and it's over.

When Mom and Dad finally talk to each other about it, the woman wants to work it through, evaluate their response and then carefully consider all of the shockwaves. The husband's ready to go because he feels like it's been resolved. He can easily grow weary of the process if he fails to anticipate his wife's need to work through all the potential ripple effects of their decision.

This scenario doesn't just apply to Moms and Dads. The process would be similar in the workplace if the boss suddenly delivered an urgent deadline or in a classroom if a student received an emergency phone call or text reporting that a loved one had been critically injured.

In all these situations the female will need to talk it through a few times because she's immediately working through all of the emotions and their potential rippling effects. A man on the other hand grasps the basic facts, identifies the problem and comes up with a solution which finishes the process.

He's ready to move on but she's not ready yet—she still wants to work it through.

BRAINY TIP

Gents, there are times this ripple can turn into a tsunami if she is operating from toxicity in her thought networks. It's almost as though to get closure on an issue the woman has to read all the pages in the book before she can put the book away; the man scans the book, and then puts the book down quickly.

However, both the man and the woman can get toxic by either refusing to read the book (deal with the issue) or the opposite; they don't put the book down—instead they bring it with them everywhere they go (won't let go of the issue).

Ladies, when you get toxic and worked up, this is the time to get the regulating help from your husband's hypothalamus. You just may have to help him along by being as clear as you can that you need help (you are good at using words even when you are worked up). And you may need to trust your husband when he tells you you're headed down a toxic road—he knows you!

Gents, when your loved one is having an emotional explosion, stay calm (because you can) and just listen offering calm, laser-focused words with plenty of eye-contact and lots of hugs. This will release oxytocin which will have potential rewarding results—especially when you hug for longer than 20 seconds! Once she is reasonable again, help her walk through the issue.

Ladies, if he gets too controlling or rushes you through too fast, use your superb linguistic and emotional skills to weave balance back in again.

FAST FACT

Her hypothalamus can quickly aggravate the argument if she turns toxic (negative). Her emotions will begin to boil up and affect her attitude, which will short circuit her integration between reasoning and emotion (function of the insula) affecting her verbal centers and a barrage of words will hit her gent.

This will affect her verbal centers and cause her to unload a flurry of words on her gent who ends up dazed and confused as she drags up twenty other issues from her thought networks.

However, if she keeps those emotions in check serotonin and oxytocin will start flowing and she will calm down.

BRAINY TIP

Gents, you can help her keep her emotions under control because of your larger hypothalamus. Ladies, just having an awareness of how this process works can help you know when you're starting down a toxic road.

Gents, if you don't stay in check, your hypothalamus, pituitary and adrenal glands (known as the HPA axis) will kick into high gear secreting too much of the hormones CRF and ACTH. These hormones will enrage the amygdala and "the beast" within will emerge.

And at that point, nothing good's going to happen in the relationship. The key to preventing these moments is to identify the first few steps down the unhealthy, toxic road.

CHAPTER 15

Memories: The Mental Baggage of Communication

Memories don't come from scrapbooks and photo albums—they're hardwired into our brains. They stay with us. They follow us everywhere we go—into our internal thought life, our relationships and all our communication.

They don't have wheels and we can't put our clothes in them—but they function just like baggage.

A memory is a thought—in fact the two are interchangeable—and the ability to access thoughts is evidence that information is physically stored in our minds. This is because thoughts/memories, aren't immaterial—they're physically present in the brain and occupy "mental" real estate.[1]

When we remember an event the nerve network where the original memory/thought is stored is activated and switched from the subconscious mind to the conscious mind. It's not just an image or a series of facts that are activated—our memories bring with them all of the original emotions and perceptions from the experience. That's why memories can be so powerful—when we dwell on them it's like we're living the moment over again and when we think, we feel.

BRAINY TIP

Ladies and gents, if you can clean up your thoughts you'll trans-
form your communication.

You think a thought before you communicate it. In fact the
communication was *first* a thought. That's why it's so important
to cultivate healthy thoughts. Healthy thoughts lead to healthy
communication; toxic thoughts lead to toxic communication.

Our thoughts are our memories—from birth to the age that we
are at today—so we have trillions of different experiences stored in
the thought networks of our subconscious minds that can shape every
thought we have.[2]

We come into communication with all our baggage, both good
and bad.

FAST FACT

Ladies and gents our recall of the past is often selective. When we
operate from bad habits (toxic thoughts) we tend to dwell on mis-
takes, pain and traumatic events from our past, which strengthen
and reinforce these toxic memories and thoughts. The presence
and influence of these toxic thoughts poison our communication
and they cause electrical chemical chaos in the brain.

BRAINY TIP

The thoughts and memories we choose to keep are critical. Stuffing memories doesn't heal our pain anymore than stuffing photographs out of sight in a drawer gets them out of our house.

God's given you the ability to choose the thoughts and memories you dwell on. When you think of how influential this is, it's as
if you have the ability to be your own neuroplastician or "mind
surgeon." Healing, forgiveness, Bible study and memorization
aren't just good "spiritual" disciplines—they can physically rewire your brain.

It's time to repack your baggage. Think hard before you hold on to that toxic thought. Watch how you think and speak about yourself and others. What words and emotions dominate your conversations with co-workers, friends and loved ones?

Thoughts (and the emotions attached to them) are the main ingredients you use to build the communication that shapes all of your relationships; so throw out the rotten ones. Find the fresh, life-giving experiences and keep them close to you.

You can do this . . . and you can start right now.

Thoughts are stored across the whole brain in branches called *dendrites*. These branches are linked together to form increasingly complex scaffolds or thought-network webs. Each element of the memory (thought)—the sights, sounds, smell, taste, actions and emotions—is encoded.

Memory involves a wide range of facets and functions, which include deeply rooted events from the past, factual information and statistics, and even things learned in the past few moments. Different areas throughout the brain are utilized to accomplish this and because of the variation in size between males and females, the resultant architecture of each person's memory building process is unique.

On average, women tend to remember details better than men. This is probably because of the different ways the two sexes organize memories. Men use the part of the brain responsible for the action of an event (the right side of the amygdala) while women use the part of the brain responsible for emotional reactions (the left side of the amygdala). [3] As you might expect, the unique design of the brain guides the way memories are stored.

However, memory is a complex process involving various structures and circuits, so for a more in-depth discussion of memory formation in both men and women, I refer you to my book *Who Switched Off My Brain? Controlling toxic thoughts and emotions. The Revised Edition.*[4]

Here's a quick overview.

The thalamus (relay station, deep in the middle of the brain) maintains activity in the brain regarding attention so the more intense our focus the better our attention and the stronger the memory. The frontal lobe (front of the brain) helps keep our attention locked in and reduces distractions; the amygdala (small almond-shaped structure deep in the middle of the brain under the temporal lobe) keeps an emotional experience alive by replaying it in a loop which helps to build the memory.

At the same time the emotional stimulation from the thought is processed along an unconscious pathway that leads to the amygdala. This produces an emotional response at the "just-aware" level; the more input we receive from the senses, the stronger the memory. In the process of building thoughts information passes through the hippocampus—a tube-like structure (looks a bit like a seahorse and is deep in your brain almost directly behind your eyes) embedded within the temporal lobes.

Experiences constantly flow through the hippocampus, some are built into thoughts and some just pass through. You control this process. It is involved in receiving information and converting it from short-term memory to long-term memory (thoughts). The main functions of the hippocampus are spatial awareness, memory formation and recall.

The hippocampus works very closely with the amygdala—this small, almond-shaped part of your brain works like a library keeping "books" that contain all the emotional information about our memories. The amygdala literally "advises" the hippocampus as to which thoughts (memories) need to be built into the thought networks in the outer part of the brain called the cortex.

For about ten minutes mental notes are made which involves circuits or memory loops between what we see and hear and the front of our brains. And then over a period of approximately 21 days the memory is consolidated from the hippocampus into the cortex. Then whatever you think about the most becomes more and more integrated into the scaffolds of the mind.

Experts show it takes up to ten years or 10,000 hours of passionately and persistently using the memory to reach a level of expertise.[5] This applies to both positive and negative memories—developing the skill required to be a great surgeon or piano player or a really bad habit like gossiping, lying or manipulating others for your own personal gain.

It can be frightening to realize that the emotional passion and energy we put into building negative toxic patterns follow us into our future. Those toxic habits we develop as an 18-year-old walk down the aisle with us and keep creating challenges in our relationships ten years later as a 28-year-old. But, these can be changed.

That's why it's so important that we recognize our toxic thoughts and patterns so we can create a healthy future—both for today AND our future.

FAST FACT

In both men and women, communication patterns can be established over a period of 21 days and then are raised to expertise level over a period of 2 years and longer through consistent use. [8]

This means we have the ability to form the nature of our communication through continuous use in the initial window of 21 days and then get expertise over the next two years. After a period of about ten years we reach a level of high expertise.

So within those first 21 days you build a memory pattern that formulates mental baggage you'll carry with you wherever you go. Your thoughts *really* matter. If they're good, this becomes a wonderful benefit. If your thoughts are bad, they poison all of your relationships for years if not dealt with.

When you keep the pattern for longer than two years you are on the way to becoming an expert in those toxic thoughts and actions. The good news is that the way you build the toxic thought is the

FAST FACT *(continued)*

same way you reverse engineer it, so, you can get rid of the baggage. (For help in this process, see *Who Switched Off My Brain? Controlling toxic thoughts and emotions. The Revised Edition.*)

BRAINY TIP

As you watch and hear and feel yourself reacting to a situation or event (you use your front part of your brain to stand outside of yourself and do this), control your reaction by making the decision to stop, repent and rewire (renew your mind).

A lot of us have developed a "toxic tolerance"—we've repeatedly used the unhealthy patterns of thought networks and harmful memories for so long (a few months, 1-2 years and beyond) that we believe they're normal. We think that's just how we are. It's not true—God's given you the ability to change . . . to renew your mind.

If you consciously catch that unhealthy, toxic memory or thought in that initial ten-minute window, even the simple decision to change will start to weaken that negative pattern.

But you will have to work for 21 days to build in the new healthy thought network in place of the old toxic one. This work is the intentional process of strengthening and reinforcing the healthy thought.

As you do this, the healthy thought or memory will become your new normal. The rewiring cycle takes about 21 days, but the more consistant you are using the new good healthy memory, the easier it will become.

The old is gone after 21 days, and you have built the new, but this needs to be built into all the complex circuits. That way of reacting will have been linked into other memories, so the traces of the old patterns may be dragged up in certain situations. Don't let the reappearance of the thought/memory discourage you—its presence doesn't ensure its power—your mind is being renewed.

It takes time to work this process all the way through the networks it has pervaded.

The complexity of the intertwining of the webs and the intricacy of the links is enormous because they are not held in a single brain area—it is a distributed storage system. Because of this massive interconnectedness, renewing our minds isn't a one-time fix. It's a lifelong process that we commit to. We're constantly renewing our minds. After those first 21 days, as a toxic link reappears, it's much easier to rewire a healthy thought in its place.[6]

The hippocampus (the long tube our experiences pass through) in men and women differs significantly in its structure, its neurochemical make-up and its reactivity to stressful situations.

BRAINY TIP

Ladies, men are less likely to express feelings verbally to the same extent that you can. They are more inclined to respond physically to memory—they may walk away, throw something or pace back and forth.

Allow them to process in a way that's consistent with their design. If they don't work it out now, this experience will turn into baggage they'll carry with them.

When adjusted for total brain size, the hippocampus is larger in women than in men. The hippocampus also has stronger connections in women into the outer cortex and to the frontal lobe, which handles decision-making, reasoning, introspection, planning and analyzing.

In addition women's brains have all these highly active XX-chromosomes in the hippocampus which allow them to build more details into their thoughts (memories) and to accurately recall the intricate details of a memory. This is especially true when the memory in question was emotionally charged. The hippocampus communicates with the amygdala regarding which memories to lock into long-term memory. Because the hyppocampus is larger in the female they connect words and feelings to thoughts more powerfully than in men.[7]

BRAINY TIP

Gents, ladies connect words and feelings to thoughts in a very powerful way. This is why they remember in such detail and with such emotional clarity every significant interaction. She wasn't taking notes of all the things you said/did . . . it's just how she's wired!

Your memories don't have the same level of emotional detail, but you can quickly recall exactly how things ended. Allow her to process through all the details without feeling threatened or inadequate. If she doesn't deal with it now, this interaction will become another piece of luggage she'll bring up later.

Ladies, he has stronger connections to the spine and action centers of the brain and therefore is more action oriented. Don't get frustrated with him when he cannot remember all the same details and emotions that remain so clear to you. He's not being lazy or disinterested—he's not designed to capture your level of detail. If you judge him that way, he'll feel disrespected or attacked. Give him space and remind him gently.

Ladies, be patient with his practical memory.

Gents, be patient with her intense memory.

Neither of you should take these differences in memory (access to thoughts in the non-conscious mind) personally. It's how you've been designed.

CHAPTER 16

He Sorts By Title, She Sorts Alphabetically

Think about a library, filled with shelves upon shelves of books neatly organized in a specific order. You walk in and easily find the book you need by simply looking up the author's last name.

But what if the books weren't organized by the author's name?

What if they were organized by book title?

If you didn't know this, you could search for hours and never find the book you need. Frustrated, you might storm out of the library, saying something like, "This place is completely disorganized!"

But in reality, the library was absolutely organized. You just never realized that the system of organization was very different from the one you were trying to operate by. It sounds absurd that anyone would ever try to find a book in a library without first understanding the organizational system, but men and women do this to each other all the time!

You see, our brains have their own libraries that use emotion, details and big pictures to organize and categorize memories. Men and women so often get used to the way that their "libraries" are organized, that they expect their mate's library to work the same way. This leads to countless misunderstandings that could be avoided if we just took the time to realize that our "libraries" are organized differently.

To truly understand how this works, we need to talk more about the amygdala. I explained how this little almond-shaped part of the brain influences the "gear-shifter," assists with hormones and helps to fuel emotion in memories. But it also comes into play in sorting your "library" as well.

The amygdala, found deep in the limbic system (the set of brain structures designated to control emotion, behavior and long-term memory that includes the hippocampus, amygdala, anterior thalamic nuclei, septum and more), rests between the right and left hemispheres of the brain—a few inches from each ear. A primary function of the amygdala is to store the emotional perceptions linked to thoughts—an emotional "library."[1]

The amygdala is also involved in thought-building, and learning to approach or avoid things based on the emotional perceptions that have been formed in the process. In this way it plays a protective role. It coordinates the stress response focusing on keeping us in stage one of stress (the good stage) and avoiding getting into stage two and three of stress (the bad stages). [2]

The amygdala alerts the cortex (the outer part of the brain where all the thoughts are stored) to size up the emotional situation to determine how much attention it needs. If the cortex decides there is reason to pay attention when the emotional intensity is high enough, it cues the cortex to alert the conscious brain.

Here's how it works: As the master of emotional perception for both males and females, the amygdala's function is to prepare for the release of chemicals that help to create memories (thoughts) of emotional experiences. If the thought is toxic, neurochemical chaos takes over. If the memory is healthy, the chemical balance is healthy.

This example may seem extreme, but it demonstrates how this process works. If a young girl was repeatedly raped as a child, she may well have formed the toxic thought (with the emotional perception) that all men are bad. That may feel like a fact to her, but the truth is that not all men are bad. So sometimes the emotional reaction from the amygdala is based on incorrect perceptions that have become toxic. This can lead to bad choices, reactions and decisions that further perpetuate toxic thought networks and unhealthy patterns of communication.

BRAINY TIP

One of the coping mechanisms you can learn to develop in order to detoxify your brain is the conscious choice not to respond immediately to emotions that you feel strongly. If you wait to respond to intense, profound emotions you give yourself a much better opportunity to discern whether those emotions are toxic or not. That doesn't mean you ignore them. You recognize the emotion, take a deep breath, and then think about the consequences for the actions you're considering.

You can begin a process of learning to let it go, like a breeze through an open window. This is your frontal lobe working with your amygdala. This healthy way of dealing with emotions is an excellent tool to help you detoxify your brain.

In this process you'll discover that ladies are better at staying calm longer than men, but when they do have an emotional outbreak, it's a big one! So we can help each other. The worst thing either of you can do for your health is to deny, block or suppress emotions, whether they are good or bad. This makes them extremely toxic throwing the design of the male/female brain that was meant for good, into complete disarray.

The amygdala connects to a number of important brain centers (including the cortex and visual cortex), which allows it to further regulate emotion and emotional behaviors, but right now, we're mostly concerned with how the amygdala affects the different male and female emotional libraries.

The amygdala occupies a significantly greater percentage of a man's brain than a female's brain and behaves differently in the male and female brain both at rest and when active.[3]

The amygdala also operates differently in men and women, which appears to reflect the arrangement of the hemispheres of the brain. The right hemisphere of the human brain deals with the big picture to the detail, while the left side is concerned with detail to the big picture. The right and left sides of the amygdala appear to work with their respective hemispheres. One side is stronger in men, and the other is stronger in women. I bet you can guess which ones, too!

Women are stronger on the left side, meaning that they remember emotional experiences in a more detailed to big picture way. Their "library" organizes memories by emotional strength and detail to the big picture, meaning a woman is much more likely to remember something emotionally important than basic factual information.

Gents, however, are much stronger on the right side, which means they're not so hot with emotional details but are good with ordering the memory. They focus on the "big picture to the detail" in a practical way rather than specific emotional experiences.

This is why couples remember shared experiences differently. The wife might remember the song that played on their first date, the food they ate at the restaurant, all the specific details of their conversation, how she felt when the violinist played that special song just for them and when he bought her the red rose and looked into her eyes. The man will simply remember that he fell in love and had a great time with his future mate . . . and that the meal was pretty good too!

BRAINY TIP

Ladies, don't let his less detailed emotional memory of important events in your relationship upset you. It doesn't mean that he doesn't care. It just means that he processes these memories differently. Just because he can't remember what you wore on your first date doesn't mean the date didn't mean anything to him!

Basically, a man's emotional library is like the preview of a movie, while a woman's emotional memory is like a DVD with the full-length movie, deleted scenes, and documentaries about the making of the movie!

A region at the front of the brain called the orbito-frontal cortex is involved in regulating and controlling emotions. Coursing through the amygdala are nerves connecting it to this orbito-frontal cortex. These connecting circuits between the orbito-frontal cortex and amygdala are important in regulating emotion, emotional perceptions and in guiding emotion-related behaviors.[4]

So the orbito-frontal cortex acts a bit like a librarian controlling the library (the amygdala).

Women have a bigger orbito-frontal cortex and smaller amygdala; men have the opposite.

This may mean that women might on average prove more capable of controlling their emotional reactions, so they would take longer to lose their temper or get irritated for example. Once again, this is on average.

But it could also have the opposite effect that when her emotions get out of control, they will be harder to get back under control.

BRAINY TIP

Ladies, because of your larger orbito-frontal cortex, you take longer on average to get toxic and worked up than men and you can also calm down quicker. This means you can also calm your man down when he gets worked up because your "calming down librarian" is bigger. However, ladies, if your mind is very toxic and chaotic this won't work so well any more, and what was meant for good does the opposite.

Gents, your smaller orbito-frontal cortex is designed to keep you primed and focused on acting quickly and efficiently in a protective sense. So you can act—do something—to calm her down. However, when your mind becomes toxic, you may lose your temper quicker, and then your smaller orbito-frontal cortex loses its focus. God has designed us so that we need to take the focus off ourselves and help each other.

FAST FACT

Ladies and gents, this points to another area where you can begin to control your toxic thoughts. The emotion you feel from the amygdala is reactive and strong enough to control and even override any inherent negative elements that there may be in a thought, because there are more connections going from the amygdala to the cortex (the outer part of your brain where your thoughts are stored) than from the cortex to the amygdala.

This ensures that the amygdala is in balance with the cortex because the cortex is so much bigger. So when the amygdala is very active it communicates with the frontal lobe and the two work together to calm you down. If you don't, negative stress will be activated.

This is the warning in your body that your thinking has become toxic and the opposite will happen. I call this out-of-balance state a "discomfort zone."

But male and female emotional libraries don't just differ when it comes to "detail to big picture" vs. "big picture to detail."

You see, a man's amygdala has more connections to the brain areas that respond to the external environment, while the woman's amygdala has more connections to brain areas that respond to the internal (mental, emotional) environment.[5]

FAST FACT

The male amygdala is connected to the visual cortex (visual stimuli) and the striatum (coordinates motor actions). Women's amygdala respond more to the insular cortex (instinct) and the hypothalamus (regulator) and other structures in the limbic system (deep seated emotional part of the brain).

BRAINY TIP

Gents, this means a woman's amygdala is more easily activated by emotional nuance. The stronger the emotional impact, the stronger the thought/memory that she builds. The female's memory circuits in the amygdala are wired for deeper emotional perceptual secrets than a man's memory circuits.

This makes a man more action-oriented and practical. This is why men are more alert to danger and concerned with protecting the people and things close to them. As a result, men often exhibit the strongest emotional responses when they feel threatened.

In a man, the more connections to the environment explains why he is always more alert to danger and on the lookout to protect, cover and do something actively about situations.

Ladies, this practical, externally-focused side of your man also explains why he tries to fix things by doing. When you have an argument and he tries to buy you flowers or fix something around the house instead of talking through it, he's not trying to avoid the problem. He's actually trying to fix it in the way that best makes sense to him.

The "doing" releases emotional energy and helps him focus. His amygdala is practical, most of the time. However, his brain circuits in the amygdala are not wired to retain information in the detailed and emotional way that a woman's is.

CHAPTER 17

She Enjoys "Multi-Tasking," He Prefers "Single-Tasking"

I'm guessing these two scenarios will sound familiar.

A woman goes to a store. While she is planning to purchase one thing in particular, she can't help but notice all the shops she encounters along the way to her original destination.

Suddenly, she feels extremely motivated to branch out and explore beyond her pre-planned purchase. Moving from shop to shop, she finds all kinds of things that she and her family want or need.

After numerous purchases, she makes her way to the store she originally planned to go to, buys what she originally planned to buy, and goes home after five, nine or fifteen hours of shopping with multiple bags on each arm!

A man goes to a store. He proceeds directly to his original destination, finds what he was looking for, buys it and returns home.

Just the length of these two descriptions tells you something about the differences between men and women!

For women, shopping is an experience that can last hours, but for men, it's a single task with a clear goal. I see these gender differences when I take Mac shopping with me. While I find various things to look at and shop for that I hadn't expected or had on a list, Mac has no desire to browse or explore for new items. He'd much rather find a place to sit and read the news and sports results on his phone.

Women enjoy shopping for all kinds of things in many different stores all in one trip because they're great at multi-tasking. Men, on the other hand, get the initial job done much faster because they are better at what we'll just call compartmentalized "single-tasking."

The usual pitfall here is for women to start blaming men for not being flexible enough and for men to start blaming women for being too easily distracted. But, as I'm sure you can guess already, these different traits actually complement each other wonderfully.

The way we "multi-task" (cross-talk) and "single-task" (focus-talk) stems in part from a section of the brain called the "corpus callosum." The corpus callosum is a thumb-sized structure that connects the two sides of the brain and helps them to work together while thinking. It integrates our thoughts. With approximately 300 million nerve fibers passing through it, the corpus callosum makes lightning-fast communication between the two sides of the brain possible. The corpus callosum is the major communication tract between the two brain hemispheres.

The corpus callosum is larger in women and smaller in men.[1] The corpus callosum also has a different shape in men and women. The shape and size of this part of the brain has a lot to do with the way we integrate and work through our tasks.

Ladies you have a larger, more bulbous-shaped corpus callosum, specifically the back part called the "splenium." Ladies you also have moderately dense tracts crossing in both directions from the left to the right side of the brain and from the right to the left side. This allows a greater degree of flexibility in thinking and integrating.

Gents, your corpus callosum is smaller, and more C-shaped. You have more fiber tracts communicating from the right to the left; but less dense tracts in the opposite direction. This means you have more asymmetry in your brain function leading to a more compartmentalized "single-tasking" approach when you think to build thoughts.

But what does this all really mean?

The C-shape allows men to be more focused, goal-oriented and "single-task" driven. The bulbous shape makes females better at multi-tasking. Men can do many different tasks but in a compartmentalized way; women multi-task in an open-ended way. This open-ended multi-tasking in women is enhanced at different stages of her cycle.[2]

Put simply, male thinking is focused and convergent; female thinking is more multi-tasked and divergent. Females can do more than one thing at a time and can have many open-ended things happening at the same time. Men do a lot of "single-tasks" meaning they will do a lot of things, but it will be open, close, open, close, open and close in a targeted, very focused way.

The fiber-density between the hemispheres also plays an important role in the differences in thinking between males and females. Recent research has discovered that the bilaterally dense fibers (from both the left to right side and right to left sides in the brain) in a woman's corpus callosum allow increased and quicker communication between the hemispheres of the brain. So a woman's brain is more bilateral enabling her to listen to, comprehend, and process up to seven auditory inputs at the same time.[3]

A man on the other hand, with his asymmetrical arrangement of fibers—the denser fibers moving from the right to the left (but less dense from left to right) will allow him to focus on each task separately and intensely.

BRAINY TIP

On a practical level, ladies when you tell your husband or male colleague seven things at once that you are happily and comfortably processing, don't be surprised when these gents react by saying "Slow down!" . . . or . . . "Tell me one-thing-at-a-time!"

That's why a woman can clean the kitchen, talk to her husband, help a child with homework and send an email all at the same time, while many men can't send an e-mail and have a conversation at the same time! He does many things with his bigger brain but one at a time. Her busy brain thinks better with multiple tasks happening at once.

So a woman's brain is busier than a man's, but gents, your asymmetry of the fibers in your corpus callosum and your bigger brain give you the ability to "single-task" which serves you very well. With your asymmetry of nerve fibers (thicker from right side of the brain to the left side of the brain), you tend to operate on one activity to whatever level of completion, then you put it aside to work on the next activity.

As we've already said, this inhibits you from doing a lot of things at once, but it means that whatever "single-task" you are working on, you are uniquely designed to do it very well.

BRAINY TIP

Ladies, because your man is goal-oriented, it's important not to interrupt his train of thought while he is talking. The design of his corpus callosum is prompting him to focus on the end goal.

So while women can on average do a lot at once, men tend on average to do what they do much quicker.

Now both of those qualities are essential for intelligent thinking. Single and multi-tasking are both critically important. So, if a male and female work together on a task, you get the best of both worlds. Each skill—multi-tasking and "single-tasking"—on their own are like the two halves of the brain separated. But together, multi-tasking and "single-tasking," creates the ideal situation.

CHAPTER 18

Emotions: He Stops, Thinks and Buries, She Never Stops

In earlier sections of this book I explained how words are expressions of thoughts. Thoughts are physical structures that are actual branches on the nerve cells in your brain, so they occupy "mental real estate."[1]

There are various chemicals and electrical-chemical reactions involved in creating thoughts. Scientists call these chemicals "molecules of emotion" because they literally represent our emotions.[2] Every thought that forms already has emotions wound into it. Thoughts are emotionally charged.

FAST FACT

Your mind is what your brain does. At a scientific level your emotions, the choices you make, the words you speak, and the actions you perform all start in the vast emotionally-laden thought-network you have creatively wired in your brain through chemical and electro-magnetic impulses.

When we think (we're always thinking consciously and subconsciously), the intertwined emotions are activated through these thought networks of the brain, which help us literally "feel" the memory. As you think you feel.

So you see, we can't talk about how men and women think differently without talking about emotion, because emotions are involved in the creation of thoughts, which trigger further emotion, which trigger further thoughts . . . you get the picture. The two are absolutely intertwined.

Every thought . . . every memory . . . is connected to emotion.

For men, emotions are compartmentalized and dealt with related to each event. The physical location of logic and spatial solutions in the brain are close to the emotional components but they function separately. This allows them to shelve emotional issues and explains why studies show that men are slower on the uptake when it comes to processing and reacting to emotions. They are able to separate events in their minds providing a different perspective on an issue.

However, for women, emotion activates all kinds of different areas of the brain: women have greater activity in both sides of the brain and in the amygdala than men.[3] Women definitely use more of their brains for emotional processing than men. This provides the other side of the perspective on an issue.

For women, emotions all meld together—emotions from different events will spill over into each other. So one event will affect the next. For men, less of the brain is lit up by emotions. Emotions are dealt with one at a time, meaning that emotions from different events will very rarely overflow into each other.

BRAINY TIP

Gents, you can talk about a negative emotional experience—work through it and then carry on the rest of your day without being affected by that negative set of emotions.

Ladies, it's harder for you to work through your emotions as quickly. If you're not careful and fail to process through the emotions you bring up, those negative experiences may color all your choices, thoughts, words and actions for the rest of the day.

FAST FACT

A woman can become genuinely emotional simply by re-telling an emotional story or event that didn't even happen to her! It doesn't take much for those parts of her brain to start firing.

So, men and women use fundamentally different emotional circuitry. Men have single focus emotion and women have multi-focus emotion.[4]

BRAINY TIP

Gents, ladies produce and recall memories more quickly with greater emotional intensity and vividness—this is why they re-member a recent argument or event in more detail. Don't take it as a personal challenge or attack—it's how she's wired!

As a result, men operate in a "stop and think" emotional pattern. God has designed men with a more action-oriented emotional system, which allows them to work through their emotions internally and then express themselves through goal-setting and action.

While this ability allows them to stop and carefully work through the issue, it also gives them a greater capacity to stop. Men have the necessary emotional wiring to stop in the middle and set a complex bundle of emotions on the shelf.

The negative side of this is that men will often bottle up their emo-tions and never work through them, which ultimately ends up creat-ing toxic patterns. Sooner or later an emotionally toxic man will lash out because he hasn't properly processed his emotions. This is because emotions are alive and living and need to be dealt with in some way—either in physical health, words and/or actions.

BRAINY TIP

Ladies, you need to help your gent express his emotions by creating a safe, loving and accepting environment to work through his issues. He needs you to encourage him to do so without feeling accused or disrespected because bottled emotions are not good for his health.

Women, instead of stopping and thinking about emotions, process them on the go, building one on top of the other. God has designed women on average to perceive, experience and remember emotional events more intensely. This means emotional attachments and verbalisations will play a strong role in their decision-making.

However, it also means that a woman can get too caught up in emotions, spiralling into a never-ending cycle of over-analysis and anxiety. This makes peaceful rest very difficult—physically and emotionally. In a particularly bad emotional spiral, not only is it difficult for a woman to calm down the thoughts in her head, but her health and sleep will be affected.

While lack of processing creates toxicity in men, over-processing can lead to toxicity in women. A woman can talk herself into an emotionally toxic black hole.

BRAINY TIP

Gents, if you feel like your lady is too emotional, remember that this is how she is wired. Getting rid of her emotions should not be the goal—instead, help her learn how to process through them in a healthy way. Help her get "unstuck." Listen and re-direct her back to healthy thoughts/emotions when necessary. When you do this, she'll be more peaceful and relaxed and your relationship will improve.

Our opposite negative emotional tendencies can create so many problems, which is why it's important for ladies and gents to watch their thoughts and process them before acting on them. When you take time to think before speaking, you are far more likely to speak in an encouraging way to your mate or son or daughter or work colleague.

FAST FACT

Both males and females have a brilliant frontal lobe (the front part of your brain) that God designed to allow us to stand outside of ourselves and observe our own thoughts, words, actions and behaviors in real time—and to control them. This is a wonderful part of the epigenetics that we discussed in Chapters Four and Five.

Gents and ladies, always stop and ask yourself these types of questions:

· What is my attitude right now?
· Am I operating in a toxic or healthy thought?
· Have I read too much into the situation?
· Is it possible that I'm creating drama and conflict in a relationship that really isn't there?
· Am I assuming attitudes and motives in other people that I have no way of actually knowing?
· What baggage have I dragged up from my subconscious to deal with this situation?

The best way to work through these kinds of questions is in a safe and trust-filled environment. I believe the lack of this kind of interaction creates so many challenges and an incredible amount of stress that could be avoided if we would stop and take the time to process our emotions in a healthy way. And a big part of this is taking the time to stop and consider the perspective of the opposite sex—it all comes down to a willingness to be less selfish and more aware of others. If we don't , things get lost in translation.

Understand that while you cannot always control events or circumstances, you can always control your reaction.

And don't forget the power of God's Word. It always helps to grab onto a Scripture that you can remember in emotionally intense situations. My personal favorite is Proverbs 3:5-6 *Trust in the Lord with all your heart and lean not on your own understanding; in all your ways acknowledge Him and He shall direct your paths.*

When those heated moments occur in marriages and relationships, it's the truth and power of God that will ultimately see you through. As we continue to dive deeper into how men and women respond to and out of emotion, let's remember that while we are made to complement each other, we are only truly complete when we live in God's truth.

CHAPTER 19

Stress:
He Needs His Space, She Needs to Talk It Through

Ninety percent of people in prison are men.

Ninety percent of people seeing therapists are women.

While at first glance these statistics might not seem connected, they are in fact closely related. At their core they both stem from an inability to handle one powerful and specific emotional reaction to toxic thinking: stress.

Consistently internalizing stress for men and women doesn't end well, because emotions have to be worked through or eventually they'll explode in a volcanic manner somewhere down the line.[1]

When the weight of stress and pressure becomes toxic and unhealthy, women will talk without thinking and men will act without thinking. I'm sure you can see how these two differ, but equally destructive results could drive men to prison and women to therapy.

I'm not equating therapy with prison—I realize prison has purely negative connotations while therapy can make very positive contributions to one's overall health—my point is stress can make a tremendous impact on the lives of both men and women.

I mentioned in the last chapter that we can't always control our circumstances, but we can control our reactions. If we can learn to help each other control how we react to stress, which is itself a reaction to toxic thinking, we'll go a long way towards bridging the gender gap.

Studies show that stress affects certain areas of the brain in completely opposite ways in men and women.[2] Under stress, men tend to withdraw socially while women seek emotional support. Men respond with "fight-or-flight" and women with "tend-and-befriend."[3]

FAST FACT

Because the "tend-and-befriend" regulatory system may protect women against stress in some ways, this pattern may provide insights into why women live an average of seven and a half years longer than men.

Let me explain what I mean, starting with the gents.

Gents, stress affects the regions of our brains associated with empathy. In your case, it causes decreased activity, which results in less empathy.[4]

Your decreased ability to process the emotions of other people means that your natural reaction will be to seek solitude to deal with your stress. You will try and work things out in your own mind until you're ready to talk about it.

FAST FACT

Ladies, a gent reacts to stress by "talking inside his head." He temporarily becomes Rodin's famous sculpture: "The Thinker." He uses his large parietal lobe to reason inside his great spatial networks, like an internal compass, and then he uses his right amygdala, which is more attuned to the outside world and has

FAST FACT *(continued)*
more connections to the visual cortex and sight and movement
areas in the brain.

BRAINY TIP

Ladies, don't be offended when the men in your life withdraw
emotionally when they're stressed out. They're not punishing
you—it's how they're wired. This is why so many men like to play
golf, go to the gym, go for a drive or flip channels. It helps them
unwind. Pressing him to talk through his feelings by repeatedly
asking, "What's wrong?" will only stress him more.

Ladies, you respond to stress in the exact opposite way. Stress causes an increase in activity in the regions of your brain that deal with empathy and emotional understanding. This leads you to protect, nurture and seek the emotional support of others when you're under stress.

This helps release oxytocin which is a bonding chemical which will help calm you down. This is true of both big pressures and little ones. This same urge motivates you to talk through problems on the phone with a variety of family and friends and to ask a stranger for directions when you're lost.

In other words ladies—you move towards people.

BRAINY TIP

Gents, this is why your lady likes to talk to you when she's stressed—
she needs help processing all the emotions that are bubbling on
the inside because of the increased stress levels. It also explains
why she'll take an unusual interest in helping others with their
problems when she's feeling pressured.

This may lead you to talking to and cuddling with your man a lot, or talking to your girlfriends. If you're a mother, you might relieve stress by tending to your children. Anytime you're stressed, your impulse will probably be to seek out others.

Personally, I love to take my children and dogs on a walk sharing our day and laughing. I also like to talk things through with Mac, but I have learned to wait until he is ready to speak and not invade his space. I have also learned that once I have spoken about something that has upset me, or that is on my mind, he likes to think of ways to solve the issues I have raised. Men like to do things. They like action. They like closure.

Now, solitude helps the gents, and interaction with others helps the ladies, but the very things that help us cope with stress can unfortunately cause very negative reactions. When both genders respond incorrectly to stress, it leads to toxic thoughts and patterns.

It's when these negative reactions take hold that we most need each other, but before we can help each other, we need to first understand the pitfalls that the opposite gender faces. We also need to make a mental note that negative reactions to stress make you sick because the brain and body are linked. Stress is the manifestation of toxic thoughts.

Ladies, time alone can really help a man de-stress as he works things out within his own mind. If this process is repeatedly interrupted, then he'll never finish working through his stress, which will lead to toxic thoughts and reactions. In order to prevent this, learn to give him his own space. If you try to make him talk about things before he's ready, it will only stress him out more.

His silent and stoic response to stress is a guy thing. Don't think he doesn't love you or that he's angry with you—it's just his way. If he's working things through with God it's fine, but if he is really just suppressing his emotions, he's in trouble.

FAST FACT

He responds to stress by withdrawing—where he either deals with the stress in his mind by compartmentalizing to find solutions (positive) which will release oxytocin or he may suppress any thinking about it (negative). He may also react aggressively with angry words (negative) or strategically with insightful words and quick solutions (positive).

So give him his space, but don't be afraid to help him process when the time comes. Wait for a signal to help him. When it looks like he's ready to talk, gently try to find out what's bothering him and how he's dealing with it.

Your empathy and communication skills and great connections to the language and reasoning centers of the brain are gifts from God that He's given you to help your husband or son or male work colleague or friend. Don't be afraid to use them.

FAST FACT

Essentially, under stress a man's brain moves into logic and spatial problem-solving. If they are working this through with God that is fine, but if they are suppressing, this is dangerous.

Now gents—it's important to know that while your lady's empathetic and emotional ways are strengths, if over-used they can leave her in a constant cycle of stress.

BRAINY TIP

Gents, be aware that the estrogen-progesterone surges that come in repeated monthly cycles from the ovaries also mean that the ladies' brain circuits are more sensitive to emotional nuance such as approval and disapproval, acceptance and rejection. But keep this information to yourself—she won't appreciate it when you blame her increased emotions on her cycle!

A woman responds to stress by talking and talking and talking to anyone who will listen. She can do this for hours with her friends and loved ones, going into all the intricate details and emotions. Of course a certain amount of talking is good, but there's a difference between processing and obsession. When your lady becomes obsessed with the stressful issue, she's just rehearsing it over and over, giving power to toxic thoughts and patterns. The talking needs to be moving in a positive direction if it's ever going to provide closure.[5]

Gents, this is where you step in. Make sure you give her space in the conversation. Let her get everything out. It may seem unstructured to you, but it really does help. Your natural instinct will be to tell her to slow down and take each problem one at a time to find a logical solution. This is great . . . but wait until she asks for your help. Until then, just show her that you are listening and sympathizing.

BRAINY TIP

Gents, you will instantly want to fix everything. Remember her wiring and let her talk her way through until she feels like she's worked through all sides of the issue. Be patient and then when she's ready, offer your valuable input.

When she reaches out to you for help, you can then guide her to a practical solution, ensuring that all her talking ends on a positive, constructive note.

BRAINY TIP

Gents, even if the issue seems solved to you, she may feel the need to bring it up again and analyze it a little more. This is normal. Once you've come to a conclusion, lovingly affirm that you've done the necessary processing and reassure her that everything's going to be okay.

Ladies, trust your man and the healthy process. After you've talked it through and come to a decision, don't keep revisiting the issue and second-guessing yourselves.

We see this difference with our sons and daughters as well where the daughters will come home from school and pour out their hearts in detail about why they feel stressed. The boys on average will answer your questions with a simple "Yes" or "No," and if things are really bad you'll only get a grunt or a sigh.

BRAINY TIP

Males are programmed to do things, so ladies, to get your sons, brothers or husbands to talk do something with them. Play a game, play with the dog together or go to the gym. While "doing" something, allow the conversation to develop naturally during the activity and you'll be surprised to watch the flood of words and the healthy management of the stress take place.

FAST FACT

A woman's highly responsive stress trigger is designed for empathy but when distorted through toxic thinking, it causes her to become anxious more quickly than a man. Anxiety can very quickly lead into depression if not managed. In fact research shows that women have twice the rate of depression and anxiety disorders compared to men.[6]

Knowing that women respond to stress by increasing activity in brain regions involved with emotion (and that these changes last longer than in men and are more pervasive) may help us begin to explain the gender differences in the incidence of mood disorders. Neuroscientists are finding that this is the case across cultures.[7]

For a woman a display of emotion is a form of communication. To a man this display of emotion makes him feel uneasy and often responsible to fix the situation. Eventually he'll feel frustrated or a measure of failure if he can't seem to calm the woman down. If he's really frustrated or stressed himself, he may get angry and tell her to stop. While that seems like a solution to him, the woman interprets this anger very negatively and likely will get even more upset. This spiral can continue and end in all kinds of unpleasant ways—he may storm off, get scared or yell louder.

God has built certain systems into the design of the brain to help us cope with stress, which become activated when we help each other. For example, when the hormone oxytocin is released in both men and women it makes us less anxious and more social. There is also a set of genes in the hippocampus of the brain that allows us to manage stress. The hormone estrogen (which is found in small quantities in men as well), also tends to enhance oxytocin resulting in a calming and nurturing feeling.[8]

We are clearly designed to help each other deal with stress. Great things happen in the brain when we reach out and help each other.

If gents and ladies respect each other's different designs but also play an active role in reaching out to each other, there's no stressful issue that can't be conquered. This approach will avoid conflict and models the servanthood that Jesus calls us to—putting each other before ourselves.

CHAPTER 20

The Rest State: He Thinks She's Babbling and She Sees "The Hibernate Look"

The brain is always busy—it doesn't turn off, but it does rest.

Neuroimaging studies show that areas of the brain light up during actively engaged tasks, other areas show a deactivation pattern, an organized rest state. In this rest state the brain is rejuvenating and preparing for the next stream of conscious processing.[1]

It's interesting to note that the male brain moves into a rest state to rejuvenate much more frequently than its female counterpart.[2] Remember . . . this doesn't mean he's switched his brain "off." His brain just needs a different type of rest and this "rest" is accomplished differently in men and women.

BRAINY TIP

Ladies, when men withdraw into their rest state they become more introverted; he's not ignoring you or being mean, he's trying to relax. He "reboots" through withdrawl.

Gents, when a women enters her rest state she's likely to be more talkative and extroverted; she's not trying to bother you, it's how she enjoys herself and gets refreshed. She "reboots" through interaction.

To sort out all the thought networks he has been building all day, a man needs to retreat, stand back and process the day and rejuvenate himself. To sort out all the thought networks she has been building all day, a woman needs to talk a lot with emotion to process the day and rejuvenate herself.

The male brain is designed to go into rest states in which it renews, recharges, and reorients itself. Females do this without going to sleep.

BRAINY TIP

Believe it or not gents, one of the ways your ladies go into a rest state is through shopping. Mac calls it RT time—retail therapy! For most ladies, shopping is like talking—it's fun, relaxing and rejuvenating especially when it has no agenda or time limit.

And ladies you can put him at ease by enjoying the process instead of feeling like you have to spend money on another pair of shoes or outfit in order to relax and have fun.

Both men and women build and receive information at an incredible pace during the day. Men especially have the ability to take in and process information throughout the day, opening and closing cycles of thought in an incredibly fast and efficient way.

But at the end of the day all of this information needs to be processed and reintegrated in order to be turned into wisdom that can be practically applied. It's a complex sorting, integrating and building process that requires physical and mental space. The whole brain is involved and it all has to do with the way his circuits are wired.[3]

This also happens periodically during the day in cycles. When you "daydream" or your mind "wanders," your default network becomes active sorting and storing the loads of information you've already absorbed.

Men tend to accomplish this by leisurely channel-surfing, flipping through a newspaper or magazine or looking at their computers or smart phones. Women on the other hand accomplish this through fun, light-hearted conversation. In this respect, this brain function is similar to the way men and women handle stress as detailed in the previous chapter.

BRAINY TIP

Ladies, early in the evening is the worst time for you to activate your prefrontal cortex and temporal lobe in order to activate your rest state. In other words, your rest state leads to lots of words and emotion—it may sound like you're babbling on for no reason.

Because of the man's approach to rest, if you jump in without allowing him to rest and process, you may be activating your rest cycle but you're keeping him from his.

Without grace and understanding, this will lead to irritability, unhealthy conflict and a really unpleasant evening for everybody!

Instead, use this time to get your thought networks lined up and coherent in your mind in order to talk to him once he is more rested. In the meantime, call a friend or family member on the phone. Find other avenues for that oxytocin through expressive bonding and talking. You could also pray in your mind and talk it through with God. Once you have given your gent space, he'll be much more prepared to listen later on. It's all about timing.

A woman sorts her day's thoughts in the opposite way: by talking things through—like emptying out your drawers and closets in the middle of the room and then going through them bit by bit until they're all tucked away. Getting it all out, so to say. The female brain, thanks to all that oxytocin, wants to bond through communication at the end of the day in order to rejuvenate. She wants to talk, using all those verbal centers, and she wants to get close to him. But if the timing is off sparks will fly. Women have more activity happening in their brains than a man when at rest.[4]

The amygdala (the almond-shaped structure that helps regulate human emotion) showed major differences at rest as well. Men's amygdala interacted more with brain regions involved with the external world, like vision and hearing; while women's amygdalae interacted more with their internal world—the organs, including those involved with reproduction and feelings.

> **FAST FACT**
>
> Bottom line we are different even at rest: ladies have a busy brain with higher blood flow and lots of connection to her emotions and feelings; men switch off and connect to the outside world.

In the beginning of my marriage, I used to say, "What's wrong?" when my husband Mac got "the hibernate look" on his face.

Mac would answer, "Nothing is wrong."

I would say, "Something is wrong! Look at your face!"

And then we would have this same silly argument in the early evening because that was when he needed space. My sixth sense was working to read his facial expressions—I just didn't have all the right information. He wasn't trying to fight or argue with me—he was trying to rest! I was invading his space and keeping him from the time he needed to sort things through.

By the same token, Mac has learned that as much as he needs his space not to be invaded, I need mine invaded!

BRAINY TIP

Ladies and gents, this is one of the most common and avoidable fights between couples. That's why the scenario of the early evening from Chapter One is so relatable.

Gents, remember women have a sixth sense to read faces and your relationship issues will get complicated when you give your lady "the hibernate look," without explaining the way your brain rests. She will think she's done something wrong or you're disappointed or upset with her.

Because of the love between a husband and wife and the chemical bond that physically exists between the man and the wife, when the female sees the "look" in the male's eyes, the mood neurotransmitters will drop. The female will consequently stress and panic, and instinctively want to restore those chemicals by talking it through. Unless the man understands this, he will become highly irritated further affecting his chemical release and disturbing his peace.

This whole unhealthy cycle can be avoided by communicating and understanding each other's needs and finding a solution that allows both the man and the woman to spend time in the rest state.

CHAPTER 21

Anger: He Boils Over Then Cools Down, She Burns Slowly

Believe it or not, there is actually a debate in academic circles as to whether men are more aggressive than women.

Depending on your upbringing you may be able to picture a man quietly reading the newspaper or a book in a recliner, dozing off and thinking contemplatively to himself (remember how his brain rests). When you think of it that way, it may appear to be a compelling argument.

But for those of you who grew up around sports, the military or other competitively intense environments this seems laughable.

You can immediately recall all kinds of vivid memories of men (husbands, fathers, brothers, cousins, neighbors, friends, co-workers, etc.) jumping around, shouting, arguing, celebrating or cheering about something you thought was silly.

The women in the other room might have been chatting and as they were getting excited their voices got louder and more animated, but those weren't necessarily angry or aggressive behaviors.

When most of us imagine an angry woman we think of the silent treatment—not screaming and yelling with violent outbursts.

The research supports this view. Studies show that troubled boys outnumber troubled girls 3:1; there are nine male killers for every female; 93 percent of the shootings in school rampages are males; 94 percent of burglaries are committed by men; male toddlers tell aggressive stories 87 percent of the time and female toddlers 17 percent of the time.[1]

However, research also shows that the majority of boys become less aggressive over time even though they are naturally less able to reign in their impulses. As a result, boys move around more in class, seem less attentive and act impulsively often calling out inappropriately in class, not because they're angry but because they have a different way of expressing their emotions.[2]

Standard psychology based on secular humanism argues that these levels of higher aggression in the male are the result of millions of years of genetic programming that have evolved as a necessary trait to survive and endure the natural selection of the evolutionary process.

That's one view, but it's not my view. A more biblical understanding of healthy aggression is what I refer to as "positive empowerment"—it is a gift God's given each of us. We've been empowered to make our own choices, and when this functions in a healthy redemptive way, the result is clear, decisive action. Positive empowerment is the confident ability to make quick decisions that protect and advance the interests of individuals, their families and their neighbors.

When you see it expressed in a healthy way, it's positively aggressive—but it's not something to be feared. Instead it creates a sense of safety and calm and it's a vital component in leadership.

Aggression was permanently distorted by the selfishness and sin that entered into man's nature when Adam and Eve disobeyed God in the garden. This same seed of mistrust, pride and self-centeredness prompted Cain to kill Abel and humanity has been dealing with it ever since. God designed us to be wired for love, naturally designed for optimism so the statistics quoted above should not be understood as God's intent but a painful reminder of our inability to deal with sin and anger through all of man's "progress" and education.

The same sin that motivated Cain to choose to kill his brother motivates men and women to kill each other all over the world through all manner of violent means.

Toxic anger and aggression are actions, words and reactions which cause the same brain areas to light up in both males and females. Even though research has shown that in general, men can be up to twenty times more aggressive than women, recent studies seem to indicate that males and females are equally as aggressive but that males are more physical and females more verbal in their aggression.[3]

We could be fooled by the female's natural tendency to avoid conflict, but when a female senses she is being left out, or that her side of the story is not being taken into consideration, the same areas that produce outward expressions of anger and aggression in a male are equally activated in a female. The difference is in the way she expresses herself.

I'm sure you'd agree that both men and women sin and respond with unhealthy anger and aggression.

BRAINY TIP

Ladies and gents, we live in a fallen world filled with sin that leads to anger, arguments and violence. But the female and male brains were not designed for continual fighting. They are hard-wired for love, not war. Constant anger, aggression and fighting damages the brain physically and emotionally.

There is a large body of research now charting how hormones affect cognition. In simple terms, your body's physiology changes according to the thoughts you think—this is the concept of epigenomes that I discussed in Chapter Five. An interesting study demonstrates how drastically this can shift in a negative direction.

A group of average happy-go-lucky male students were found to be more likely to mix a brutally spiked drink for a stranger after handling a gun than playing a board game. Their aggressive urges were related to an abnormal rise in testosterone that resulted from handling the gun and their corresponding thoughts.[4]

MRI scans showed that brain areas keeping aggression and impulsive behavior in check were relatively larger in women than in men. Female brains have a significantly greater volume than males in the front part of the brain behind the forehead (the orbital-frontal cortex), which is responsible for making cool-headed decisions. This is especially significant in its proportion to the amygdala, an almond-shaped structure deep inside the brain that stimulates the fight-or-flight reaction that triggers and releases the adrenal glands.

The implication here is that in an emotionally charged situation, women are better equipped to keep a tighter rein on their tempers than men.[5]

BRAINY TIP

Gents, ladies have a bigger braking mechanism than you. She will try to defuse a volatile situation rather than fly off the handle. But once she does lose it, she's much more difficult to slow down.

FAST FACT

Because of the differences in the make-up of the male and female brains, men and women experience anger differently. Men on average get fired up quickly, boil over but then also cool back down in a short period of time. Women on the other hand burn slowly on overage—they take longer to get upset but once they're fired up—it's much more difficult for them to calm down.

Researchers also found that the amygdala, which also processes emotional memories, acts differently in men and women.[6] The right side of men's amygdala, which is more in tune with the outside world and communicates with regions that control sight, such as the visual cortex, and motor coordination (also the striatum deep inside the basal ganglia) fires up a lot when emotional.

Women, on the other hand, activate the left side of the brain, which concentrates more on the body's inner environment and is connected to the insular cortex, where sensory information is translated into emotional experiences, and to the hypothalamus, the master regulator of such basic functions as metabolism.

BRAINY TIP

Teaching men and women that we're the same makes the problem worse, not better. It makes the goal of changing our behavior based on willpower instead of understanding one another through celebrating and accounting for one another's differences. Less comparing . . . more understanding.

FAST FACT

The amygdala functions differently in men and women. Gents focus outward to an action/big picture reaction and are more tuned into the outside world. Women focus inward to a detailed picture and are more in tune with the inner world.

When men are presented with an emotionally provocative stimulus, part of the motor system is activated. This makes men more active in resolving the situation by acting on the environment.[7]

But in women, the hypothalamus is activated, which controls, amongst other functions, emotions, digestion and sleep, so it may not be surprising that when a woman is really upset she feels weak and nauseated and can't sleep or eat.[8]

BRAINY TIP

Ladies and gents, your reaction to an argument or a fight is different. Don't try and assume the other person's feelings based on his or her behavior. The same emotional response in the brain motivates men to take action and women to walk away.

He needs to fix it, she's sick to her stomach and can't eat or sleep.

FAST FACT

The right-left differences in amygdala division explain why women remember every excruciating detail of the situation (what they were wearing, background noises, how hot or cold it was, where they were standing or what they were looking at . . .) without remembering the outcome while men don't remember any details but they immediately recall what they wanted to do in that moment.

When males and females get into an argument, cortisol, which is a really important chemical but should only be released into the body by the adrenal glands in small intermittent amounts, is released in abundance.

Cortisol takes about twelve hours to subside in a female and about one hour in a male. The female brain, however, becomes more stressed in an argument than the male brain causing a female to over-react. This releases more chemicals at a higher rate than in the male brain that makes a female feel terrible.[9]

A fight for a female is on a par with having a seizure.

BRAINY TIP

Gents, you can go from zero to a fight and back again very quickly. Your lady can't—just the thought of a fight stresses her out. She will try anything to defuse a conflict (until it's her only choice) because discord puts her at odds with her natural wiring. She sees conflict as threatening, a potential "big problem." You don't see arguments this way—sometimes you may even enjoy it because of the response it creates in your brain.

Ladies, your bigger prefrontal cortex gives you the advantage in sparring with your words, but his bigger amygdala means the impact of your words are going to really hit him hard and fuel the fire!

The male amygdala also has many testosterone receptors, which can increase the anger response in males when his thoughts are becoming toxic.

Women have an extra intriguing brain circuit that controls the anger response by reflecting first. Anger moves through the insula (gut-feel) first, then to the larger prefrontal cortex, next to the anterior cingulate gyrus, and finally to the verbal circuit. For the male brain, anger is a much shorter and more intense route straight from the amygdala to the prefrontal cortex.[10]

The female brain does not like conflict and will generally try to avoid it. The anticipation and fear of angering the other person and losing the relationship causes such a strong neurochemical change in the female brain—specifically involving serotonin, dopamine and norepinephrine—the impact is almost like a seizure.

Women avoid anger like men avoid emotion.

BRAINY TIP

Gents, if you want to calm her down, here's the secret: she needs to talk it through and to be listened to. This doesn't mean she's right or that she automatically wins every argument, but it does mean in order to process she needs to connect with you.

The connection that results from talking it through and knowing that you've listened to her activates the pleasure centers in a female brain. This causes a major dopamine and oxytocin rush, which provides a huge neurological reward. Dopamine is a neurochemical that stimulates the motivation and pleasure circuits in the brain. So, if you want to calm your wife, girlfriend or sister down, let her talk it through and make a genuine connection with her.

Women may try to avoid an angry confrontation, but when it does happen . . . watch out! Once anger gets to the verbal section of the anger circuit, it releases a flood of words that even the most verbally-gifted man will have a hard time matching. On average, men speak fewer words and have less verbal fluency than women, so a barrage of angry and confusing words will increase their amygdala reaction making the male become even more frustrated and even angrier.

Typically the result is a knock-down, drag out, everybody ends up hurt argument. Sometimes it's a shouting match, other times its a cold war that ends up with one or both parties completely shutting down through the use of that age old weapon: "the silent treatment."

FAST FACT

Gents, your lady doesn't look for a fight, but when she's in a fight, she's like a cat. This is because a woman will prolong a fight because she's actually trying to stop the fight. That sounds like a complete paradox. However, because of the excess chemicals that are flowing, and the seizure-like effects they create, women get all confused, so often as a woman is trying to stop a fight, she may actually make it worse.

Males, in fact, have the stronger ability to stop any arguments because of the focused nature of their brain—they are able to get closure and shift out of the argumentative state more easily.

When you find yourselves in the early stages of a fight or an argument, slow down and think about what's happening in the brain.

The man's brain circuits push him frequently and quickly to angry and aggressive actions, which trigger a response from the women's circuit. At first she may try to stay calm—but then her verbal section is engaged which leads to snide verbal jabs which only causes the man to escalate his reactions. She may withdraw out of fear and stress or she may go right at him with a flurry of words and arguments.

By this stage the stress response is shifting to stage two and loads of cortisol is being released. Here's a big reason men and women respond so differently to this kind of experience: while a man's cortisol levels can return to normal in an hour, the same process can take up to twelve hours for a female![11]

BRAINY TIP

Most men deal with arguments by raising their voices or arguing directly. Once it's over it's over, a woman may still be upset, but the man has moved on emotionally. If he sees the woman is still upset he may try to fix it with a peace offering like flowers, a card or a gift.

Ladies, this is not the time to give a cold shoulder—don't leave him hanging . . . respond to his attempts at reconciliation. Men are not wired for intense, prolonged deep conversations or emotional arguments that drag on and on. Don't manipulate the situation in order to preoccupy his attention and focus.

Gents, when your lady is under pressure in an argument and she feels she is not being heard or understood she will argue, cry or say something that will astound you. Most of the time she didn't mean a word of it. It's not you—she's just processing—so gents don't take it personally .

Unless these significant differences are understood and used to shape expectations, they can lead to ongoing hurt and disappointment, which will threaten the health and vitality of any male/ female relationship.

Arguing will quite simply leave a man and woman's brains in a neurochemical fracas—and it's worse for a woman than it is for a man.

The feeling of safety is built into the brain's wiring, but scans show that women's brains activate more when it comes to the anticipation of fear and pain. We are wired for love, but the brain *learns* fear when its pleasure-reward circuits fire incorrectly. The brain also *learns* about what is dangerous when its fear circuits are activated.

Because of the larger prefrontal cortex and anterior central gyrus (ACG) in women, the fear circuit is more amplified and she consequently finds it harder to control her fears once they are built into the networks of her mind. This results in anxiety—which is four times more common in women than in men.

But this anxiety, and cortisol levels in general, can be kept under control rather easily in women: shower them with smiles, compliments and love. This is a practical and scientific example of what the Bible tells us in 1 John 4:18a: *There is no fear in love. But perfect love drives out fear* (NIV).

Men (because of the design of the larger parietal lobe and a more externally focused amygdala) need to feel that they are providing for and protecting their loved ones. One thing that frequently leads to arguments is when a woman, with all good intentions tells her man how to solve problems that he is already busy working on. An aggressive attempt by a woman to resolve a problem without his input/leadership is often interpreted as a lack of trust or respect in the man's abilities. Whether or not the perception is true, the chances are good that he will lash out.

BRAINY TIP

Gents, don't assume that a woman's input is automatically a disrespectful slight against your leadership or an indictment of your ability. Accepting her help is not an admission of failure. Instead, it can be a great asset. Don't be afraid to ask for help—listening to and considering her perspective won't make her love and respect you less, it will strengthen her feelings toward you.

Ladies, choose your words carefully when offering input. If your tone is critical or even slightly disrespectful, you're going to trigger an aggressive response, even if you end up complimenting him. His mind will be focused on where you started, not where you finished.

Gents, you need to understand that when your lady offers an opinion, she's not calling you weak. Her objective is not to make you feel bad or disrespect your worth as a man. She's trying to help you.

There is an interesting study that shows how vivid the effect of mental stress from arguments between couples can negatively affect healing.

Researchers gave small suction blisters on the skin of married couples. They were then asked to discuss a topic (some couples were neutral, some disputed) for thirty minutes. The researchers then monitored the status and health of the wounds over a period of several weeks.

They found that the couples that had especially sarcastic and argumentative discussions healed 40 percent slower than those who didn't.[12]

Negative anger is a part of life—and if you're in it long enough, sooner or later it comes into play in every relationship. Your goal isn't to suppress it, ignore it or hope that it goes away on its own. Avoiding conflict completely is just as toxic and unhealthy in the long run as constantly bickering and tearing each other down.

Ephesians 4:26 says, *In your anger do not sin: Do not let the sun go down while you are still angry* (NIV). You're going to get angry, but there's a healthy way to deal with it that will ultimately make your relationships more honest and intimate.

Understanding your unique design and the differences in your brains are a big part of it. Remember, men you heat up and cool down so much more quickly than she does. And ladies, as that cortisol is working its way through your system, if you've resolved your disagreement, drop it. Don't start a new fight while you're cooling down from the last one!

When you can recognize your differences and shape your expectations, you're free to receive the benefits that properly processed anger can provide—greater understanding, greater honesty, greater connections, greater health and most of all, greater love for one another.

CHAPTER 22

Empathy: Discovering the Power of Mirror Neurons

I love a good story.

It doesn't matter if I'm having coffee with a friend, going to the movies with my husband Mac, watching TV with my family or listening to a great preacher or communicator.

A great story draws you in—as you hear about the characters and you follow the ups and downs of the plot, you find yourself hanging on every scene all the way until the end.

And when it's a truly great story, the entire experience stays with you.

That's because every great story makes us care—it's as if every experience, every heartache, every emotion is actually happening to us.

Great stories—whether it's an inspiring story from Scripture that happened thousands of years ago, a classic romantic movie from the 1950s, or a funny anecdote a friend told us yesterday—cause us to *empathize*.

Empathy is the wonderful God-given ability to identify with, and vicariously understand, the internal experiences of another person.

It is a beautiful human characteristic that increases compassion and understanding, shifts perspective and leads to deeper and more meaningful relationships.

Empathy makes communication more genuine and valuable. It creates an atmosphere where forgiveness flows more freely, where we consider how our actions make others feel and where we're able to work through misunderstandings before they become full-blown fights.

Empathy is the result of many regions of the brain collaborating and working together, which makes sense considering how big empathy is. The strongest evidence suggests the participatory involvement of the medial frontal lobes, the right parietal region, the temporal lobe and the amygdala. In fact research shows that acts of empathy and altruism decrease stress, increase longevity, boost the immune system and increase happiness, joy and peace![1]

Prior research has also shown the crucial role of the insula in helping us simulate the experiences of others, while the temporal pole has been shown to be important for understanding the emotions of others. The ACG (anterior central gyrus) is also involved in the way our feelings affect our judgments and decisions. This circuit contributes to empathy and social understanding.

The collaborative nature of the neuroscience behind empathy is a reflection of the collaborative nature of empathy itself. It is a whole brain and whole person affair. And to top this off God adds maleness and femaleness to the empathy dimension. This is why I like to be sure to bring home the importance of all of us developing our empathy nature.

As early in the process of thought development as the convergence of the five senses in the brain, we see an immediate difference in empathy in the male and female brains.[2]

Research was done using fMRI in males and females to see if they process empathy differently. They found stronger activity in females in the right inferior frontal cortex. This region is also one of the regions with mirror neurons. One of the most important distinctions between male and female strategies for assessing emotions was the way each gender used mirror neurons.

Mirror neurons (nerve cells) are truly incredible. They're another tangible example of God's great love for us that he demonstrated in our design. Mirror neurons help us to process and vicariously identify with what someone else is feeling or doing. These tiny little miracles are the key to our incredible capacity to empathize with others.[3]

We are designed to understand, love and help each other. This is not an accident. It stands in direct contrast to evolutionary theory and natural selection. It's a reflection of God's character that He intentionally wove into our design.

You and I have been hard-wired with the capacity to experience powerful compassion for others.

Essentially a mirror neuron is a group of nerve cells that fires both when someone does something and when we observe the same action performed by another.[4] The neuron "mirrors" the behavior of the other, as though the observer were actually carrying out the action or performing the behavior. They help us understand the undercurrents between us that govern so much of human behavior. Mirror neurons allow one person to experience what another is going through without actually duplicating the actions or circumstances.

BRAINY TIP

Ladies and gents, mirror neurons are the reason you feel each other's pain and the pain of your children and friends and even watching TV and movies—both emotional and physical pain. You can deepen your love for each other by increasing your awareness and paying closer attention to the impact that your behavior has on your loved ones.

Up to 30 percent of the brain is suspected to consist of these miraculous mirror neurons found in the frontal lobe and the parietal lobe of the brain. We have the tools and the capacity—mirror neurons and the empathy circuit—to empathize with each other.[5] The question is, are we using what we've been given?

Reading and observing each other's body language, tuning into their attitudes, listening to both the content and the context of their words, and intimately sharing in their experiences are all ways we empathize with others through the use of our mirror neurons.

When one person sees another expressing an emotion the areas of the brain that are associated with feeling that emotion are activated. This makes emotions transmittable. This emotion mirroring is thought to be the basis of empathy.[6]

Imitation and emulation occur through mirror neurons and this is how we spread mannerisms, interests, values, skills and information through our family cultures as we watch one other.

FAST FACT

Mirror neurons are so powerful that we are even able to mirror or echo each other's intentions. This explains why we cannot hide an attitude from each other, even when we think we're being sneaky. Attitudes are contagious.

As we watch and interact with each other, we influence emotional states, attitudes and behavior and this can physically be observed inside our brains. We can mirror each others' thought processes without consciously having to work it out because of these amazing mirror neurons.

The mirror neurons also whip up the emotions between us so as one partner gets worked up this transmits to the other partner as well. However, as we understand this process we give ourselves a much better opportunity to stop and calm down instead of mirroring the unhealthy emotions of others.

Scientists have already determined there is a gender difference in the human mirror neuron system, with female participants in significant studies showing stronger motor resonance (action) than in males.[7] This makes women want to hug, pickup, and touch. As I've mentioned earlier, parts of the limbic cortex (which regulates emotional responses) are larger in women and they also have a greater density of neurons in parts of the brain associated with language processing and comprehension.

Females seem to recruit regions containing mirror neurons to a higher degree than males. Males rely more on the left temporoparietal region to empathize, so they empathize differently.[8]

Since mirror neurons have been found in areas of the brain associated with language, intrapersonal and interpersonal thinking, these different areas are bigger in females. Because of this females have an increased ability to express their feelings of empathy through both their communication and actions.

Males rely more on the left temporoparietal region to empathize, so they empathize less through communication and more through practical action. They show their concern and empathy by doing practical things to solve the problem.[9]

I see this in my marriage. When I'm plugging away at work, writing a book and speaking at conferences, I still have my responsibilities as a mother of four teenagers, and household tasks like cleaning and laundry. I know that Mac has feelings for me not because he tells me, but because he jumps right in and shows me. He'll ensure that I get to sleep in late after staying up late writing, and then he'll even bring me breakfast in bed. This helps me realize that he understands and feels what I'm going through.

You can see these same differences in empathy as two parents watch their child playing sports.

When a child gets injured Mom wants to run out onto the field, hold her and tell her it's going to be all right. On the other hand, Dad quickly evaluates the level of injury and then springs into action to get ice, band-aids or his phone out to call the doctor.

This isn't just a hypothetical story I came up with for the book—this exact scenario recently happened to our family and I made a mental note to put it in this book.

One of the girls' on my daughter's soccer team fell badly and dislocated her kneecap—a serious and extremely painful injury. Within seconds the women were running to comfort and nurture the fallen player (to hug her, tell her "It's going to be okay," pick her up, cry with her, etc.).

The men followed a few seconds later because they were first waiting for her to get up and walk it off. But once they heard this brave young lady cry out in pain they sprung into action.

Immediately they all grabbed their cell phones to call for help anticipating the practical needs as they began formulating and implementing a collective plan. A chiropractor issued instructions on how to position her and then phoned a medical colleague—a female orthopedic surgeon who walked him through the procedure to get the knee cap back in place.

I happened to be right next to the phone so I could hear the warm, comforting words that accompanied the orthopedist's instructions. She wasn't just giving medical instruction—she was empathizing. The male chiropractor was just as empathizing, but his passionate desire to help this young lady led him to focus and clearly articulate exactly what needed to take place. "I'm going to straighten your leg . . . it may hurt . . ." (a serious understatement) and with a practical couple of swift moves he brilliantly realigned her kneecap.

At the same time, the injured girl's father was calling his wife to inform her of what had taken place—he was giving factual updates because she needed emotional context and reassurance.

In the meantime the poor child was freezing, so while this very practical male empathy was quickly and aggressively pursuing the solution, the female nurturing empathy was responding with an equal, yet different, force.

One of the female teachers had cupped the injured young lady's head lovingly and was praying for her and comforting her with loving words of assurance. I ran to find her a blanket as it was a freezing January morning and she was rapidly turning blue. Another mom propped her head up comfortably with a jersey and held her hand. The coach (also a female) got the rest of the team praying—her teammates were already in tears for their wounded friend. Even the opposing team instinctively responded with concerned looks, tears and prayers.

In contrast, a male coach was contributing according to his pattern by giving the girls on both teams practical instructions regarding what was going to happen next.

All of the men and women I described were fully engaged with the situation, empathizing with the needs of the injured young lady, but the way they experienced this was different. It would be wrong for either group to assume that their concern or care for the situation was insignificant or unjustified because it wasn't their own; everyone's empathy circuits were in high gear to solve the problem.

FAST FACT

The male and female brains are both designed to empathize—but they do so differently.

Men tend to empathize strategically to understand or anticipate what others are going to do. Women empathize to increase their connection, consensus and collaboration.

This ability to understand one another is one of the main benefits empathy and mirror neurons provide. Male empathy is strategic and intentional and sometimes competitive in trying to understand what others are going to do; women's empathy is to get closeness, consensus and collaboration. Overall empathy is the desire to understand and serve others and is built into men and women.

Another aspect of empathy and mirror neurons is the ability to feel the pain another is feeling. For example, brain areas activated when one is in pain are also activated when one observes another's emotional and physical pain. The anterior insula and anterior cingulate are activated in both cases, and higher empathy scores are correlated with greater activation. Seeing another person in pain could lead one to avoid a dangerous activity without having to actually experience it.[10]

Because of this unique brain design females use different strategies to assess emotion than males. Men more often use the left cognitive hemisphere in empathy and women the more emotional parts such as the mirror neurons in the right hemisphere.

FAST FACT

Brain imaging research is showing that the mere act of observing or imagining another person's emotional state automatically activates similar brain patterns in the observer. The mirror-neuron system (MNS) allows us to read facial expression and understand what that person is feeling.

When we are looking at an infant or another person we care about, ladies will resonate with that feeling a lot longer than men. This is not to say that men don't do this. They do.

Men start out very quickly by getting a big picture quick flash of what's going on. Then they switch into another system called the temporal parietal junction system, which allows them to start searching their entire brain circuitry for ways to fix the problem. We saw this play out in the story of the soccer injury.

Empathy provides an advantage in learning by helping improve communication, understanding, and imitation: we can learn from each other.

BRAINY TIP

The mirror neurons, it would seem, break down the barrier between the self and others. God wants us to love our neighbor the way we love ourselves and this amazing little facet of creation gives us a powerful tool in this process.

Be intentional—use your mirror neurons to identify and understand what others are feeling so you can love them the way God has called you to!

CHAPTER 23

Love & Sex: All You Need Is . . . *Oxytocin?*

Genesis 2:22 says, The LORD God fashioned into a woman the rib which He had taken from the man, and brought her to the man, *and they felt the special, euphoria that only comes from a rush of phenylethlylamine and dopamine, followed by the desire to bond and the good feelings caused by oxytocin and dopamine.*

Okay. Not really.

But I'm a scientist—I can't help but see these marvelous hormones working their magic in the brain and marvel at the beauty of how God has designed us!

I'm sure you've never read this passage the way that I just wrote it. It may not be how the Bible describes the first encounter between Adam and Eve, but God definitely made the male and female brains to communicate in the very special state we call "being in love."

The science behind the process of being in love only supports and confirms the truth we find in God's Word. That's why I can confidently say that both Adam and Eve felt the effects of dopamine, oxytocin and many other brain chemicals when they met for the first time.

I realize this isn't the most romantic way to describe how we fall in love. Somehow I don't think the classic Beatles song, "All You Need is Love," would have been such a huge hit if the lyrics had been, "All You Need is Oxytocin." But that's exactly what's happening.

I'm sure you've felt the effects of love before. Your heart races. Maybe you feel tingly all over. You can't eat and you sometimes stare into space with a silly smile on your face. You don't walk you float, because it feels like your feet aren't touching the ground. This isn't just "puppy love" or being overly sentimental.[1]

FAST FACT

Brain-imaging studies of women in love show increased activity in many areas specifically instinct, attention and memory circuits. Men show more activity in high-level visual processing areas.

The brain circuits "in love" show reduced activity in the amygdala (the perceptual warning system of the brain) and the ACG (the anterior cingulate gyrus/the "gear-shifter") which combine to form the critical thinking and worry center. This means that all wariness is switched off—believe it or not, science confirms love's ability to keep us "in the clouds."

God specifically wired your brain to feel this way.

The First Six Months

Scientists have documented the flood of chemicals that affect the brain when two people fall in love. Talking through all of these chemicals would take a while, but together, they all have the same collective result—it's clear that God designed us to move into a state of euphoric energetic happiness, constantly thinking about our beloved and craving their presence.[2]

When you first fall in love, the surge of these chemicals is huge while the attraction is occurring, while the bonding is taking place. So that "chemical attraction" that we thought was maybe just a fallacy, is an actual fact. In fact the love-struck male releases vasopressin into the brain which produces a laser-like focus on his beloved. Females secrete oxytocin. These both increase dopamine, the pleasure and focus neurotransmitter.

BRAINY TIP

Because of the spiritual, emotional and chemical bond between a man and a woman we have the power to build each other up or tear each other down. This causes real structural change in our brains in a positive or negative direction—it's up to us.

Throughout this book we've talked about how as men and women, we need each other. God himself confirmed this when, before creating Eve, He said, *"It is not good for the man to be alone; I will make him a helper suitable for him"* (Genesis 2:18 NIV).

God made us to complete each other, and scientifically, this is more obvious than ever when we observe how the brain behaves when we "fall in love." God created you and your love to stimulate a specific response in each other. In fact, when you fall in love, the chemicals in your brain create an emotional and physical longing in you for that person.

When you and your love are apart, you will literally, physically "feel" their absence. But when you are together, a positive chemical reaction occurs. This is more than the poetic language and metaphors we use to describe these incredible feelings and emotions—it's also scientific fact.

FAST FACT

Being in love creates a positive chemical reaction that causes you to be physically healthier than feeling alone. A lack of love and affirmation can literally make you sick.

When you first fall in love, these chemicals overrun your brain, creating an impact similar to addiction—not to a substance but to another person. The addiction is so strong, that it's even been compared to taking drugs—but it's obviously a lot healthier and a lot safer. This healthy addictive effect also helps to lay down shared memories.[3]

FAST FACT

Researchers are even finding that the intense passionate feelings of love can provide amazingly effective pain relief, similar to painkillers or such illicit drugs as cocaine. When people are in this passionate, all-consuming phase of love, their moods change in ways that have a positive impact on pain by reducing it.[4]

It turns out that the areas of the brain activated by intense love are the same areas that drugs use to reduce pain.[5] When thinking about your beloved, there is intense activation in the reward area of the brain—the same area that lights up when you take cocaine, the same area that lights up when you win a lot of money. These scientists are hoping that a better understanding of these neural-reward pathways that get triggered by love could lead to new methods for reducing pain.

Chemicals are released and exchanged in the male and the female brains when they talk, kiss and touch. These chemicals interchange and react, and a chemical imprint forms in each other's brains. So there is literally a chemical representation of you in the brain of the one you love.

BRAINY TIP

Love reduces pain! Don't resist feeling and expressing love for others because there are tremendous physical benefits when you do.

Interestingly enough, when you first fall in love, the surge of these chemicals is abnormally high. The hormones act as neurochemical glue—building a love connection and drawing you and your love together in a close bond as you launch deeper into greater levels of intimacy in your relationship.

BRAINY TIP

Ladies, you were designed to create a response in your gent;
gents you were created to respond to her. We are delightfully and
complementarily different.

Teenage Love, Loss and Your Brain

The emotional/chemical bonding that love produces in our brains is
wonderful when you're married, but it can be dangerous for teenagers
who are casually dating.

Before the age of approximately 18, a twenty-second hug can trigger a series of chemical reactions and sexual arousal.[7] Teenagers don't
have mature "extension cords" running from the amygdala to the prefrontal cortex, so their ability to control their passion is limited. The
good news is personal convictions, a clear understanding of the wisdom found in God's Word and strong parental guidance can "wire
in" thought networks to help the teenagers in their decision-making
while in this developmental stage.[8]

Sexual activity among teens is so common because once triggered,
the intensity of their passionate impulses in so many cases outweighs
their ability to control them. Most young people fail to realize the significance and the potential long-term relational challenges that come
as a result of multiple sexual relationships and the multiple chemical
bonds in your brain that form through this process.

Because the brain is designed for one partner, confusion will arise
when these same bonds are formed with multiple partners.[9]

Falling in love has a massive chemical influence on our brains that
impacts us at a physical level. Because of this, the death of a spouse
is especially traumatic and painful because of the neurochemical
bonds deep inside the brain. The mourning and sadness that follows

transcends emotions and impacts the widow or widower at a physical level.

When these neurological bonds are broken they produce physical pain in both the brain and body as a result of the massive amounts of bonding chemicals that accompany a long-term, loving relationship.[10]

It takes time for the chemical bond to dissolve. The deep limbic system misses the person's voice, touch and smell. Thinking of all the good memories that have been shared over the years helps with the healing process because of the chemicals that are re-activated. A similar process takes place during divorce but can be more complex and difficult because it often lacks the same level of closure.

By the same token, this chemical bond vibrates and it attracts. And this is why, when you are away from your life partner—if they have to go on a business trip or he or she is away for too long during the day—you physically feel the longing.

The "Cooling Down" Phase

The first six months of a new relationship are very passionate because of the excessive amount of chemicals being secreted to create the bond. After about six months, the patterns have to start stabilizing, because if you have too much of those chemicals flowing at that rate for too long, the relationship will go haywire—too much passion and attachment eventually leads to unhealthy, co-dependence and even paranoia.

Eventually, the chemicals will have to back off to more normal levels. Typically, this "cooling down" period happens about six months in. A lot of relationships and marriages hit a bit of shaky ground during this period. The first serious argument usually occurs.

Without a proper understanding of the cooling down phase's purpose, and without proper communication, this simple, insignificant argument can set a toxic precedent for the marriage or relationship.

So, understanding love from an additional neurological perspective sheds new light and meaning on these issues and can counter a lot of the potential problems that could creep in.[11]

BRAINY TIP

Approximately six months into the relationship, bad habits and toxic patterns can be set up unless the couple understands what is happening in their brains and why. These patterns of relating can continue through the marriage unless reversed.

This cooling down period is incredibly important—it means that you've entered a new and more mature phase of the relationship. The passion's not leaving . . . instead, it's increasing in depth.

In marriage, if you are willing to accept these growing pains, you will find yourself in a much more committed and solid relationship. You need the chemical link in your brain between you and your spouse to stabilize and move into a longer-lasting state, otherwise the marriage will suffer long-term. Without this stability, bad habits and toxic patterns will develop that can continue throughout the entire marriage.

It's at this point that you can really start to develop habits that will keep that spark of love alive in your hearts . . . and in your brains . . . for years to come.

Maintain that Chemical Bond!

Remember the Beatles song I mentioned, "All You Need is Love?" To keep the love alive in your marriage, you *really* do need oxytocin.

Oxytocin, created in the hypothalamus and secreted by the pituitary (it's also secreted by ovaries and testes) of the brain, causes relaxation, fearlessness, bonding, and contentment in both males and females. It's the main chemical that draws couples together again and again.[12]

If after years of marriage, you feel like the "spark" is missing between you and your spouse, this means you're both suffering from oxytocin deprivation, which really means that you both need to work on openly expressing love to each other. The brain's attachment system needs activation almost daily to maintain its proper effects.

Too many couples become lazy in love, waiting for "good feelings" to flourish on their own and then wondering why their marriage is unhappy. Instead of waiting for the feeling, your relationship will be much stronger when you repeat the healthy patterns of expression and loving communication that release the oxytocin. At this stage its vital to remember that your commitment creates the feelings, not the other way around.

BRAINY TIP

The more you connect via phone calls, notes, text messages, smiles, holding hands, hugs and so on the stronger your love for each other will grow.[13]

When you verbalize and physically express how you feel about each other, you strengthen your relationship not just emotionally, but physically and chemically as well.

And if you're a parent, remember that the relationship patterns you model are being consistently observed and will be implemented. This is a very significant way that you can train your children for healthy relationships—show them what it looks like in the way that you interact with your spouse.

Our children gave us a great compliment recently. They saw another couple and said, "Wow Mom, that man doesn't look at her the way Dad looks at you." This obviously makes me very happy, but both Mac and I will tell you that our love for each other doesn't just happen on its own. We make an effort to connect every single day. These little, seemingly unimportant connections strengthen our chemical bond by raising our oxytocin levels.

Want to know the best part? This is possible for any couple. You can do this right now if you want. All it requires is a commitment on your part to understand and meet your mate's needs.

We can't talk about our mates' needs without talking about sex. I'm sure I've got your attention now.

A woman is only ready for sex when her amygdala (the emotional alert center of the brain) and ACG switch into low gear. That doesn't mean she needs to lose her mind before she can be intimate with her husband—she just needs to relax. Any worry about the children, work, what she has to do tomorrow, etc. will quickly get her out of the mood.[14]

Stress increases a male's desire for sex because it's an action, and as we've seen "doing" helps a man process stress. However, stress decreases a female's desire for sex. This is thought to be because the stress hormone, cortisol, blocks oxytocin action in the female brain.[15]

Women require an extra neurological step of calming down and switching off. There has to be peace in the relationship before a woman can have sex. She cannot have any annoyance or anger towards her husband. The best sex operates on love. Love is forgiving, kind and holds no memory of wrongs. Fighting, criticizing—any form of strife can throw out a woman's neurological clock for up to 24 hours.

Testosterone stimulates sexual desire in both males and females. It is produced in the adrenal glands and testes in the male, and in the adrenal glands and ovaries in the female. Testosterone activates the hypothalamus. Men have ten to a hundred times more testosterone than women.[16]

Gents, let's say that you decided to kiss your wife, just to show her that you love her. When you kiss, you pass testosterone on to your wife, which increases her feelings towards you. The moment that you kiss, there's an immediate exchange of postural, physical and chemical information. Testosterone is nature's aphrodisiac.

I remember explaining this once to a church in South Africa, when one of the pastors started laughing out loud. I asked him what was so funny and he told me he'd just turned to his wife and said, "You know how I got you? I backwashed testosterone into your Coke!"

FAST FACT

Testosterone, vasopressin, dopamine and oxytocin are made in the pituitary and hypothalamus. The male brain uses vasopressin mainly for social bonding and parenting; the female uses primarily oxytocin and estrogen. In both males and females oxytocin results in relaxation, fearlessness, bonding and contentment. The brain's attachment system needs activation almost daily to maintain oxytocin's effects over the long term.

BRAINY TIP

These hormones are like neurochemical glues that build the love circuits and draw you together. In this process bonding occurs and you enter a deeper relationship.

The brain's attachment system needs activation almost daily to maintain these effects over the long term. Here are a few quick ways to encourage this process.

Ladies, your man needs to be physically touched two to three times more frequently than you do in order to maintain the same levels of oxytocin.[17]

To him, this communicates affirmation and appreciation—two of his biggest needs. He needs to be honored for who he is, not for who you want him to be. He needs to be praised for his successes and encouraged when he fails. This admiration brings him fulfillment in your relationship.

Ladies if you are not happy, this makes your gent feel like a failure. So, commit to honoring, affirming and respecting him, and I can almost guarantee that you will see a change. Make him your king and he will make you his queen.

Gents, your lady wants love, romance and attention. She wants you to listen to her without always having to offer solutions. She desires to be valued, and if you treat her as an exquisite, priceless treasure, it will make a positive and healthy difference in your marriage.

A woman thrives when she is loved by a man who is committed to her for life. Hold her, hug her, listen to her, and tell her that you love her every day.

These are just a few ways that you can strengthen your chemical bond with your spouse, but it's just the beginning—thank each other constantly, express your emotions to each other, connect through phone calls, notes, smiles, hugs and kisses. When you verbalize and physically express how you feel about each other, you strengthen your relationship.

And don't worry—you don't have to do all the work. God has already designed your brains to kick in and help you bond with your spouse.

CHAPTER 24

Gray and White Matter: He's Like a Supercomputer, She's Like the Internet

In the late 1990s, the media sensationalized a few gender-related brain studies, giving new life, momentum and attention to a centuries-old debate.

Who's smarter: *Men or women?*

According to these studies, men have physically larger brains, with four billion more brain cells than women. Also, the size of a woman's brain shrinks during pregnancy.

Conclusion: Men must to be smarter . . . *right?* Not so fast.

Brain science shows us that, when it comes to intelligence, bigger is not necessarily better. The fact that the typical male brain is 8-10 percent larger than a typical female brain doesn't mean that men are smarter.

Now ladies, before you get too puffed up, I'd like to quickly point out that women are not smarter than men. In fact, the entire gender intelligence argument misses the point. It's not the size of the brain that determines intelligence, but rather the "equipment" found within the brain and the connections among and within this "equipment."

That "equipment," specifically, would be the volume of gray and white brain matter. The regions of gray and white brain matter, located throughout the brain, control intelligence, but in very different ways.[1] Gray matter grows when we think, while white matter becomes thicker and more "myelinated" when we think. Myelination is the insulation around the nerve that enables the information (in the form of electro-magnetic impulses) to travel through the brain.

The more insulation, the faster the impulse travels and the quicker and more efficiently we think.[2]

More myelin turns the small country road into a multi-lane super-highway so communication in the brain speeds up, gets stronger and becomes more accurate. This increases fluidity of thoughts and movement.

It's like upping your brain's bandwidth to a high-speed T3 line.

Thought networks, which involve circuits made up of hundreds of thousands of fibers and synapses, will increase in intelligence in pro-portion to the amount of gray matter and how thick the myelin of the white matter becomes. As I said earlier and cannot emphasize enough, this in turn depends on how hard we think and how deeply we chal-lenge ourselves to persevere and push through and beyond in a targeted struggle. These two factors play a massive role in how we improve our own intelligence and the intelligence of our relationships.

Myelin makes sure that the electrical impulse travels at the right speed and arrives at the right time at the cell body so that branches can grow at the synapse of the cell body and hold the memory. The cell body and branches growing off it are the gray matter.[3]

So the faster the speed, the more branches, the greater the learning, the better the thought/memory—all of this works together to increase your intelligence.

Patterns of gray matter and white matter in the brain will determine not only a person's intelligence, but also a person's unique strengths and weaknesses. We actually wire in weaknesses by toxic thinking. We build gray matter and add more insulating layers of myelin around the white matter each time we think, so we are influencing the development of our own intelligence all the time. And what's more, the research shows that these gray and white area patterns are different in everyone.[4]

This explains why one person can be good at mathematics and not so good at spelling, and another person of equal intelligence is a brilliant writer but struggles with math. Intelligence is a combination of giftings and the applied commitment to develop those gifts and abilities to their highest potential.

You are wired in a direction but it's up to you to take that direction and push towards becoming "genius." Genius is not effortless performance but struggling in targeted ways at the edge of your ability.[5]

BRAINY TIP

Quite simply, practice makes perfect, ladies and gents. So the harder and more regularly you practice using your gift in your relationships, the happier and more intelligent you will be.

As we think, we change the amounts and patterns of gray matter and white matter and this differs in every single one of us (a topic I cover in greater depth in my book, *The Gift In You, Discover new life through gifts hidden in your mind*). Overall there are more generic differences between men and women, distinctly different ways men and women create this "brain-architecture."

Intelligence in males and females appears to be based on the volume of gray matter and white matter and how these differing types of matter are used to affect our thought networks in varying ways.

Ladies and gents, I'm here to tell you that we're all gifted with intelligence, and different kinds of intelligence at that. Men and women can both be geniuses. One doesn't have to be smarter than the other.

Intelligence between genders isn't competitive—it's *complementary* and exponentially so. You could say that male and female intelligence works a lot like the relationship between supercomputers and the internet.

191

> **FAST FACT**
> Gray matter is like a supercomputer and white matter is like the Internet.

Let's take a deeper look at our Creator's design.

The Supercomputer: Men and Gray Matter

A supercomputer is a powerful computer that can process large quantities of data of a similar type very quickly.

Gents, your strengths lie in gray matter, of which you have six and a half times more of than women.[6] This gray matter functions like numerous supercomputers.

The gray matter clusters into information processing centers throughout the brain. Each center is amazingly focused, functioning like a supercomputer built to perform one specific task. A man's brain will work with one data center at a time, solving one problem before moving to the next.

Gents, because of this, your intelligence is very compartmentalized.

If nerve networks are like trees, then you move from treetop to treetop, functioning on one tree at a time. You are excellent at detaching from one task and moving on to the next. Your ability to strategize and problem-solve is unparalleled.

The Internet: Women and White Matter

As you probably already know, the internet is a vast network that links smaller networks together forming a web of information that can be quickly accessed.

Now ladies, we're the pros when it comes to white matter. We have ten times more white matter than men!

White matter consists of interconnected fibers called neuropil. These fibers connect all the gray matter—the supercomputer centers in your brain. Now, you don't have supercomputers as powerful as the gents, but your supercomputers are much more interconnected. They work together.

If he works from one supercomputer at a time, then you function like the internet, connecting countless computers together at once.

White matter is also coated with myelin, which allows you to connect everything together at lightning fast speeds. Myelin makes sure that electrical impulses travel quickly and efficiently throughout the brain, swapping and storing information in the different computers.

Your mind is speeding through these different computers, pulling up different windows and opening numerous sites, all at the same time. Gents, this might seem like a big mess to you, but trust me, this organized chaos works for us.

And ladies, remember the nerve network trees? Gents operate in the treetops, one tree at a time, but you work at the tree trunks and the roots, essentially connecting to an entire forest at once. This makes you very introspective and intuitive. Men also use white matter, but differently to females; females also use gray matter, but differently to males.

Other research shows that the nerve cells in the cortex (the outer part of the brain—gray matter) of females are packed more closely together![7] This means women's circuits cycle wide and fast as they analyse multiple things at once—high bandwidth at lightning speed—and the more we talk the faster we get.

BRAINY TIP

Gents, this has to do with communication speed and how quickly women can shift between topics in multiple conversations without finishing each thought or story. Don't let it bother you.

Ladies, don't be surprised when gents are determined to have focused, purposeful conversations that resolve all the loose ends. It's how they're wired.

Gents may have more powerful processing centers, but the female brain is more integrated and appears to function more holistically.

How It All Fits Together

So where does this leave us? It's clear that when it comes to intelligence, men and women excel in different ways. Once we start comparing and competing with one another, we've lost sight of the brilliant plan and design that we've been created for.

We need each other: we are exponentially better together.

Without supercomputers, the internet couldn't exist. But in our modern, technologically advanced world, a computer won't even come close to realizing its full potential without a basic internet connection. It's only when we put the two together that we find a great formula for relational success . . . only then can we enhance each other's intelligence.

FAST FACT

Ladies and gents, God has created two different types of brains designed for equally intelligent behavior.

This means gents tend to excel in tasks requiring more local processing, while women tend to be above-average at integrating and assimilating information from distributed gray-matter regions in the brain.

Females have about fifteen percent more blood flow on average in their brains. This can be seen on PET scans as fifteen percent more areas lighting up in a woman's brain than a man's brain when dealing with emotions and memory and language.[8]

FAST FACT

This faster blood flow to the ladies' brains is an advantage when it comes to the interconnectedness of female intellectualizing across the tree trunks. Gents don't need as much speed in blood flow as they intellectualize differently in pockets across the treetops.

These are two very different neurological pathways and mental styles that still result in equivalent overall performance in intelligence tests. Difference is good.

Men and women both have incredible potential for intelligence. Many geniuses are *men* . . . and many are *women*. Their unique contributions and skill sets share similarities but there's no objective metric that would allow us to measure and declare a definitive winner.

It's like asking, "Who's smarter: Albert Einstein or Mother Teresa?" There's no way to answer that question. Both of them made historic contributions that changed the world through their unique gifts.

Science shows no difference in general intelligence between men and women. Men and women both perform equally on a huge variety of cognitive tests. We can reach pretty much the same answers . . . we just take different neural circuits to get there.[9]

Our differences in gray and white matter are really just two sides of the same coin. No single structure within the brain will determine intelligence. We have different strengths, and while we may be unique, we are equally intelligent (see Chapter One).

So gents, with your supercomputers, you excel in areas requiring specific information processing—like math problems. Ladies, with your interconnected network, you excel in areas that require integrating and assimilating information—like language and communication.[10] This does not mean ladies can't excell in math and men in language —remember the "1-Factor."

These two distinct types of intelligence are even evident in small children. Girls prefer humanlike dolls that they can talk to, while boys prefer more mechanical toys like LEGOs that they can take apart and fit together any way they please.[11]

FAST FACT

Ladies and gents, the designs of the brain differ to meet informa-tion. Ladies will use the interconnectedness (cross-signaling) of their brains to get to an answer—this shows up on a PET (positron emission tomography) scan as a larger area of activation.

Gents lateralize and compartmentalize making them more fo-cused. This shows up on a PET scan as pockets of activation.

When it comes to making decisions, the most important question to a woman is, "Which option is the most comfortable?"

BRAINY TIP

Ladies, you're better at making decisions regardless of con-text, prioritizing your personal preferences. Familiarity becomes your guide.

Gents, the most important question to you is, "Which option will work and which one won't?" You're better at considering context and working towards a target or end goal.

Any of these methods, if left unchecked, would end in disaster. Ladies, if we made all the decisions, little would get done. Gents, if you made all the decisions, communication and emotional interaction would plummet.

FAST FACT

Decision-making and judgement are strongly influenced by emotions, which drive actions. Emotions give power to a decision. Negative moods become a toxic block to a good decision in both males and females. Researchers can actually see this on fMRI scans where the parts of the frontal lobe (the ventrolateral prefrontal cortex) have to work harder when a person is in the wrong mood.

BRAINY TIP

Toxic moods affect our ability to think clearly and make good decisions. Good decisions don't just happen—you prepare for them by carefully checking your attitude. Healthy attitudes lead to good, healthy decisions. This applies to both males and females.

And in the same way, those destructive toxic decisions can be traced back to toxic attitudes.

Every good relationship starts with the intentional choice to monitor and guard your own attitude. You have more control over that than any other factor in your relationships.

We can help each other. We need it. We're so much stronger when we live this way.

Don't worry about who is the most intelligent. Realize that when it comes to making smart decisions, the only correct strategy is one that implements both perspectives.

Remember, the internet without computers is pointless, and one computer on its own will never reach its full potential. Let's connect the two together and see what we can accomplish.

When we do, we'll find it's far greater than anything we could accomplish on our own.

CHAPTER 25

Spatial Perception: He Uses a Compass, She Paints a Picture

The next time you need directions, instead of using your GPS or Google Maps, ask a man and a woman for help. Chances are the responses will be very different.

Most likely the man will give you exact names and numbers of streets and freeways while the woman will probably say something like, "Look for the Target on the right hand side—the one across the street from Panera and Barnes & Noble. Once you get there . . . make a right."

The man gives you the facts like a compass. The woman paints a picture for you of what you'll experience along the way.

Men and women manage spatial perception very differently—this affects how they estimate time, judge their own speed, judge the speed of other objects, carry out mental calculations, learn mathematics, and coordinate and visualize objects.

Men typically have stronger spatial abilities, or ability to mentally represent a shape and its dynamics. Research has discovered that women have a thicker parietal region of the brain, which seems to restrict her ability to mentally rotate objects—an aspect of spatial ability.[1]

Spatial ability is enhanced by the hormone testosterone and suppressed by the hormone estrogen.[2] This infusion of male hormones spurs the development of spatial skills like navigation, imagining how three dimensional objects move in space, and aiming at targets and seeing problems from different angles. These are all areas that on average show a male advantage appearing as early as five months and across cultures.[3]

FAST FACT

Spatial-mechanical functioning is evident as early as five months old. It makes boys want to move objects through the air such as action figures, balls, airplanes, their little sisters, or just moving their arms and legs.

Girls do not have the same amount of exposure to testosterone as boys and are on average better at language, communication, computation, verbal memory and dealing with feelings.[4]

BRAINY TIP

Don't compare yourself to each other. It's not a competition—it's completion. God didn't create us to engage in a battle of the sexes.

His perfect design allows gents, with more cortical areas devoted to spatial experience, to turn their life experiences into physical spatial responses—strategic action. Ladies, with more cortical areas for verbal experience, will tend to turn experience and process experience through and into emotive verbal responses.

God's not asking us to decide which one is better—He's asking us to enjoy the wonderful results when these two perspectives come together and beautifully complement one another.

The higher testosterone in men tips the male brain towards data-driven and spatial problem-solving one-thing-at-a-time and away from understanding emotion and intention in others.

FAST FACT

With stronger connection pathways between the cerebellum and the verbal and emotional areas in the brain, women rely more on multi-tasking and emotive verbal processing.

With stronger connection pathways between the cerebellum and spatial areas in the male brain, men lean towards spatial action processing.

Men gravitate towards action-oriented conversation; women gravitate towards multi-task conversations involving emotion.

A recent study demonstrated this idea in a practical way. Men and women were both placed in the same maze and were closely observed. Using brain-imaging techniques, scientists discovered that men found their way out using the left hippocampus, a memory storage region that also governs spatial mapping in the physical environment.

Women used their right parietal and prefrontal cortex, which are linked to visual identification and reasoning. The women's use of the prefrontal cortex, say researchers, suggests that they relied on landmarks and pictured the objects in their minds, while the men used both landmarks and geometric cues, like shapes and angles, to escape the maze.[5]

FAST FACT

Women "see" landmarks and orient direction based on color, sound and shape—they paint a picture. They may get confused or turned around when it comes to the specific navigation, but they feel their way to their intended goal.

Men are more inclined to follow the compass/GPS directions no matter where it leads them. Their confidence in the data will lead them to continue even when it doesn't feel right because they expect their surroundings to ultimately conform to the information.

Remember, we're speaking in generalities here. I know there are some women whose sense of direction is great—but the brain science tells us they're very adept at using landmarks, colors and shapes well—my eldest daughter is this way.

My sense of direction leaves a lot to be desired, but I still process spatial perception the same way as my daughter—we're both employing the same neural pathways—she's just much better at it.

Mac on the other hand looks at a Google map, has a conversation with his GPS telling her he prefers his way (but he still has it on to consider the data), drives to a place once and knows it. His sense of direction is stunning to me. He uses Euclidian space (geometry), including compass points and distances brilliantly.

We live in Texas where one street/highway can have four or five different names. There are all kinds of crazy access roads and the map looks more like a plate of spaghetti than a nice, clean grid. Even the GPS gets confused at times! Unless I've been there before, I won't go without him—it's too easy for me to get lost, end up late and miss my appointment.

I understand not all couples are this way. That's not the point I'm trying to make. We have a friend whose wife has a much stronger sense of direction but their approach is consistent with these differences in the brain. Her sensory navigation happens to be better than his geometric methods.

The area of the brain called the parietal lobe (top back) integrates signals from many of the senses. More specifically the lower area is called the inferior-parietal lobule (IPL), which is bigger in men than women, especially on the left side.[6] This part is thought to control mental mathematical ability, spatial perception, the ability to sense relationships between body parts, and to mentally rotate three-dimensional figures.

This probably explains why men frequently perform higher in mathematical tasks than women. Interestingly, this is the same area of Einstein's brain that was discovered to be abnormally large.[7]

This spatial ability mixed with testosterone is satisfied in sports. In fact, formal sports similar to what we know today started around the 1800s. Physical activity is very important for males and females but is essential for males to keep their hormones balanced and aggression in check and to satisfy their natural spatial inclination.

BRAINY TIP

Ladies, just watch how your gent loves watching sports—just because he enjoys it doesn't mean he's avoiding you or being lazy. Sports stimulate the male brain like shopping stimulates the female brain. Men are fascinated with estimating distance, angles speed and direction. It relaxes and challenges their mind and de-stresses them.

On average men are excellent at seeing in three dimensions and women are excellent at seeing in two dimensions. Boys will do better than girls on three-dimensional video games by a ratio of 4:1.[8] Men have the ability to see something that is two-dimensional (like a map) as three-dimensional in their minds. Women battle with this and will cope better with a map that has three dimensions like trees and mountains and other landmarks on them. Men are also superior at converting verbal instructions into a visual picture in their mind—a skill that is much more difficult for a woman.[9]

BRAINY TIP

Gents, when you give a map to your lady, make it three-dimensional by adding landmarks.

Spatial tests reflect differences in men and women's preferred cognitive strategies. For instance, when asked to visually compare two figures in their minds, boys may be more inclined to rotate one mentally until it resembles the other.[10]

Girls may be more likely to compare features of the two objects point by point because she has mirror image spatial ability on both sides of the brain. Because of this she will stop talking while she orients and tries to find her way.[11]

BRAINY TIP

Gents, she's not nagging you about the house for the fun of it. She can't miss it. Her point-to-point matching causes her to see that crumb on the kitchen counter, the thin layer of dust, the messy desk and the mixed-up couch cushions!

Women find it easier to calculate math problems out loud because the verbal expressions as well as the auditory stimulation from hearing themselves talk it through matches the way their brain circuits are designed.

Males on the other hand like to work the math calculation out in their heads specifically in the larger parietal lobe of their brains, and are not as good at verbalizing math calculations out loud. This is why a female who loves math—who mastered the exercises and techniques through lots of verbalization and practicing out loud—will often make a better math teacher than a man.

A woman's process of learning math lends itself to teaching others to a much greater extent than her male counterparts. Years of practice and repetition build strong teaching scaffolds into their brains which allow them to continue to grow and improve as they teach the math to their students.

Male math teachers often don't give sufficient explanations to students because the math is quite literally "all in their heads." Years of silently visualizing their processes create an isolated learning environment. Inviting a struggling math student into this fast-moving, intuitive context often makes grasping new concepts very difficult.

Again, this is a general summary of the scientific data, not a rule—there are certainly wonderful male math teachers who are able to create amazing learning environments that out perform their female associates.

BRAINY TIP

Gents, it's not unusual for you to demonstrate spatial expertise in mazes, estimating angles, algebraic equations, calculating directions and projecting time and yet struggle to find an item in your closet, on your desk or in the fridge that's right in front of you.

This is because the right side of your brain develops faster than the left side and is filled with amazing connections. You also have a larger parietal lobe.

Ladies, your spatial thinking and perceptions are functionally "point-to-point." This means you match and feel your way around looking for those easily identifiable landmarks—even in math. Finding them gives you a calming confidence that you're on the right track.

On average, it's much more difficult for ladies to rotate maps or do math in our heads so we have to rely on our eyes. That helps us get our bearings, gain confidence and get the feeling that everything is alright.

Ladies, don't try to make your sense of direction more "manly." Work within your unique design—lean on those landmarks, talk yourself through it.

A woman may often criticize a man's driving as overly aggressive because she does not possess his spatial ability to make the necessary decisions and judgements on the road. When he's focused and has planned the route and potential obstacles in his mind before he needs to alter his speed or direction he can safely drive from point A to point B.

Once a woman becomes familiar and comfortable with a route, she may assume she can increase her aggressiveness because she has a great feel for where she's at and where she's going. However, because she still does not share the male's ability to visualize traffic flow in her mind's eye, this may prove risky and dangerous.

These differences are also evident in parallel parking. A study commissioned by an English defensive driving school showed that men in the United Kingdom averaged a whopping 82 percent accuracy while women struggled with just 22 percent accuracy in the same situations. Only 23 percent of women were able to get it right on the first attempt.[12]

A similar study done in 2009 by Ruhr University argued that a driver's gender may affect parking ability. According to the research, female drivers took an average of twenty seconds longer to park than male drivers, yet were still less likely than men to park accurately.[13]

BRAINY TIP

Ladies, don't be threatened or insecure about your driving. Be grateful for and appreciate your gent's advantages in this area—I know I do.

Unless your gent has a bad driving record, sit back and trust in his superb spatial ability while driving and parallel parking. His eyes are better designed for long distance vision over a narrower field of vision, especially at night. You add this to his great spatial ability and your gent is able to identify oncoming traffic much more quickly.

I have one last thought on driving that may help parents. At the age of sixteen, neither boys nor girls have all the required tools developed in their brains to drive with the highest degree of safety and skill. It is far wiser to wait till they are eighteen to drive when the brain is more equipped to meet the challenges that driving presents.

Research also shows that the majority of traumatic brain injuries occur from car accidents between the ages of sixteen to eighteen.

This superior spatial ability that God hard-wired into the male brain is helpful for more than just driving. A man can often sort through a long, rambling, emotionally-fuelled conversation and find the core issue in order to solve it like a puzzle. Obviously, this is the best case scenario.

If the man tries to cut the woman off, if he seems distant or uninterested, there's going to be trouble. But if he's forced to sit there and listen, talk about it himself, and process the scenario to death, he will start showing signs of irritability, become physically fidgety or lose eye contact and stare off into space.[14]

Men delay emotional reactions because they literally process them through their superior spatial skills. Research shows that men can take up to seven hours longer than women to process emotional data.[15] In the right environments, this can free them to act calmly and clearly before they get caught up in emotions. Of course, men can have quick emotional reactions and women can have delayed emotional reactions, but the data shows these patterns to be the average norm.

BRAINY TIP

Ladies' delayed emotional reaction is a God-given design for men. If both of you are trapped in your emotions, it's very easy to react in a toxic or unhealthy manner. When your gent starts to get upset and passionately responding out of his emotions, don't talk him into a deeper frenzy. Instead, give him some room to work it through in his head.

Your gent needs this emotional protection for his mental health. As much as the talking relieves stress for us, the focused spatial thinking in his mind relieves stress and gives him healthy perspective.

We are actually designed to de-stress each other, which we can do when we recognize and respect our differences.

Women are more able to put their feelings into words in the moment, and they'll often keep talking all the way through until they've processed all the different emotions they're experiencing. This process won't be nearly as helpful for a man. If they are willing to participate, it will take them longer to get there . . . if they're able to get there in that context at all.

BRAINY TIP

In the middle of an intense emotional experience, ladies want to sit down and talk. Some men may want to talk about their feelings (not nearly as long) but most men would rather go to the gym. Not to avoid the issue—but to really get their minds around it.

Ladies, if your gent gets all fidgety, loses eye contact with you, interrupts you, abruptly ends the conversation and walks off, take this as a signal that he needs space to process. Don't corner him— your ability to give him room will prevent arguments and allow him to contribute great insight once he's had time and *space* to work on it.

There is more circuitry in the male brain for the spatial and physical processing of emotional stimuli, which leads them to process more with the amygdala and brain stem. This creates strong physical response to feeling.

That's why a man is much more likely to pace, run, jump, wave his arms or smash something when he's processing intense emotions.

The male brain is uniquely engineered to evaluate and understand objects, how they relate to other objects and how objects can provide solutions to problems. Because of this his brain is essentially programmed in "fix-it" mode. A man will therefore try to fix situations, including emotional circumstances, using his outstanding spatial abilities, which often manifest themselves physically. This exertion allows him to let off steam, release tension, relax and rotate all the various problems in his mind.

Women express feelings while men release them through spatial rumination and physical expression.

BRAINY TIP

Ladies, instead of giving your gents a "Honey-do" list one moment and then asking him to talk about his feelings later, remember his "doing" and his "feeling" work together.

After realizing this, I often say to Mac: "Darling I need your help. I need you to do something for me!" He loves it. He's designed to express his emotions by "doing." He'll respond with a big smile and say, "For you I will climb the highest mountain and swim the deepest sea!"

There is evidence that the male brain has higher activity in one side than the other and relies on specialized brain regions when performing a task.[16]

Women, meanwhile, have high activity in both hemispheres regardless of the task, resulting in greater communication between the two. Women also enlist more brain regions to process information.[17]

When at rest, the male mind appears to be more attuned to the external world, while female brains are more attuned to the internal world.[18]

In the world today where equal opportunity in the classroom and the workplace has become an obsession endangering the individual uniqueness of the male and female, many results remain unchanged.

Spatially structured, highly competitive, results-oriented and project-focused fields are *still* dominated by men. And in the same way, nurturing, networking, compassionate, conversational, cooperative, and people-oriented professions are *still* dominated by women.

Even as influential leaders in our culture labor to convince us that we're interchangeable parts, these differences emerge. They don't need to threaten us. They don't diminish us or box us in. We're all unique.

209

Being a woman isn't all that defines me—it's one aspect of a much more complicated and supernatural design.

Remember your "I-Factor," develop your skills, celebrate your differences and learn to enjoy others. Once you do, you'll experience a whole new measure of joy and freedom in life.

His brain and her brain are simply not the same—and it's by design. You weren't created to compete, but to serve and love one another, and solve the mystery.

Conclusion

Men and women are different. Both the physical anatomy and functional strategy of our brains are different. We can't attribute this to social engineering, cultural norms or our up-bringing.

We've been created different—it's in our fundamental design.

Our parents, our communites, and the cultural context of our childhood and adolescence certainly have a prominent developmental role in each of our lives. But your brain has been fashioned in a specific way that shapes your "true you" long before any of these other factors have had the opportunity to exercise their influence on you.

Scripture and science agree on this point.

In Psalm 139 David writes, *You made all the delicate, inner parts of my body and knit me together in my mother's womb. Thank you for making me so wonderfully complex! Your workmanship is marvelous—how well I know it* (Psalm 139:13-14 NLT).

David recognized and celebrated the complexity and uniqueness of his Creator's craftsmanship. Understanding and walking in this powerful truth had a transforming power on David's relationships. It created security and trust in God, it helped him to have a true servant's heart, and it led him to place a high value on the life and worth of others.

When God told Jeremiah, *"Before I formed you in the womb I knew you, before you were born I set you apart"* (Jeremiah 1:5 NIV). He wasn't singling out the prophet as the only one who's uniquely designed and known long before he was born.

Later, in one of the most famous passages in all of Scripture, Jeremiah would relay this message from God to His people: *"For I know* the plans I have for you," declares the Lord, "plans to prosper you and not to harm you, plans to give you a hope and a future" (Jeremiah 29:11 NIV).

Deep down we know this is true. You know you're not an accident. Although at times you may struggle with understanding the specifics of God's will, you believe God has a wonderful plan for your life. This world may try to convince you that only fools believe such a grandiose, sovereign idea. Science is actually showing us that we are optimistic by design; science is catching up with Scripture.

Our culture prides itself in permitting you to believe whatever you want to believe. Until of course, what you believe offends someone else. The only person who is unequivocally wrong is the one who stands up and claims to have objective truth that affects someone else.

This philosophical approach to life has dominated gender studies in recent history, creating a persuasive argument to turn from what Scripture, science and the truth resonate in our heart.

It doesn't take a PhD, a theologian or an expert to realize that men and women are different. Children understand this in a profound way from an early age. We don't need to don lab coats and step into clinical labs to study male/female behavior in rats and monkeys to confirm the fundamental differences between genders designed by our Creator. However, the science coming out of these endevours provide tangible sign posts or clues to help solve the mystery of he said/she said.

This shouldn't make us feel negative, challenged or threatened. How we react to this fundamental truth is so important. We don't have to fear this idea as a license for abuse or a guarantee of conflict.

Instead, we can celebrate it.

Many influential leaders and teachers and philosophers try to fight this way of thinking. They build campaigns to convince the culture at large of a much different narrative. They attempt to shape cultural norms to create an atmosphere that goes beyond equality to indistinguishable gender uniformity—but the results of this process are damaging.

I'm not referring to normal curious expressions like a little boy playing with dolls or little girls building LEGOs, and playing cops and robbers. Instead I'm referring to curbing ambitions, reshaping values and encouraging experimentation in the interest of "life experience." Instead of developing and creating confidence and security in their unique "I-Factor" plus maleness or femaleness, this approach only produces confusion and discouragement.

There are consequences to denying the natural differences in brain structure and function to offset historic abuse. The answer to patterns of societal disadvantage for women is not to train them to compete like men.

The true answer is to give women the freedom to be fully female as God intended. Not to ridicule them or put them in small, generalized boxes, but to help them understand the marvelous and complex ways that the Creator has designed them (like David said).

Women aren't the only ones who need this help. Men have so many competing voices vying to define what manhood is all about, but none of those concepts can compare to the brilliant, strategic design of the One who created them.

We shouldn't be threatened by this—we should celebrate it.

Men and women perceive the same world though different eyes. If the world were a puzzle, men are interested in building the puzzle; women are interested in how each piece relates to the others.

We need to make the effort to educate ourselves on the unique and wonderfully complementary differences between us that make us better together. We need to stop competing and start celebrating one another.

We'll solve the puzzle more quickly, and more joyfully, when we work together. And we can do this—*that's what this book is all about.*

One hundred to one hundred fifty years ago the observation that men and women were different would have been an obvious statement.

Eighty to one hundred years ago the male was seen as physically and intellectually superior to the female.

Fifty to eighty years ago a movement started that argued that women were every bit the equal of a man, and could do every task as well, given the opportunity. Feminism aimed not to simply open new doors of opportunity for women, but to kick them down when necessary. It wouldn't stop until every "glass ceiling" was shattered.

Twenty to forty years ago we were told that the only differences between men and women were environmental—the result of their social conditioning and the influence of outside factors. Under the right conditions, there would be no difference. This was promised as true success because according to this line of thought, the notion of "difference" was responsible for the abuse women suffered.

Ten to twenty years ago science began to tell us a different story. And interestingly enough, this new narrative wasn't really new. The research and scientific findings lined up with what God had suggested all along.

Males and females are not interchangeable, nor environmentally programmed, but distinctly and mysteriously different in a positive and complementary way. There is an intimate separateness between them. An astounding amount of data continues to emerge and reiterate this transforming truth.

If we had listened more closely, we could have saved ourselves both time and pain. There's a remarkable difference in the way men and women relate the stories of their lives.

Men emphasize turning points, achievements, life-altering decisions, and the progress in completing goals. They move from headline to headline.

When a woman tells her story, the experience is completely different. It's filled with rich character details, back-story, vivid emotions and sensory perceptions, and highly nuanced relational intrigue that bounces from one character to the next until a narrative mosaic emerges.

Independently both accomplish the intended result—they communicate the story. But when trust and understanding grows to the point where these two approaches come together, something beautiful, supernatural and miraculous takes place. The result is profound—both plot and character come together to form something neither could accomplish on their own. The solved mystery is exponential.

This is just one of the many ways that our differences in design can move from competition to completion.

My goal and my prayer for you is not merely to understand or to increase your education. My deep desire is that all of your relationships would improve. Your communication would be more gracious, rich and meaningful.

And your ability to avoid offense and stress would increase as you generously forgive, listen, love and serve others.

To that end here are five truths I would like to leave you with:

1. There is no superior/inferior hierarchy between men and women.

Our brains are hardwired differently, and these anatomical variations in architecture and function illuminate some of the reasons why men and women are exquisitely different. We're equal—designed to improve, strengthen, complement, and complete one another according to God's design.

2. Every one of us—both male and female—is unique, created with our own "I-Factor."

Science and research has incredible capacity to show us trends in data. These generalities are superbly useful as they help us make sense of big picture concepts. In some cases, they even help us understand specific individuals—but not all individuals.

Don't use the lessons in this book as a broad brush to explain why a member of the opposite sex behaves the way he or she does. Remember, your goal isn't to prove how smart you are. I'm not giving you the ammunition you need to win the argument. My goal is much more important.

I want you to recognize your own uniqueness and in doing so, the uniqueness of others. When you combine this with an increased appreciation for the distinct design features of the male/female brain, you will have more love and understanding in all your relationships—neighbors, co-workers, friends, siblings, parents and yes, spouses.

3. The female brain is hard-wired toward nurturing, peace-making and emotions.

A woman's brain has phenomenal capability in her linguistic and communicative skills, human relations, the ability to carry out detailed and pre-planned tasks, a tremendous capacity for deep empathetic nurturing relationships and friendships, and an almost phenomenal capacity to read minds and emotions.

This doesn't mean a man is incapable of these outcomes, but a woman is designed with built-in advantages in each of these areas.

4. The male brain is hard-wired for problem-solving, systematic thinking, and achieving results.

A man's brain is brilliantly wired for focus and problem-solving, for diffusing out the meaning from a massive amount of information, for keenly systematizing sequences of events, for orienting in space and visualising objects in three dimensions, for judging time, speed and distance, and for lovingly providing the covering for his dear ones.

As I said before, this doesn't mean a woman is incapable of these outcomes, but a man is designed with built-in advantages in each of these areas.

5. Loving, meaningful relationships require work. You have to fight for them!

The greatest test of love is how willing you are to fight for it.

Quitting is agonizing, but it's easy. Relationships aren't. You have to fight for them. But you can't use the weapons that most people associate with fighting. Your greatest weapons in your fight for your relationships are compassion, empathy, understanding, patience, forgiveness, kindness, honesty, commitment and courage. These aren't common qualities, but they are our natural design; each of us has the capacity to walk in them as we manage our expectations and ask God to guide us through this process.

We are intimately designed to nourish others and to be nourished ourselves—and this is not always easy given our essentially selfish but not natural design, through bad choices to get our own needs met.

Males and females both have to do their parts. This transcends all types of relationships—it's just as true for co-workers, friends, neighbors, parents and siblings as it is for husbands and wives.

Men and women need to stop being so harsh, and stop spending so much energy being frustrated by our differences. Yes they exist. Brain science and Scripture show us very clearly that women and men handle life differently. Don't waste your time trying to figure out who's right or which way is the right way.

That's a game no one can win. Instead of fighting and competing, put on your dancing shoes. You were designed for it.

There is a natural rhythm—like a dance—between males and females. If men and women could both understand better how their brains work differently, they could take advantage of these natural rhythms to relate better—they could dance in step.

Enjoy the dance—you were created for it.

ACKNOWLEDGEMENTS

We live in a relational world, and we are uniquely designed to relate. I want to acknowledge all the amazing people, male and female, I have been privileged to relate to over the years: my husband, my four children, my family, my friends, my patients and clients, my colleagues, my pastors and my mentors. All these enriching relationships have contributed in multiple ways to my work and research. I could not have written this book without you! In fact, in the same vein as the famous Swiss Cognitive Psychologist, Jean Piaget, who observed his own children in developing his theory, I often joke in my lectures and seminars that my family—in fact, everyone I relate to—are my "lab rats!"

I also want to give special acknowledgement to the people who have directly made this book happen:

Mac, my incredible and wonderful husband, you were the perfect "lab rat"—patiently putting up with statements from me like "Wow, what you have said explains the research perfectly; let me put that in my book!" and "Ha the research is true—look at what you just did! Let me put that in my book!" "Now that is such a 'man statement' . . . you guessed it—let me put that in my book!" And my four amazing and supportive children (**Jessica, 20; Dominique, 16; Jeffrey, 14 and Alexy, 13**) got in on the act with statements like: "Mom, Dad's saying a 'man thing.'" That is, until I started commenting on their behaviors and reactions and how they were so male and female! I found myself watching male/female reactions at sporting, school and church events; I even watched myself and found my book helping me! And that leads me to another very important acknowledgement: **Jed, my editor,** male editor I emphasize (my publishers were just making sure I wouldn't be biased)! This is the first time I have worked with a male editor, and I wasn't so sure at first because, in typical male style, he didn't communicate as much as I was used to with my previous female editors. But he was brilliant! He helped make my sometimes too "sciency" writing easy to read and humorous; he's the reason I said above that my own book was helping me! He also made sure that the male perspective was correctly represented! And Jed had a superb and professional creative team helping him keep me on track. They handled everything, from the conceptual stages to the editing and proofing to final layout . . . I call them "**Team Inprov**" (**Jimmy, Terry, Jon), and** coordinated by **Amy** who helped keep my reference list at a few hundred and not a few thousand! . . . I think we should put her in charge of the budget. And in the middle of all this was my faithful assistant, **Kayla**, who ran between us all, making sure I got done what was needed and Team Inprov got done what they needed to do. She encouraged us all along the way. And finally, to all the **researchers** out there who have contributed such a body of knowledge to this interesting field.

APPENDIX

There are five images of the brain that Dr. Leaf uses for her lecture series in this appendix. You can reference these when she refers to the different parts of the brain.

Golgi stain of the "magic-trees" of the mind or thoughts grouping together like trees in a forest.

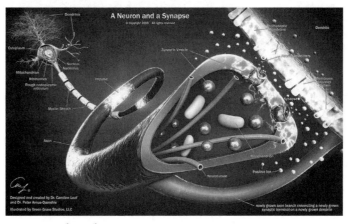

An active thought.

A well-developed toxic thought: a schematic representation.

A well-developed healthy thought: a schematic representation.

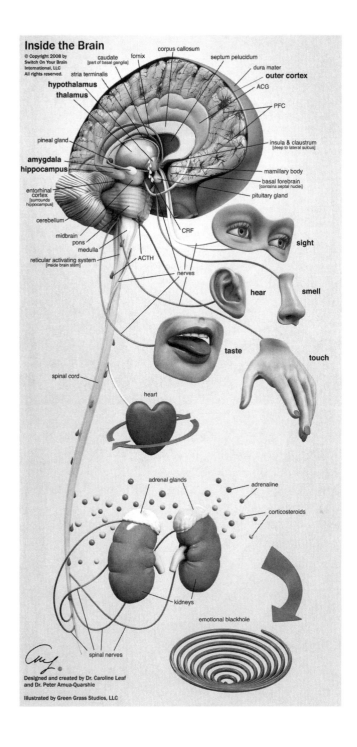

Inside the Brain

caudate [part of basal ganglia]

fornix

corpus callosum

septum pelucidum

stria terminalis

dura mater

outer cortex

hypothalamus

ACG

thalamus

PFC

pineal gland

insula & claustrum [deep to lateral sulcus]

amygdala

hippocampus

mamillary body

basal forebrain [contains septal nuclei]

entorhinal cortex [surrounds hippocampus]

pituitary gland

cerebellum

CRF

sight

midbrain

pons

medulla

reticular activating system [inside brain stem]

ACTH

nerves

hear   **smell**

taste   **touch**

spinal cord

heart

adrenal glands

adrenaline

corticosteroids

kidneys

emotional blackhole

spinal nerves

Designed and created by Dr. Caroline Leaf and Dr. Peter Amua-Quarshie

Illustrated by Green Grass Studios, LLC

END NOTES

Introduction

1. · Church, D. 2009. <u>The Genie in Your Genes</u>. 2nd Ed. Energy Psychology Press. Santa Rosa, CA.

· Dossey, L. 2006. "The Extraordiany Healing Power of Ordinary Things." Harmony, NY.

· Greenfield, S. 2000. <u>The private life of the brain</u>: Emotions, consciousness, and the secret of the self. John Wiley & Sons, Inc. NY.

· Kandel, E. 1998. "A new intellectual framework for psychiatry?" <u>American Journal of Psychiatry</u>. 155, pp. 457.

· Kempermann, G. & Gage, F. 1999. "New nerve cells for the adult brain." Scientific American. 280, pp 48.

· Leaf , C.M. 1997. "The Mind Mapping Approach: A model and framework for Geodesic Learning." Unpublished D. Phil Dissertation, University of Pretoria. Pretoria, SA.

· Leaf, C.M. 1997. "The Development of a Model for Geodesic Learning: The Geodesic Information Processing Model." <u>The South African Journal of Communication Disorders</u>. Vol. 44. pp. 53-70.

· Leaf, C.M. 1997. "The Move from Institution Based Rehabilitation (IBR) to Community Based Rehabilitation (CBR): A paradigm shift." <u>Therapy Africa</u>. 1 (1) August 1997, p. 4.

· Leaf, C.M. 2009. <u>The Gift in You: Discover new life through gifts hidden in your mind</u>. Inprov. Dallas, TX.

· Lipton, B. 2008. <u>The Biology of Belief: Unleashing the power of consciousness, matter and miracles</u>. Mountain of Love Productions. USA.

· Lipton, B.H., Bensch, K.G. et al. 1991. "Microvessel Endothelial Cell Transdifferentiation: Phenotypic Characterization." <u>Differentiation</u>. 46:117-133.

· Rossi, E. 2002. "The psychobiology of gene expression". Norton, NY.

· Ratner, C. 2004. "Genes and psychology in the news." <u>New ideas in Psychology</u>.

Chapter 2: Embrace the Mystery

1. · Diamond, M. & Hopson, J. 1999. "How to Nurture Your Child's Intelligence, Creativity and Healthy Emotions from Birth through Adolescence." <u>Magic Trees of the Mind</u>. Penguin. USA.

· Dispenza, J. 2007. "Evolve Your Brain: The science of changing your brain." Health Communications, Inc. FL.

· Kandel, "A New Intellectual Framework for Psychiatry."

· Kandel, E.R., Schwartz, J.H, Jessell, T.M. (Eds.) 1995. <u>Essentials of Neural Science and Behavior</u>. Appleton & Lange. USA.

· Kandel, E.R., Schwartz, J.H, Jessell, T.M. (Eds.) 2000. <u>Principles of Neural Science</u>. 4th Ed. McGraw-Hill. NY.

· Kandel, E.R. 2006. <u>In Search of Memory: The emergence of a new science of mind</u>. W.W. Norton & Company. NY.

· Springer, S.P & Deutsch, G. 1998. <u>Left Brain, Right Brain</u>. W.H. Freeman & Company. NY.

2. · Brizendine, L. 2007. <u>The Female Brain</u>. Transworld Publishers. UK.

· Brizendine, L. 2010. <u>The Male Brain</u>. Three Rivers. NY.

· Darlington, C. 2009, <u>The Female Brain</u>. 2nd Ed. CRC. FL.

· Epstein, R. 2010. "How Science Can Help You Fall in Love." in Scientific American Mind. Jan/Feb 2010. 26-33.

- Gurian, M. 2003. <u>What Could He Be Thinking?</u> St. Martin's Press. NY.
- Harley, W.J. 2001. <u>His needs Her needs</u>. Revell. MI.
- Kimura, D. 2000. <u>Sex and Cognition</u>. MIT. USA.
- Moir, J. & Jessel, D. 1991. <u>Brain Sex</u>. Dell Publishing. NY.
- Pinker, S. 2008. <u>The Sexual Paradox</u>. Scribner. NY.
- Sax, L.M. 2005. <u>Why Gender Matters</u>. Broadway Books. NY.
- Witelson, S. F. 1978. "Sex differences in the neurology of cognition: psychological, social, educational and clinical implications." In Sullerot, E. (ed). Le Fait Feminin, Paris. Fayard: 287-303.
- Witelson, S. 2005. "Deep, Dark Secrets of His and Her Brains." http://www.latimes.com/news/printedition/la-sci-brainsex16jun16,0,1790519.story.
- Witelson, S. 2007. "Sandra Witelson: Neuroscience, biological basis for cognition in male and female brains." http://www.science.ca/scientists/scientistprofile.php?pID=273.
- Witelson, S. 2011. "It's Partly in Your Head." http://online.wsj.com/article/SB10001424052748704013604576246612976236624.html.

3.
- Fine, C. 2010. <u>Delusions of Gender</u>. W.W. Norton & Company. NY.
- Kaiser, A., Haller, S., Schmitz, S. & Nitsch, C. 2009. On sex/gender related similarities and differences in fMRI language research. In <u>Brain Research Reviews</u>. 61(2): 49-59.
- Lehrer, J. August 17,2008. Of course I love you, and I have the brain scan to prove it—We're looking for too much in brain scans. In <u>Boston Globe</u>. K1.

4. Lim, K. & Basser, P. "Development of higher-resolution diffusion tensor imaging techniques." http://www.technologyreview.com/biomedicine/16473/page1/.

5.
- Brizendine, <u>The Female Brain</u>.
- Brizendine, <u>The Male Brain</u>.
- Darlington, <u>The Female Brain</u>.
- Gurian, <u>What Could He Be Thinking?</u>
- Kimura, <u>Sex and Cognition</u>.
- Sax, <u>Why Gender Matters</u>.
- Vilain, E. "Biology in Sex and Gender: Expert Interview Transcript." http://www.learner.org/courses/biology/units/gender/experts/vilain.html.

Chapter 3: The "I-Factor"

1. Leaf, <u>The Gift in You</u>.

Chapter 4: More Than Your Genes

1.
- Parker, S. 2007. <u>The Human Body</u>. Dorling Kindersley Limited. London.
- Ridley, M. 2006. <u>Genome</u>. Harper Perennial. NY.

· Ward, D. 2001. "Ohio State University Genome Map Reveals Many Additional Probable Genes." http://researchnews.osu.edu/archive/genome.htm.

2. · Arnold, A.P. 2004. "Sex chromosomes and brain gender." Nature Reviews Neuroscience. 5(9) pp. 701-708.

· Arnold, A.P. http://faculty.bri.ucla.edu/institution/personnel?personnel_id=45271.

· Parker, The Human Body.

· Ridley, Genome.

· Ward, http://researchnews.osu.edu/archive/genome.htm.

3. · Arnold, "Sex chromosomes and brain gender."

· Arnold, http://faculty.bri.ucla.edu/institution/personnel?personnel_id=45271.

· Parker, The Human Body.

· Ridley, Genome.

· Ward, http://researchnews.osu.edu/archive/genome.htm.

4. · Arnold, "Sex chromosomes and brain gender."

· Arnold, http://faculty.bri.ucla.edu/institution/personnel?personnel_id=45271.

· Baron-Cohen, S. 2003. The Essential Difference: The Truth about the Male and Female Brain. Basic Books. NY.

· Brizendine, The Female Brain.

· Carrel. L. & Huntington. F.W. 2005. "X-inactivation profile reveals extensive variability in X-linked gene expression in females." Nature. 434(7031) pp. 279-80.

· De Vries, J. et al. 2002. "A model system for study of sex chromosome effects on sexually dimorphic neural and behavioral traits." Journal of Neuroscience. 22(20) pp.9005-14.

· Dewing, P. & Vilain. E. et al. 2003. "Sexually dimorphic gene expression in mouse brain precedes gonadal differentiation." 118 (1-2) pp 82-90.

· Larrimore, W. & Larrimore, B. 2008. His Brain Her Brain. Zondervan .USA.

· Marano, H.E. 2003. "The New Sex Scorecard: Men and women's minds really do work differently—but not on everything." July/August 2003. Psychology Today. psychologytoday.com/articles/pto-20030624-000003.html.

· Moir & Jessel, Brain Sex.

· Ridley, Genome.

· Ward, http://researchnews.osu.edu/archive/genome.htm.

5. Ward, http://researchnews.osu.edu/archive/genome.htm.

6. Parker, The Human Body.

7. · Brizendine, The Female Brain.

· Kimura, Sex and Cognition.

· Parker, The Human Body.

· Sax, Why Gender Matters.

8. Yang, X., Lusis, J. & Drake, T. 2006. "UCLA Study Finds Same Genes Act Differently In Males and Females." Science Daily. University of California. Los Angeles, CA. http://www.sciencedaily.com/releases/2006/07/060707190114.htm.

9. Yang, Lusis, & Drake. http://www.sciencedaily.com/releases/2006/07/060707190114.htm.

10. · Sax, Why Gender Matters.
    · Yang, Lusis, & Drake. http://www.sciencedaily.com/releases/2006/07/060707190114.htm.

11. · Church, The Genie in Your Genes.
    · Lipton, The Biology of Belief.
    · Lipton & Bensch. Differentiation.

12. · Blair, J. 2000. Who gets sick? Peak. Houston, TX.
    · Church, The Genie in Your Genes.
    · Greenfield, The private life of the brain.
    · Lipton, The Biology of Belief.
    · Lipton & Bensch, Differentiation.
    · Ratner, New ideas in Psychology.
    · Rossi, The psychobiology of gene expression.
    · Wright, W. 1998. Born that way: Genes, Behavior, Personality. Knopf. NY.

13. · Benson, H. 2010. Relaxation Revolution. Simon & Schuster. NY.
    · Church, The Genie in Your Genes.
    · Kandel, "A New Intellectual Framework for Psychiatry."
    · Lipton, The Biology of Belief.
    · Lipton & Bensch, Differentiation.
    · Nelkin, D. 1995. The DNA Mystique. Freeman. NY.
    · Ratner, New ideas in Psychology.
    · Rossi, The psychobiology of gene expression.

14. · Benson, Relaxation Revolution.
    · Church, The Genie in Your Genes.
    · Grauds, C. 2005. The Energy Prescription. Bantam. NY.
    · Kandel, "A New Intellectual Framework for Psychiatry."
    · Lipton, The Biology of Belief.
    · Lipton & Bensch, Differentiation.
    · Nelkin, The DNA Mystique.
    · Newberg, A. & Waldman M.R. 2010. How God Changes Your Brain. Ballantine Books Trade Paperbacks. NY.
    · Ratner, New ideas in Psychology.
    · Rossi, The psychobiology of gene expression.

15. · Church, The Genie in Your Genes.

· Epigenetics. 2004. http://www.sciencemag.org/feature/plus/sfg/resources/res_epigenetics.dtl.

· Epigenetics. 2006. http://discovermagazine.com/2006/nov/cover.

· Epigenetics. 2006. http://www.ehponline.org/members/2006/114-3/focus.html.

· Lipton, The Biology of Belief.

· Lipton & Bensch, Differentiation.

Chapter 5: Genes, Epigenomes, Trees & The Power to Choose

1. · Leaf, "The Mind Mapping Approach."

· Lipton, The Biology of Belief.

· Lipton & Bensch, Differentiation.

· Norretranders, T. 1998. The User Illusion: Cutting Consciousness Down to Size. Penguin Books. NY.

2. · Leaf, C.M. 2007. "Who Switched Off My Brain? Controlling Toxic Thoughts and Emotions." DVD series. Switch on Your Brain. Johannesburg, SA.

3. · Bultman, S. J., Michaud, E. J. & Woychik, R. P. 1992. Molecular characterization of the mouse agouti locus. Cell 71:1195-1204.

· Doidge, N. 2007. The Brain that Changes Itself: Stories of personal triumph for the frontiers of brain science. Penguin Books. USA.

· Leaf, "Who Switched Off My Brain?" DVD series.

· Lipton, The Biology of Belief.

· Lipton & Bensch, Differentiation.

· Nathanielsz, P.W. 1999. Life in the Womb:The Origin of Health and Disease. Promethean Press. Ithaca, NY.

· Siegal, D.J. 1999. The Developing Mind: How Relationships and the Brain Interact to Shape Who We Are. Guilford. NY.

4. · Church, The Genie in your Genes.

· Doidge, The Brain that Changes Itself.

· The Economist. 2006. Learning without learning. (23) pp. 89.

· Felliti, V.J. et al. 1998. "Relationship of childhood abuse and household dysfunction to many of the leading causes of death in adults. The adverse child experiences study (ACE)." American Journal of Preventative Medicine. (4) 245.

· Lipton, The Biology of Belief.

· Lipton & Bensch, Differentiation.

· Steinberg, D. 2006. "Determining nature vs. Nurture: molecular evidence is finally emerging to inform the long-standing debate." Scientific American Mind. pp. 12.

· Szyf, Moshe. 2009. "Epigenetics." http://www.the-scientist.com/article/display/5583/.

· Weinhold, R. 2006. "Epigenetics is the science of change." Environmental health perspectives. 114 (3).

5. · Church, <u>The Genie in your Genes</u>.

    · Doidge, <u>The Brain that Changes Itself</u>.

    · The Economist. <u>Learning without learning</u>.

    · Felliti, <u>American Journal of Preventative Medicine</u>.

    · Lipton, <u>The Biology of Belief</u>.

    · Lipton & Bensch, <u>Differentiation</u>.

    · Steinberg, "Determining nature vs. Nurture."

    · Szyf, Epigenetics.

    · Waterland, R.A. & Jirtle, R.L. 2003. <u>Transposable Elements</u>: Targets for early nutritional Effects on Epigenetic Gene Regulation Molecular and Cellular Biology. (23) pp. 5293-5300.

    · Weinhold, "Epigenetics is the science of change."

6. · Doidge, <u>The Brain that Changes Itself</u>.

    · Felliti, <u>American Journal of Preventative Medicine</u>.

    · Szyf, <u>Epigenetics</u>.

    · Waterland & Jirtle, <u>Transposable Elements</u>.

7. · Church, <u>The Genie in your Genes</u>.

    · Doidge, <u>The Brain that Changes Itself</u>.

    · Lipton, <u>The Biology of Belief</u>.

    · Lipton & Bensch, <u>Differentiation</u>.

    · Nathanielsz, <u>Life in the Womb</u>.

    · Siegal, <u>The Developing Mind</u>.

Chapter 6: Vision: He Sees Tan, She Sees Relaxed Khaki

1. · Hurlbert, A.C. & Ling, Y. 2007. "Biological components of sex differences in color preference." Current Biology. (170) pp. 623-25.

    · Sax, <u>Why Gender Matters</u>.

2. Guiffre, G.L. et al. 2007. "Changes in color discrimination during the menstrual cycle." <u>Opthalmologica</u>. (221) pp. 47-50.

3. · Darlington, <u>The Female Brain</u>.

    · Kimura, <u>Sex and Cognition</u>.

    · Sax, <u>Why Gender Matters</u>.

4. · Carrel & Huntington, <u>Nature</u>.

    · De Vries, "A model system for study of sex chromosome effects on sexually dimorphic neural and behavioral traits."

    · Dowd, M. 2005. "X-celling over men." <u>New York Times</u>. 434(7031) pp 279-280.

- Larrimore & Larrimore, <u>His Brain Her Brain</u>.
- Marano, "The New Sex Scorecard."

5.
- Kaplan, E. & Benardete, E. 2001. "The Dynamics Of Primate Retinal Ganglion Cells." Progress in Brain Research. (134) pp 17-34.
- Meissirel, C. et al. 1997. "Early Divergence of Magnocellular and Parvocellular Functional Subsystems in the embryonic Primate Visual System." Proceedings of the National Academy of Sciences. (94) pp. 5900-5905.
- Sax, <u>Why Gender Matters</u>.

6.
- Kaplan & Benardete, "The Dynamics Of Primate Retinal Ganglion Cells."
- Meissirel, "Early Divergence of Magnocellular and Parvocellular Functional Subsystems in the embryonic Primate Visual System."
- Moir & Jessel, <u>Brain Sex</u>.
- Sax, <u>Why Gender Matters</u>.

7.
- Kaplan & Benardete, "The Dynamics Of Primate Retinal Ganglion Cells."
- Kimura, <u>Sex and Cognition</u>.
- McGuiness, D. 1976. "Sex Differences in Organisation, Perception and cognition." Exploring Sex Differences. Lloyd, B. & Archer, J. (eds). Academic Press. London. pp. 123-55.
- Meissirel, "Early Divergence of Magnocellular and Parvocellular Functional Subsystems in the embryonic Primate Visual System."
- Moir & Jessel, <u>Brain Sex</u>.
- Sax, <u>Why Gender Matters</u>.

8.
- Kaplan & Benardete, "The Dynamics Of Primate Retinal Ganglion Cells."
- Kimura, <u>Sex and Cognition</u>.
- McGuiness, "Sex Differences in Organisation, Perception and cognition."
- Meissirel, "Early Divergence of Magnocellular and Parvocellular Functional Subsystems in the embryonic Primate Visual System."
- Moir & Jessel, <u>Brain Sex</u>.
- Sax, <u>Why Gender Matters</u>.

9.
- Connellan, J. & Baron-Cohen, S. et al. 2000. "Sex Differences in Human Neonatal Social Perception." <u>Infant Behavior and Development</u>. (23) pp. 113-18.
- Hanlon, Thatcher & Cline, <u>Developmental Neuropsychology</u>.
- Hoff Somers, C. 1994. <u>Who Stole Feminism?</u> Simon & Schuster. NY.
- Lutchmaya, S., Baron-Cohen, S. & Raggat, P. 2002. "Fetal Testosterone and Eye Contact in 12 -Month-Old Infants." <u>Infant Behavior and Development</u>. (25) pp. 327-35.
- McClure, E. 2000. "A Meta-Analytic Review of Sex Differences in Facial Expression Processing and Their Development in Infants, Children and Adolescents." <u>Psychological Review</u>. 126 pp. 424-53.
- Sax, <u>Why Gender Matters</u>.

10.
- Connellan & Baron-Cohen, "Sex Differences in Human Neonatal Social Perception."

- Hanlon, Thatcher & Cline, <u>Developmental Neuropsychology</u>.
- Hoff Somers, <u>Who Stole Feminism?</u>
- Lutchmaya, Baron-Cohen & Raggat, "Fetal Testosterone and Eye Contact in 12 -Month-Old Infants."
- McClure, "A Meta-Analytic Review of Sex Differences in Facial Expression Processing and Their Development in Infants, Children and Adolescents."
- Sax, <u>Why Gender Matters</u>.

11. · Connellan & Baron-Cohen, "Sex Differences in Human Neonatal Social Perception."
- Hanlon, Thatcher & Cline, <u>Developmental Neuropsychology</u>.
- Hoff Somers, <u>Who Stole Feminism?</u>
- Lutchmaya, Baron-Cohen & Raggat, "Fetal Testosterone and Eye Contact in 12 -Month-Old Infants."
- McClure, "A Meta-Analytic Review of Sex Differences in Facial Expression Processing and Their Development in Infants, Children and Adolescents."
- Sax, <u>Why Gender Matters</u>.

12. · Kimura, <u>Sex and Cognition</u>.
- Hall, J. 1984. <u>Nonverbal Sex Differences</u>. John Hopkins. Baltimore.

13. Kimura, <u>Sex and Cognition</u>.

Chapter 7: Hearing: He Hears the Boom, She Hears the Footsteps

1. · Kimura, <u>Sex and Cognition</u>.
- McGuinness, D. 1972. "Hearing: individual differences in perceiving." <u>Perception</u>. 1 pp.465-473.

2. · Cassidy, J. & Ditty, K. 2001. "Gender Differences Among Newborns on a Transient Otoacoustic Emissions Test for Hearing." <u>Journal of Music Therapy</u>. 38 pp.28-35.
- Cone-Wesson, B. & Ramirez, G. "Hearing Sensitivity in Newborns Estimated from ABR's to Bone-Conducted Sounds." <u>Journal of the American Academy of Audiology</u>. 8 pp. 299-307.
- Kimura, <u>Sex and Cognition</u>.
- McGuinness, "Hearing."
- Witelson, S., Glezer, I. & Kigar, D. 1995. "Woman Have Greater Numerical Density of Neurons in the Posterior Temporal Lobe." Journal of Neuroscience. 15 pp. 3418-28.

3. Kimura, <u>Sex and Cognition</u>.

4. · Kansaku, K. & Kitazawa, S. 2001. "Imaging Studies on Sex Differences in the Lateralization of language." <u>Journal of Neuroscience Research</u>. (41) 4 pp. 333-337.
- Larrimore & Larrimore, <u>His Brain Her Brain</u>.
- Pease, A. & Pease, B. 2003. <u>Why Men Don't Listen and Women Can't Read Maps</u>. Pease International. Great Britain.

5. · Darlington, <u>The Female Brain</u>.

- Kimura, <u>Sex and Cognition</u>.
- Pease & Pease, <u>Why Men Don't Listen and Women Can't Read Maps</u>.

6.
- Darlington, <u>The Female Brain</u>.
- McGuinness, "Hearing."

7.
- Darlington, <u>The Female Brain</u>.
- Kimura, <u>Sex and Cognition</u>.
- Halpern, D. 1993. "Sex, Brains and Hands—Gender Differences in Cognitive Abilities." <u>Skeptic</u>. Vol. 2. No. 3. pp. 96-103. http://www.skeptic.com/eskeptic/05-03-15/.
- Halpern, D. 2000. <u>Sex differences in Cognitive Abilities</u>. Lawrence Erlbaum Associates. New Jersey.
- McGuinness, "Hearing."

Chapter 8: Touch: Hugs and Handshakes

1.
- Diamond, M. 1984. "Cortical change in response to environmental enrichment and impoverishment." Brown, C. (Ed.) <u>The Many Facets of Touch</u>. Skillman, Johnson & Johnson. N.J.
- Hatfield, R. 1994. "Touch and Human Sexuality." in Bullough, V. , Bullough B. & Stein, A. (Eds.). <u>Human Sexuality: An Encyclopedia</u>. Garland Publishing, NY. http://faculty.plts.edu/gpence/PS2010/html/Touch%20 and%20Human%20Sexuality.htm.
- Merzenich, M.M. 2001. "Cortical Plasticity Contributing to Chilhood Development." in McClelland, J.L. & Siegler R.S. (Eds.). <u>Mechanisms of Cognitive Deleopment: Behavioural and neural perspectives</u>. Lawrence Eribaum Associates. Mahwah, NJ.
- Spitz, R. A. 1945-49. <u>The Psychoanalytic Study of the Child</u>. Vols. 1-4. International Universities Press. New York.
- Spitz, R. A. 1947. "Hospitalism: A follow-up report." in Fenichel, D., Greenacre, P. & Freud, A. (Eds.). <u>The Psychoanalytic Study of the Child</u>. 2 pp. 113-117. International Universities Press. New York.
- "Touch is Great!" http://www.touchisgreat.com/pb/wp_0ac8b62c/wp_0ac8b62c.html.

2.
- Larrimore & Larrimore, <u>His Brain Her Brain</u>.
- Moir & Jessel, <u>Brain Sex</u>.
- Pease & Pease, <u>Why Men Don't Listen and Women Can't Read Maps</u>.

3.
- "It's the Truth—Pain Hurts Women More than Men." 2005. News Medical. www.news-medical.net/?id=11498.
- Weiss, S. 2007. "Psycho physiologic and behavioral effects of tactile stimulation on infants with congenital heart disease." Research in Nursing and Health. (15) 2 pp. 93-101.

4.
- Doidge, <u>The Brain that Changes Itself</u>.
- Uvnas-Moberg, K. 2011. "Oxytocin: World's expert talks about this calming hormone." http://www. lifesciencefoundation.org/cmoxytocin.html.

5.
- Freeman, W.J. 1995. <u>Societies of Brains: A study in the neuroscience of love and hate</u>. Lawrence Eribaun Associates. Hillside, NJ.
- "Women need that healthy touch." Times Online. http://www.timesonline.co.uk/tol/news/uk/article413100.ece.
- Uvas-Moberg, "Oxytocin."

6. Freeman, <u>Societies of Brains</u>.

7. · Larrimore & Larrimore, <u>His Brain Her Brain</u>.
· Moir & Jessel, <u>Brain Sex</u>.
· Pease & Pease, <u>Why Men Don't Listen and Women Can't Read Maps</u>.
· Willis, F. & Briggs. 1992. <u>Journal of Non-verbal Behavior</u>. "Relationship and Touch in Public Settings." 16(1) pp. 55-63.

8. · Hall, J.A. & Veccia, E.M. 1990. More "Touching" Observations: New Insights on Men, Women and Interpersonal Touch. <u>Journal of Personality and Social Psychology</u>. 59, 1155-1162.
· Moir & Jessel, <u>Brain Sex</u>.
· Singly, S. 2004. "Touching Behavior." http://www.uhh.hawaii.edu/academics/hohonu/writing.php?id=50.

9. · "It's the Truth." www.news-medical.net/?id=11498.
· Weiss, "Psycho physiologic and behavioral effects of tactile stimulation on infants with congenital heart disease."

10. Brizendine, <u>The Female Brain</u>.

11. · Diamond, M. 1984. "Cortical change in response to environmental enrichment and impoverishment."
· Hatfield, "Touch and Human Sexuality."
· Merzenich, "Cortical Plasticity Contributing to Chilhood Development."
· Spitz, <u>The Psychoanalytic Study of the Child</u>.
· Spitz, "Hospitalism: A follow-up report."
· "Touch is Great!" http://www.touchisgreat.com/pb/wp_0ac8b62c/wp_0ac8b62c.html.

12. · Iacoboni, M. 2009. <u>Mirroring People</u>. Picador. NY.
· Rizzolatti, G & Arbib, M. 1998. "Language within our grasp." Trends in neuroscience. 21 pp.188-94.

13. · Iacoboni, <u>Mirroring People</u>.
· Rizzolatti & Arbib, "Language within our grasp."

14. · Hall & Veccia, More "Touching" Observations: New Insights on Men, Women and Interpersonal Touch.
· Hatfield, "Touch and Human Sexuality."
· Moir & Jessel, <u>Brain Sex</u>.
· Singly, "Touching Behavior."
· Touch. <u>Journal of Personality and Social Psychology</u>. 59, 1155-1162.

Chapter 9: Non-Verbal Communication: More Than Words

1. · Parker, <u>The Human Body</u>.
· Hall, J. 1978. "Gender effects in decoding nonverbal cues." <u>Psychological Bulletin</u>. 85(4) pp. 845-857.

· Hall, J & Carter. et al. 2000. **"**Gender differences in nonverbal communication of emotion." Gender and Emotion: social psychological issues. Fischer, A. (ed) pp. 97. Cambridge University Press. UK.

2. · Darlington, The Female Brain.

   · Kimura, Sex and Cognition.

   · Larrimore & Larrimore, His Brain Her Brain.

   · Moir & Jessel, Brain Sex.

3. · Brizendine, The Female Brain.

   · Pinker, The Sexual Paradox.

4. · Brizendine, The Male Brain.

   · Brizendine, The Female Brain.

   · Gurian, What Could He Be Thinking?

   · Kimura, D. 2002. "Sex Differences in the brain: Men and Women Display Patterns of Behavioral and Cognitive Differences That reflect Varying Hormonal Influences on Brain Development." Scientific American.

Chapter 10: He Speaks in Headlines, She Tells Every Detail

1. · Leaf, "The Mind Mapping Approach."

   · Leaf, C.M. 2007 Who Switched Off My Brain? Controlling Toxic Thoughts and Emotions. Switch on Your Brain, USA. Dallas. TX.

   · Leaf, C.M. 2009 Who Switched Off My Brain? Controlling Toxic Thoughts and Emotions. Revised Edition. Inprov. Dallas, TX.

2. · Kimura, D. 1993. "Neuromotor mechanisms in human communication." Oxford University Press. NY.

   · Kimura, D. 2002 "Women's advantage on verbal memory is not restricted to concrete words." Psychological Reports. (91) pp.1137-1142.

   · Kimura, D. 2008. "An Alternative to the Broca/Wernicke Hypothesis Of Speech Representation In The Brain." http://www.sfu.ca/~dkimura/Publications/An%20Alternative%20to%20the%20BrocaWernicke%20 Hypothesis%20of%20Speech%20Representation%20in%20the%20Brain.pdf.

3. · Gurian, What Could He Be Thinking?

   · Kimura, "Neuromotor mechanisms in human communication."

   · Kimura, "Women's advantage on verbal memory is not restricted to concrete words."

   · Kimura, "An Alternative to the Broca/Wernicke Hypothesis Of Speech Representation In The Brain."

   · Leaf, "The Mind Mapping Approach."

   · Parker, The Human Body.

   · Pinker, The Sexual Paradox.

   · Sax, Why Gender Matters.

   · Witelson, Sex differences in the neurology of cognition.

   · Witelson, "Deep, Dark Secrets of His and Her Brains."

· Witelson, "Sandra Witelson."

· Witelson, "It's Partly in Your Head."

4. Pennebaker, J.W. & King, L.A. 1999. "Linguistic styles: Language use as an individual difference." *Journal of Personality and Social Psycholog.* 77, 1296-1312. A series of studies that reveal how language use reflects personality, health, and social behaviors.

5. · Brizendine, The Male Brain.

· Brizendine, The Female Brain.

· Darlington, The Female Brain.

· Gurian, What Could He Be Thinking?

· Harley, His needs Her needs.

· Kimura, Sex and Cognition.

· Moir & Jessel, Brain Sex.

· Pinker, The Sexual Paradox.

· Sax, Why Gender Matters.

· Witelson, Sex differences in the neurology of cognition.

· Witelson, "It's Partly in Your Head."

6. · Gefen, D. 1997. Gender differences in the perception and use of email: An extension to the technology acceptance model. MIS quarterly. 21(4).

· Gurian, What Could He Be Thinking?

· Karten, N. 2002. Communication Gaps and How to Close them. Dorset House Publishing. NY.

· Larrimore & Larrimore, His Brain Her Brain.

· Roter, D. & Hall, J. et al. 2002. "Physician Gender Effects in medical Communication: A Meta-analytic view." JAMA. 288(6) pp. 756-764.

· Tannen, D. 1990. You Just Don't Understand: Men and Women in Conversation. Harper, NY.

7. · Darlington, The Female Brain.

· Kimura, Sex and Cognition.

· Pinker, The Sexual Paradox.

· Schlaepfer, TE., Harris, G.J., Aylward, E.H., McArthur, H.C., Peng, L.W., Lee, S. & Pearlson, G.D. "Structure differences in the cerebral cortex of normal male and female subjects." Psychiatry Research—Neuroimaging. 61:129-135, 1995.

· Witelson, Sex differences in the neurology of cognition.

8. · Andreano, J. & Cahill, L. 2009. "Sex influences on the neurobiology of learning and memory." Learning Memory. 16 pp.248-266. http://www.learnmem.org/cgi/doi/10.1101/lm.918309.

· Brizendine, The Male Brain.

· Brizendine, The Female Brain.

· Cahill, L. 2004. "Sex-related hemispheric Lateralization of Amygdala Function in emotionally Influenced Memory: An fMRI investigation." Learning Memory. 11 pp.261-266. http://www.learnmem.org/cgi/doi/10.1101/lm.70504.

· Cahill, L. 2005. "His Brain Her Brain." Scientific American. 292 (5) pp. 40-47.

· Cahill, L. 2006. "Why sex matters for neuroscience." <u>Nature Reviews</u>. 7 pp. 477-484.

· Kimura, <u>Sex and Cognition</u>.

· Larrimore & Larrimore, <u>His Brain Her Brain</u>.

· Moir & Jessel, <u>Brain Sex</u>.

· Pinker, <u>The Sexual Paradox</u>.

· Sax, <u>Why Gender Matters</u>.

9. · Hanlon, Thatcher & Cline, <u>Developmental Neuropsychology</u>.

· Pinker, <u>The Sexual Paradox</u>.

· Sax, <u>Why Gender Matters</u>.

10. · Taha, H. 2006. "Females superiority in Phonological and lexical processing." The Reading Matrix. 6(2).

· Witelson, Glezer & Kigar, "Woman Have Greater Numerical Density of Neurons in the Posterior Temporal Lobe."

11. · Brizendine, <u>The Female Brain</u>.

· Kimura, <u>Sex and Cognition</u>.

· Larrimore & Larrimore, <u>His Brain Her Brain</u>.

· Moir & Jessel, <u>Brain Sex</u>.

· Pinker, <u>The Sexual Paradox</u>.

· Sax, <u>Why Gender Matters</u>.

· Wagemaker, H. 2006. "Are Girls Better Readers? Gender differences in reading Literacy in 32 countries." International Association for the Evaluation of Educational Achievement. 6(2).

12. · Brizendine, <u>The Male Brain</u>.

· Brizendine, <u>The Female Brain</u>.

· Darlington, <u>The Female Brain</u>.

· Kimura, <u>Sex and Cognition</u>.

· Larrimore & Larrimore, <u>His Brain Her Brain</u>.

· Moir & Jessel, <u>Brain Sex</u>.

· Pinker, <u>The Sexual Paradox</u>.

· Sax, <u>Why Gender Matters</u>.

13. · Kimura, <u>Sex and Cognition</u>.

· Schlaepfer, Harris, Aylward, McArthur, Peng, Lee & Pearlson, "Structure differences in the cerebral cortex of normal male and female subjects."

· Taha, "Females superiority in Phonological and lexical processing."

· Witelson, <u>Sex differences in the neurology of cognition</u>.

· Witelson, Glezer & Kigar, "Woman Have Greater Numerical Density of Neurons in the Posterior Temporal Lobe."

14. · Darlington, <u>The Female Brain</u>.

   · Kimura, <u>Sex and Cognition</u>.

   · Moir & Jessel, <u>Brain Sex</u>.

   · Pinker, <u>The Sexual Paradox</u>.

   · Sax, <u>Why Gender Matters</u>.

   · Schlaepfer, Harris, Aylward, McArthur, Peng, Lee & Pearlson, Structure differences in the cerebral cortex of normal male and female subjects.

   · Taha, "Females superiority in Phonological and lexical processing."

   · Witelson, <u>Sex differences in the neurology of cognition</u>.

   · Witelson, Glezer & Kigar, "Woman Have Greater Numerical Density of Neurons in the Posterior Temporal Lobe."

   · Witelson, "Deep, Dark Secrets of His and Her Brains."

   · Witelson, "Sandra Witelson."

   · Witelson, "It's Partly in Your Head."

15. · Andreano & Cahill, "Sex influences on the neurobiology of learning and memory."

   · Cahill, "Sex-related hemispheric Lateralization of Amygdala Function in emotionally Influenced Memory: An fMRI investigation."

   · Cahill, <u>Nature Reviews</u>.

   · Cahill, L. 2005. "His Brain Her Brain." Scientific American. 292 (5) pp. 40-47.

   · Darlington, <u>The Female Brain</u>.

   · Kimura, <u>Sex and Cognition</u>.

   · Moir & Jessel, <u>Brain Sex</u>.

   · Pinker, <u>The Sexual Paradox</u>.

   · Sax, <u>Why Gender Matters</u>.

   · Schlaepfer, Harris, Aylward, McArthur, Peng, Lee & Pearlson, "Structure differences in the cerebral cortex of normal male and female subjects."

   · Taha, "Females superiority in Phonological and lexical processing."

   · Witelson, <u>Sex differences in the neurology of cognition</u>.

   · Witelson, Glezer & Kigar, "Woman Have Greater Numerical Density of Neurons in the Posterior Temporal Lobe."

   · Witelson, "Deep, Dark Secrets of His and Her Brains."

   · Witelson, "Sandra Witelson."

   · Witelson, "It's Partly in Your Head."

16. · Halpern, <u>Sex Differences in Cognitive Abilities</u>.

   · Shaywitz, B. et al. 1995. "Sex Differences in the Functional Organization of the Brain for Language." Nature. 373 pp. 607-609.

   · Springer & Deutsch, <u>Left Brain, Right Brain</u>.

17. · Andreano & Cahill, "Sex influences on the neurobiology of learning and memory."

- Cahill, "Sex-related hemispheric Lateralization of Amygdala Function in emotionally Influenced Memory: An fMRI investigation."
- Cahill, Nature Reviews.
- Cahill, "His Brain Her Brain."
- Darlington, The Female Brain.
- Halpern, Sex Differences in Cognitive Abilities.
- Kimura, Sex and Cognition.
- Moir & Jessel, Brain Sex.
- Pinker, The Sexual Paradox.
- Sax, Why Gender Matters.
- Shaywitz, "Sex Differences in the Functional Organization of the Brain for Language."
- Witelson, Sex differences in the neurology of cognition.
- Witelson, "Deep, Dark Secrets of His and Her Brains."
- Witelson, "Sandra Witelson."
- Witelson, "It's Partly in Your Head."

18.
- Benbow, C. 2000. "Sex Differences in Mathematical Reasoning Abilities at Age 13: Their Status 20 Years Later." Psychological Science. 11(6).
- Feingols, A. 1994. "Gender Differences in Personality: A Meta-Analysis." Psychological Bulletin. 116(3) pp. 429-456.
- Plomin, R. et al. 1998. "Genetic Influence on Language Delay in Two-Year old Children." Nature Neuroscience. 1(4) pp. 324-328.

19.
- Cancian, F.M. 1985. "Gender Politics: love and power in the public and private spheres." Gender and the life Course. Rossi, A. (ed.). Aldine, NY.
- Hite, S. 1987. The Hite Report: Women and Love. Alfred A Knopf. NY.
- Larrimore & Larrimore, His Brain Her Brain.
- Moir & Jessel, Brain Sex.
- Pease & Pease, Why Men Don't Listen and Women Can't Read Maps.

20.
- Brizendine, The Male Brain.
- Brizendine, The Female Brain.
- "Women need that healthy touch." Times Online.

21.
- Else-Quest, N. M., Hyde, J. S., Goldsmith, H. H. & Van Hulle, C. 2006. Gender differences in temperament: A meta-analysis. Psychological Bulletin. 132, 33-72.
- Hyde, J. S. 2005. "The gender similarities hypothesis." American Psychologist. 60, 581-592.
- Moir & Jessel, Brain Sex.
- Pinker, The Sexual Paradox.

22.
- Drakich, D. & Drakich, J. 1993. "Understanding Gender Differences In Amount of talk: A Critical Review of Research." Gender and Conversational Interaction. Tannen, D. (ed.). Oxford University Press. NY.

- Gurian, <u>What Could He Be Thinking?</u>
- Lieberman, M. 2006. "Sex Differences in "Communication Events" Per Day?" http://itre.cis.upenn.edu/~myl/languagelog/archives/003894.html.
- Lieberman, M. 2007. "Sex-linked lexical Budgets." http://itre.cis.upenn.edu/~myl/languagelog/archives/003420.html. http://www.google.com/search?hl=en&client=safari&rls=en&sa=X&ei=1R3ITYO CD5S5tgeq1eW0BA&ved=0CBUQBSgA&q=http%3A//.cis.upenn.edu-my/language+log/archives/003420.html.&spell=1.
- Mehl, M.R. & Vazine, S. 2007. "Are Women Really More Talkative Than Men?" <u>Science.</u> 317(5834) pp.82.
- Schute, N. 2007. "Chatty Cathy, Chatty Charlie: Surprise! A Study finds males talk just as much as females." Us News and World Report. http://www.sciencedaily.com/releases/1999/05/990518072823.htm.

23.
- Cameron, D. 1998. "Gender, Language and discourse: A review essay." Signs. 23(4) pp. 945-973.
- Cameron, D. 2005. "Language, gender and Sexuality: Current issues and new directions." <u>Applied Linguistics.</u> 26(4) pp 482-502.
- Drakich & Drakich, <u>Gender and Conversational Interaction.</u>
- Hyde, "The gender similarities hypothesis."
- Leaper, C. & Ayres, M. 2007. "A Meta-Analytic Review of Gender Variations in Adults' Language use: Talkativeness, Affiliative Speech, and Assertive speech." Personality and Psychology Review. 11(4) pp. 328-363.
- Sunderland, J. 2006. <u>Gender and Language: an Advanced Resourcebook.</u> Routledge, London.

24.
- Berger, E. 2007. "Men talk as much as women, study says." Houston Chronicle. http://www.chron.com/disp/story.mpl/chronicle/4947103.html.
- Bryner, J. 2007. "The Last Word: Men Talk as Much as Women." Live Science. http://www.livescience.com/7330-word-men-talk-women.html.
- Holleran, S. & Whitehead, J. et al. 2010. <u>Social Psychology and Personality Science.</u> 2(1) pp. 65-71.
- Mehl, M.R. & Pennebaker, J.W. et al. 2001. "The Electronically Activated Recorder (EAR): A Device for Sampling naturalistic daily activities and conversations." <u>Behavior Research Methods, Instruments and Computers.</u> 33 pp. 517-523.
- Mehl, M.R. & Pennebaker, J.W. 2003. "The sounds of social life: A psychometric analysis of students daily social environments and natural conversations." <u>Journal of Personality and Social Psychology.</u> 84 pp. 857-870.
- Mehl & Vazine, "Are Women Really More Talkative Than Men?"
- Newman, M.L. & Groom, C.J. et al. (in press) "Gender Differences in language use: An analysisi of 14000 text samples." <u>Discourse Processes.</u>

25.
- Berger, "Men talk as much as women, study says."
- Bryner, "The Last Word: Men Talk as Much as Women."
- Lieberman, "Sex-linked lexical Budgets."

Chapter 11: The "Gear-Shifter"

1.
- Gazzaniga, M. 2008. "Human: The Science behind What Makes Us Unique." Harper Collins. NY.
- Kosslyn, S. & Koenig, O. 1995. "Wet mind: The New cognitive Neuroscience." Free Press. NY.

· Leaf, <u>Who Switched Off My Brain?</u>

· Leaf, <u>Who Switched Off My Brain?</u> Revised Edition.

· Ramachandran, V. 2011. <u>The Tell-Tale Brain</u>. WW Norton & Company.

· Restak, R. 2000. "Mysteries of the Mind." <u>National Geographic Society</u>. Washington D.C.

· Rubin, M. & Safdieh, J. 2007. <u>Netter's Concise Neuroanatomy</u>. Saunders Elsevier.

· Springer & Deutsch, <u>Left Brain, Right Brain</u>.

2. · Amen, D. 1998. <u>Change Your Brain Change Your Life</u>. Three Rivers Press. NY.

· Eisenberger, N. & Lieberman, M.D. 2003. "Does rejection hurt? An fMRI study of Social Exclusion." <u>Science</u>. 10 pp.290-292.

· eScience News. 2011 "Acute pain is eased with the touch of a hand." http://esciencenews.com/articles/2010/09/23/acute.pain.eased.with.touch.a.hand.

· Howard, P. 2006. <u>The Owner's Manual For The Brain</u>. Bard Press. Austin, TX.

· Kross, E. & Berman, M. et al. 2011. "Social rejection shares somatosensory representations with physical pain." <u>PNAS</u>. 108(15) pp. 6270-6275.

· Panksepp, J. 2003. "Feeling the Pain of Social Loss." <u>Neuroscience</u>. 302(5643) pp.237-239.

· Roizen, M. & Mehmet, C. 2008 <u>You: The Owner's Manual</u>. Collins.

· ScienceDaily. 2011. "Study Illuminates the 'Pain' of Social Rejection." http://www.sciencedaily.com/releases/2011/03/110328151726.htm.

3. · Amen, <u>Change Your Brain Change Your Life</u>.

· Howard, <u>The Owner's Manual For The Brain</u>.

· Roizen & Mehmet, <u>You</u>.

· Pert, C. et al. 1973. "Opiate Agonists and Antagonists Discriminated by Receptor Binding in the Brain." <u>Science</u>. (182): 1359-61.

· Pert, C.B. 1997. <u>Molecules of Emotion: Why you feel the way you feel</u>. Simon and Schuster. UK.

4. · Beaton, D. 2003. "Effects of Stress and Psychological Disorders on the Immune System." Rochester Institute of Technology. http://www.personalityresearch.org/papers/beaton.html.

· Carson, R.C., Butcher, J.N. & Mineka, S. 2002. "Fundamentals of abnormal psychology and modern life." Allyn and Bacon. Boston.

· eScience News. 2011. "Mindfulness meditation training changes brain structure in 8 weeks." http://esciencenews.com/articles/2011/01/21/mindfulness.meditation.training.changes.brain.structure.8.weeks.

· Jones, J. 2003. Stress responses, pressure ulcer development and adaptation. <u>British Journal of Nursing</u>. 12, 17-23.

· Leaf, <u>Who Switched Off My Brain?</u>

· Leaf, "Who Switched Off My Brain?" DVD series.

· Leaf, <u>Who Switched Off My Brain?</u> Revised Edition.

· Salzano, R. 2003. "Taming Stress." <u>Scientific American</u>. 289, 88-98.

· Schwarts, T. 2003. "Psychologist and scientist Suzanna Segerstrom '90 studies optimism and the immune system." <u>Chronicle</u>. Lewis & Clark College. Portlan, OR. http://legacy.lclark.edu/dept/chron/positives03.html.

Chapter 12: The Sixth Sense:
She Reads the People, He Reads the Room

1. · Ackermann, H. & Riecker, A. 2010. "The contribution(s) of the insula to speech communication: a review of the clinical and functional imaging literature." Brain Structure Function. 214 pp. 5–6. doi:10.1007/ s00429- 010-0257-x.

· Blakeslee, S. 2007. "The Insula - body in the brain." http://www.ithou.org/node/1595.

· Blakeslee, S. 2007. "A Small Part of the Brain, and Its Profound Effects." The New York Times. http://www. nytimes.com/2007/02/06/health/psychology/06brain.html.

· Brass, M. & Haggard, P. 2010. "The hidden side of intentional action: the role of the anterior insular cortex." Brain Structure and Function. 214 pp.5–6. doi:10.1007/s00429-010-0269-6.

· Craig, A.D. 2010. "Barrow scientist leads insula research." eScience News. http://esciencenews.com/ articles/2010/07/07/barrow.scientist.leads.insula.research.

· Craig, A.D. 2010. "Once an island, now the focus of attention." Brain Structure and Function. 214 pp. 395-396.

· Craig, A.D. 2006. "Interoception and Emotion: A Neuroanatomical Perspective" Lewis et al. (eds) The Handbook of Emotion. 3rd Ed. Ch. 16. http://brainimaging.waisman.wisc.edu/~perlman/papers/ EmotionTheory08/InteroceptionandEmotion.pdf.

2. · Allman, J. 2007. "A Small Part of the Brain and Its Profound Effects." http://www.biopsychiatry.com/tobacco/ insula.htm.

· Allman, J. 2011. "Mechanisms of Economic and Social Decision-Making." http://www.allmanlab.caltech.edu/ research.html.

· Allman, J. & Woodward, J. 2008. "What are Moral Intuitions and Why should we care about them? A Neurobiological Perspective." Philosophical Issues. 18(1) pp. 164-185.

3. · Ackermann & Riecker, "The contribution(s) of the insula to speech communication."

· Blakeslee, "The Insula - body in the brain."

· Blakeslee, "A Small Part of the Brain, and Its Profound Effects."

· Brass & Haggard, "The hidden side of intentional action."

· Craig, A.D. 2006. The Handbook of Emotion.

· Craig, "Barrow scientist leads insula research."

· Craig, "Once an island, now the focus of attention."

4. · Ackermann & Riecker, "The contribution(s) of the insula to speech communication."

· Allman, "A Small Part of the Brain and Its Profound Effects."

· Allman, "Mechanisms of Economic and Social Decision-Making."

· Allman & Woodward, "What are Moral Intuitions and Why should we care about them?"

· Blakeslee, "The Insula - body in the brain."

· Blakeslee, "A Small Part of the Brain, and Its Profound Effects."

· Brass & Haggard, "The hidden side of intentional action."

· Craig, The Handbook of Emotion.

· Craig, "Barrow scientist leads insula research."

· Craig, "Once an island, now the focus of attention."

3. · Brizendine, <u>The Male Brain</u>.

· Brizendine, <u>The Female Brain</u>.

· Moir & Jessel, <u>Brain Sex</u>.

· Pinker, <u>The Sexual Paradox</u>.

· Uvas-Moberg, "Oxytocin."

Chapter 13: Pain in Your Brain

1. · Ackermann & Riecker, "The contribution(s) of the insula to speech communication."

· Allman. "A Small Part of the Brain and Its Profound Effects."

· Allman. "Mechanisms of Economic and Social Decision-Making."

· Allman, & Woodward, "What are Moral Intuitions and Why should we care about them?"

· Blakeslee, "The Insula - body in the brain."

· Blakeslee, "A Small Part of the Brain, and Its Profound Effects."

· Brass & Haggard, "The hidden side of intentional action."

· Craig, "Barrow scientist leads insula research."

· Craig, "Once an island, now the focus of attention."

· Craig, <u>The Handbook of Emotion</u>.

2. · "It's the Truth - Pain Hurts Women More than Men." www.news-medical.net/?id=11498.

· Moir & Jessel, <u>Brain Sex</u>.

· Paulson, P. & Minoshima, S. et al. 1998. "Gender differences in pain perception and patterns of cerebral activation during noxious heat stimulation in humans." <u>Pain</u>. 76(2) pp.223-229.

· Reinisch, J. 1974. "Fetal Hormones, The Brain, and Human Sex Differences: A heuristic, integrative Review of the recent Literature." Archives of Sexual Behavior. 3(1) 51-90.

3. Cahill, "Sex-related hemispheric Lateralization of Amygdala Function in emotionally Influenced Memory: An fMRI investigation."

4. · Amen, <u>Change Your Brain Change Your Life</u>.

· Eisenberger & Lieberman, "Does rejection hurt?"

· Howard, <u>The Owner's Manual For The Brain</u>.

· Roizen & Mehmet, <u>You: The Owner's Manual</u>.

5. · Leaf, <u>Who Switched Off My Brain?</u>

· Leaf, "Who Switched Off My Brain?" DVD series.

· Leaf, <u>Who Switched Off My Brain?</u> Revised Edition.

6. · Ackermann & Riecker, "The contribution(s) of the insula to speech communication."

   · Blakeslee, "The Insula - body in the brain."

   · Blakeslee, "A Small Part of the Brain, and Its Profound Effects."

   · Brass & Haggard, "The hidden side of intentional action."

   · Craig, "Barrow scientist leads insula research."

   · Craig, "Once an island, now the focus of attention."

   · Craig, The Handbook of Emotion.

   · Eisenberger & Lieberman, "Does rejection hurt?"

   · eScience News. "Acute pain is eased with the touch of a hand."

   · Howard, The Owner's Manual For The Brain.

   · Kross & Berman, PNAS.

   · Ramachandran, The Tell-Tale Brain.

   · Roizen & Mehmet, You: The Owner's Manual.

7. Singer, T. 2004. "Empathy for Pain Involves the Affective but not Sensory Components of Pain." Science. 303 pp. 1157-1162.

8. · Darlington, The Female Brain.

   · Kimura, Sex and Cognition.

9. · "Endorphin and enkephalim." http://www.discoveriesinmedicine.com/Com-En/Endorphin-and-Enkephalin.html.

   · Nicoli, R. & Siggins, G. et al. 1977. "Neuronal actions of endorphins and enkephalins among brain regons: a comparative microiontopho retic study." PNAS. 74(6) pp. 2584-2588.

Chapter 14: Here Come the Hormones!

1. · Brizendine, The Male Brain.

   · Brizendine, The Female Brain.

   · Gazzaniga, "Human: The Science behind What Makes Us Unique."

   · Pert, "Opiate Agonists and Antagonists Discriminated by Receptor Binding in the Brain."

   · Pert, Molecules of Emotion.

   · Restak, "Mysteries of the Mind."

2. · Brizendine, The Male Brain.

   · Brizendine, The Female Brain.

   · Darlington, The Female Brain.

   · Diamond, M. 1988. Enriching Heredity: The impact of the environment on the brain. Free Press. NY.

   · Diamond, Magic Trees of the Mind.

   · Diamond, M., Scheibel, A., Murphy, G. & Harvey, T. 1985. "On the Brain of a Scientist: Albert Einstein." Experimental Neurology. 88(1):198-204.

- Kimura, <u>Sex and Cognition</u>.
- Kirschbaum, C. & Kudielka, B. et al. 1999. "Impact of Gender, Menstrual Cycle Phase, and Oral Contraceptives on the Activity of the Hypothalamus-Pituitary-Adrenal Axis. <u>Psychosomatic Medicine</u>. 61 pp. 154–162.
- Moir & Jessel, <u>Brain Sex</u>.
- Pinker, <u>The Sexual Paradox</u>.
- Witelson, <u>Sex differences in the neurology of cognition</u>.
- Witelson, "Deep, Dark Secrets of His and Her Brains."
- Witelson, "Sandra Witelson."
- Witelson, "It's Partly in Your Head."

3. Nishizawa, S. & Benkelfat, S. et al. 1997. "Differences between males and females in rates of serotonin synthesis in human brain." <u>PNAS</u>. 94(10) pp. 5308-5313. USA. http://www.ncbi.nlm.nih.gov/pmc/articles/PMC24674/.

4.
- Witelson, "Deep, Dark Secrets of His and Her Brains."
- Witelson, "Sandra Witelson."
- Witelson, "It's Partly in Your Head."

5.
- Brizendine, <u>The Male Brain</u>.
- Brizendine, <u>The Female Brain</u>.
- Kimura, <u>Sex and Cognition</u>.
- Darlington, <u>The Female Brain</u>.
- Moir & Jessel, <u>Brain Sex</u>.
- Pinker, <u>The Sexual Paradox</u>.

6.
- Brizendine, <u>The Male Brain</u>.
- Larrimore & Larrimore, <u>His Brain Her Brain</u>.
- Pert, "Opiate Agonists and Antagonists Discriminated by Receptor Binding in the Brain."
- Pert, <u>Molecules of Emotion</u>.

7.
- Economist. 2004. "I get a kick out of you: Scientists are finding that, after all, love really is down to a chemical addiction between people." http://www.oxytocin.org/oxytoc/love-science.html.
- Francis, D. & Young, L. et al. 2002. "Naturally Occurring Differences in Maternal Care are Associated with the Expression of Oxytocin and Vasopressin (V1a) Receptors: Gender Differences." <u>Journal of Neuroendocrinology</u>. 14 pp. 349–353. http://www.dafml.unito.it/anatomy/panzica/neuroendo/articolipdf/2002FrancisJNeuroEndo.pdf.
- Insel, T. & Huilhan, T. 1995. "A gender-specific mechanism for pair bonding: Oxytocin and partner preference formation in monogamous voles." Behavioral Neuroscience. 109(4) pp. 782-789 doi: 10.1037/0735-7044.109.4.782. http://psycnet.apa.org/psycinfo/1995-43085-001.

Chapter 15: Memories:
The Mental Baggage of Communication

1. · Leaf, Who Switched Off My Brain?
   · Leaf, "Who Switched Off My Brain?" DVD series.
   · Leaf, Who Switched Off My Brain? Revised Edition.

2. · Leaf, Who Switched Off My Brain?
   · Leaf, "Who Switched Off My Brain?" DVD series.
   · Leaf, Who Switched Off My Brain? Revised Edition.
   · Meyer, J. 1995. Battlefield of the Mind. Faith Words. NY.

3. · Bauer, P. J. 1993. "Memory for Gender-Consistent and Gender-Inconsistent Event Sequences by Twenty-Five-Month-Old Children." Child Development. 64 pp. 285–297. doi: 10.1111/j.1467-8624.1993.tb02910.x.
   · Cahill, "Sex-related hemispheric Lateralization of Amygdala Function in emotionally Influenced Memory: An fMRI investigation."
   · Herlitz, A. 2008. "Psychologists Explore Possibility Of Gender Differences In Memory, Findings Favor Females." http://www.medicalnewstoday.com/articles/98144.php.
   · Leaf, Who Switched Off My Brain?
   · Leaf, "Who Switched Off My Brain?" DVD series.

4. · Coyle, D. 2009. "The Talent Code." Bantam Books. USA.
   · Ericsson, A. et al. 1993. "The Role of Deliberate Practice in the Acquisition of Expert Performance." American Psychological Association. 100(3) pp. 363-406.
   · Ericsson, K. & Lehmann, A. 1996. "Expert and Exceptional Performance: Evidence of Maximal Adaption to Task Constraints." Annual Review of Psychology. 47. http://www.questia.com/googleScholar. qst?docld=5000321924.
   · Fields, R.D. 2008. "White matter matters." Scientific American. pp. 54-61.

5. · Diamond & Hopson, Magic Trees of the Mind.
   · Kandel, "A new intellectual framework for psychiatry?"
   · Leaf, Who Switched Off My Brain?
   · Leaf, "Who Switched Off My Brain?" DVD series.
   · Leaf, Who Switched Off My Brain? Revised Edition.

6. · Brizendine, The Male Brain.
   · Brizendine, The Female Brain.
   · Darlington, The Female Brain.
   · Dowd, "X-celling Over Men."
   · Hendrich, B, D., Plenge, R.M. & Willard, H.F. 1997. "Identification and characterization of the human xist gene promoter: implications for models of X chromosome inactivation." Nucleic Acids Research. 25(13) pp. 2661-2671.

· Kimura, <u>Sex and Cognition</u>.

· Larrimore & Larrimore, <u>His Brain Her Brain</u>.

Chapter 16: He Sorts by Title, She Sorts Alphabetically

1. · Cahill, "Sex-related hemispheric Lateralization of Amygdala Function in emotionally Influenced Memory: An fMRI investigation."

   · Damasio, A. R. 1999. <u>The Feeling of What Happens: Body and motion in the making of consciousness</u>. Harcourt, Brace & Company. NY.

   · LoPresti, M.L., Schon, K. et al. 2008 " Working memory for social cues recruits orbitofrontal cortex and amygdala: A functional magnetic resonance imaging study of delayed matching to sample for emotional expressions." <u>The Journal of Neuroscience</u>. 28(14) pp. 3718-3728.

   · Restak, K. 1979. <u>The Brain: The last frontier</u>. Doubleday. NY.

   · Restak, "Mysteries of the Mind."

   · Restak, R. 2009. <u>Think Smart: A neuroscientists prescription for improving your brain performance</u>. Riverhead Books. NY.

2. · Davis, M. & Wheelen, P.J. 2001. "The amygdala, vigilance and emotion." <u>Molecular Psychiatry</u>. 6 pp. 13-34.

   · Packard, M.G. & Cahill, L. 2001. "Affective modulation of multiple memory systems" Current Opinion in Neurobiology." 11 pp. 752-756. http://bobhall.tamu.edu/epsy602/Topics/Articles/PackardandCahill.pdf.

   · Vasdarjanova, A., Cahill, L. & McGaugh, J.I. 2001. "Disrupting basolateral amygdala function impairs unconditional freezing and avoidance." <u>European Journal of Neuroscience</u>. 14 pp. 709-718.

3. · Amen, D. 1998. <u>Change Your Brain Change Your Life</u>. Three Rivers Press. NY.

   · Brizendine, <u>The Male Brain</u>.

   · Brizendine, <u>The Female Brain</u>.

   · Cahill, "Sex-related hemispheric Lateralization of Amygdala Function in emotionally Influenced Memory: An fMRI investigation."

   · Gur, R.E. & Gur, R. 1990. "Gender differences in regional cerebral blood flow" Schizophrenia bulletin." 16(2).

   · Larrimore & Larrimore, <u>His Brain Her Brain</u>.

4. · Cahill, "Sex-related hemispheric Lateralization of Amygdala Function in emotionally Influenced Memory: An fMRI investigation."

   · Kalin, N.H. 2001. "The primate amygdala mediates acute fear but not the behavioral and physiological component of anxious temperament." <u>The Journal of Neuroscience</u>. 21:2067-74. www.biopsychiatry.com/amygdala.htm.

5. University of California, Irvine. 2006. "Researchers: even at rest, men's and women's brains behave differently." PHYSorg.com. http://www.physorg.com/news63301200.html. http://www.sciencedaily.com/releases/2006/04/060404090204.htm.

Chapter 17: She Enjoys "Multi-Tasking," He Prefers "Single-Tasking"

1. · Darlington, <u>The Female Brain</u>.

· Johnson, S.C., Farnworth, T. et al. 1994. "Corpus callosum surface area across the human adult life span: Effect of age and gender." <u>Brain Research Bulletin</u>. 4 pp. 373-377.

· Kontos, D., Megalooikonomou, V., Gee, & James, C. "Morphometric analysis of brain images with reduced number of statistical tests: a study on the gender-related differentiation of the corpus callosum." <u>Artificial Intelligence in Medicine</u>. 47(1) pp. 75-86.

· Kimura, <u>Sex and Cognition</u>.

· Lee, DJ., Chen, Y et al. 2002. "Corpus callosum: musician and gender effects." <u>Neuroreport</u>. 14(2) pp. 205-209.

· Moir & Jessel, <u>Brain Sex</u>.

· Pinker, <u>The Sexual Paradox</u>.

· Springer & Deutsch, <u>Left Brain, Right Brain</u>.

· Witelson, S. F. 1989. "Hand and sex differences in the isthmus and genu of the human corpus callosum: A postmortem morphological study." <u>Brain</u>. 112, 799-835.

2. · Darlington, <u>The Female Brain</u>.

· Johnson & Farnworth, "Corpus callosum surface area across the human adult life span."

· Kimura, <u>Sex and Cognition</u>.

· Kontos, Megalooikonomou, Gee, & James, <u>Artificial Intelligence in Medicine</u>.

· Lee & Chen, "Corpus callosum."

· Moir & Jessel, <u>Brain Sex</u>.

· Pinker, <u>The Sexual Paradox</u>.

· Springer & Deutsch, <u>Left Brain, Right Brain</u>.

· Witelson, "Hand and sex differences in the isthmus and genu of the human corpus callosum."

3. Kansaku & Kitazawa, "Imaging Studies on Sex Differences in the Lateralization of Language."

Chapter 18: Emotions: He Stops, Thinks and Buries, She Never Stops

1. · Church, <u>The Genie in Your Genes</u>.

· Doidge, <u>The Brain that Changes Itself</u>.

· Leaf, "The Mind Mapping Approach."

· Leaf, <u>Who Switched Off My Brain?</u>

· Leaf, <u>Who Switched Off My Brain?</u> Revised Edition.

· Mrsic-Flogel, T. 2011. "Connectomics: Mapping the Brain's Complexity." http://starson.starsconfidential. com/2011/04/11/connectomics-mapping-the-brains-complexity/.

2. · Pert, "Opiate Agonists and Antagonists Discriminated by Receptor Binding in the Brain."

· Pert, Molecules of Emotion.

3. · Brizendine, The Male Brain.

· Brizendine, The Female Brain.

· Darlington, The Female Brain.

· Gurian, What Could He Be Thinking?

· Kimura, Sex and Cognition.

· Pinker, The Sexual Paradox.

· Sax, Why Gender Matters.

· Witelson, "Deep, Dark Secrets of His and Her Brains."

· Witelson, "Sandra Witelson."

· Witelson, "It's Partly in Your Head."

· Witelson, S.F., Szechtman, H. & Nahmias, C. 2004. "Sex differences in functional activation patterns revealed by increased emotion processing demands." Neuroreport. 15, 219-223.

4. · Cahill, L., Uncapher, M. et al. 2004. "Sex-Related Hemispheric Lateralization of Amygdala Function in Emotionally Influenced Memory: An fMRI Investigation." Learning and Memory. 11(3) pp. 261–266.

· Canli, T. & Desmond, J.E. et al. 2002. "Sex differences in the neural basis of emotional memories." Proceedings of the National Academy of Sciences of the United States of America. 99 (16) pp. 10789-10794.

· Darnall, B.D. & Suarez, E.C. 2009. "Sex and gender in psychoneuroimmunology research: Past, present and future." Brain, Behavior, and Immunity. 23(5) pp. 55-604.

· Darlington, The Female Brain.

· Pinker, The Sexual Paradox.

· Wrase, J., Klein, S. et al. 2003. "Gender differences in the processing of standardized emotional visual stimuli in humans: a functional magnetic resonance imaging study." Neuroscience Letters. 348(1) pp. 41-45.

Chapter 19: Stress: He Needs His Space, She Needs to Talk it Through

1. · Church, The Genie in Your Genes.

· Leaf, Who Switched Off My Brain?

· Leaf, "Who Switched Off My Brain?" DVD series.

· Leaf, Who Switched Off My Brain? Revised Edition.

· Lipton, The Biology of Belief.

· Petrie, K.J., Booth, R.J. & Pennebaker, J.W. 1998. "The immunological effect of thought suppression." Journal of Personality and Social Psychology. 75 pp. 1264-1272.

· Pert, "Opiate Agonists and Antagonists Discriminated by Receptor Binding in the Brain."

· Pert, Molecules of Emotion.

2. · Mather, M., Lighthall, N.R. et al. 2010. "Sex differences in how stress affects brain activity during face viewing." NeuroReport. 21 (14) 933 DOI: 10.1097/WNR.0b013e32833ddd92.

· Roberts, T.A. & Pennebaker, J.W. 1995. "Women's and Men's strategies in perceiving internal state." Zanna, M. (ed). Advances in Experimental and Social Psychology. 27 pp. 143-176.

· University of Southern California. 2010. "Why We Fight: Men Check Out in Stressful Situations, While Women Show Increased Brain Coordination When Looking at Angry Faces." Science Daily. http://www.sciencedaily.com/releases/2010/09/100928135056.htm

3. · Taylor, S.E. 2006. "Tend and befriend: Biobehavioral Bases of Affiliation Under Stress." Current Directions in Psychological Science. 15(6) pp. 273-277.

· Taylor, S.E., Gonzaga, G. et al. 2006. "Relation Of Oxytocin To Psychological stress and Hypothalamic-Pituitary-Adrenocortical PA axis Activity in Older women." Psychosomatic Medicine. 68 pp. 238-245.

· Taylor, S.E. 2010. "Mechanisms linking early life stress to adult health outcomes." PNAS. USA. 107(19) pp. 8507-8512.

4. · Brizendine, The Male Brain.

· Brizendine, The Female Brain.

· Darlington, The Female Brain.

· Kimura, Sex and Cognition.

· Larrimore & Larrimore, His Brain Her Brain.

· Mather & Lighthall, "Sex differences in how stress affects brain activity during face viewing."

· Moir & Jessel, Brain Sex.

· Pert, "Opiate Agonists and Antagonists Discriminated by Receptor Binding in the Brain."

· Pert, Molecules of Emotion.

· Pinker, The Sexual Paradox.

5. · Damasio, A. & Damasio, H. 2006. "Minding the Body." Daedalus. 135 pp. 15–22.

· Lighthall, N.R., Mather, M. et al. "Acute stress Increases sex differences in risk seeking in the balloon analogue risk task." PLoS. 14(70) pp.e6002 doi1371/journal.pone.0006002.

· University of Pennsylvania: School of Medicine. 2007. "Brain Imaging Shows How Men And Women Cope Differently Under Stress." Science Daily. http://www.sciencedaily.com/releases/2007/11/071119170133.htm.

6. · Neumann, I.D. 2008. "Brain oxytocin: A key regulator of emotional and social behaviours in both females and males." Journal of Neuroendocrinology. 20 pp. 858–865.

· Taylor, S.E., Klein, L.C. et al. 2000. "Biobehavioral responses to stress in females: Tend-and-befriend, not fight-or-flight." Psychological Review. 107 pp. 411–429.

· Wang J.J., Korczykowski et al. 2007. "Gender difference in neural response to psychological stress." Social Cognitive and Affective Neuroscience. 2 pp. 227–239.

7. · Campbell, A. 2008. "Attachment, aggression and affiliation: The role of oxytocin in female social behavior." Biological Psychology. 77 pp. 1–10.

· Girdler, S.S., Jamner, L.D. et al. 1997 "Hostility, testosterone, and vascular reactivity to stress: Effects of sex." International Journal of Behavioral Medicine. 4 pp. 242–263.

· Kudielka, B.M. & Kirschbaum, C. 2005. "Sex differences in HPA axis responses to stress: a review." Biological Psychology. 69 pp. 113–132.

· Sanders, G., Freilicher, J. et al. 1990. "Psychological stress of exposure to uncontrollable noise increases plasma oxytocin in high emotionality women." Psychoneuroendocrinology. 15 pp. 47–58.

· Van Stegeren, A.H., Wolf, O.T. et al. 2008. "Salivary alpha amylase and cortisol responses to different stress tasks: Impact of sex." International Journal of Psychophysiology. 69 pp. 33–40.

· Wang J.J., Korczykowski. et al. 2007. "Gender difference in neural response to psychological stress." Social Cognitive and Affective Neuroscience. 2 pp. 227–239.

· Zimmer, C., Basler, H.D. et al. 2003. "Sex differences in cortisol response to noxious stress." Clinical Journal of Pain. 19 pp. 233–239.

Chapter 20: The Rest State: He Thinks She's Babbling and He Sees "The Hibernate Look"

1. · Begley, S. 2010. "The Hidden Brain: What scientist can learn from 'nothing'." Newsweek. www.newsweek.com/2010/05/31/the-hidden-brain.html.

· Dastjerdi, M., Foster, B. et al. 2010. "Differential electrophysiological response during rest, self-referential, and non-self referential tasks in human posteromedial cortex." www.pnas.org/cgi/doi/10.1073/pnas.1017098108.

· Gur, R. et al. 1995. "Sex differences in regional cerebral glucose metabolism during a resting state." Science. 267(5197) pp. 528-531.

· Kimura, Sex and Cognition.

· Mantini, D., Perucci, M.G. et al. 2007. "Electrophysiological signatures of resting state networks in the human brain." Proceedings of the National Academy of Sciences USA. 104(320 pp. 13170-13175.

· Pinker, The Sexual Paradox.

· Raichle, M. E. & Gusnard, D.A. 2005. "Intrinsic brain activity sets the stage for expression of motivated behavior." The Journal of Comparative Neurolology. 493 pp. 167-176.

· Tian, L., Wang, J. et al. 2011. "Hemisphere-and gender reated differences in small world brain networks: a resting-state functional MRI study Neuroimage." 54(1) pp. 1 91-202.

2. · Raichle & Gusnard, "Intrinsic brain activity sets the stage for expression of motivated behavior."

· University of Montreal. 2010. "Does sex matter? It may when evaluating mental status." Psychology and Sociology. http://www.sciencedaily.com/releases/2010/11/101118123840.htm.

3. · Gur, R. et al. 1995. "Sex differences in regional cerebral glucose metabolism during a resting state." Science. 267(5197) pp. 528-531.

· Gur, R.C., Turetsky, B.I. et al. 1999. "Sex differences in brain gray and white matter in healthy young adults." Journal of Neuroscience. 19 pp. 4065-4072.

· Gur, R.C., Alsop, D. et al. 2000. "An fMRI study of sex differences in regional activation to a verbal and a spatial task." Brain and Language. 74 pp. 157-170.

Chapter 21: Anger: He Boils Over Then Cools Down, She Burns Slowly

1. · Baillargeon, R.H. et al. 2007. "Gender differences in physical aggression: A prospective population-based survey of children before and after 2 years of age." Developmental Psychology. 43(1) pp. 13-26. doi:10.1037/0012-1649.43.1.13.

   · Brizendine, The Male Brain.

   · Brizendine, The Female Brain.

   · Johnson, D. McDermott, R. et al. 2006. "Overconfidence in wargames: experimental evidence on expectations, aggression, gender and testosterone." Proc Biol Sci. 273(1600) pp. 2513-2520 doi: 10.1098?rspb.2006.3606.

   · Pinker, The Sexual Paradox.

2. · Brizendine, The Male Brain.

   · Johnson & McDermott, "Overconfidence in Wargames."

   · Pinker, The Sexual Paradox.

3. · Burton, L., Hafetz, J. & Henninger, D. 2007. "Gender Differences in Relational and Physical Aggression." Soical Behavior and Personality. 35(1), 41-50.

   · Burton, L., Hafetz et al. 2008. "Aggression, gender-typical childhood play, and a prenatal hormonal index." Social Behavior and Personality.

   · Deloris, 2009. "Gender Differences and Aggression:Males and females are different when it comes to expressing aggressive behaviors." http://socyberty.com/psychology/gender-differences-and-aggression//.

   · Reidy, D.E., Sloan, C. et al. 2008. "Gender role conformity and aggression: influence of perpetrator and victim conformity on direct physical aggression in women Personality and individual differences." 46(2) pp. 231-235.

   · Simmons, R. 2002 Odd Girl Out: The Hidden Culture of Aggression. Harcourt Trade. USA.

4. · Brener N.D., Simon TR, Krug E.G., Lowry R. 1999. "Recent trends in violence- related behaviors among high school students in the United States." JAMA. 282:440—446.

   · Lowry R., Powell K.E., Kann L., Collins J.L., Kolbe L.J. "Weapon-carrying, physical fighting, and fight-related injury among U.S. adolescents." Am J.

   · Pinker, The Sexual Paradox.

5. Gur, R.C., Gunning-Dixon, F. et al. 2002. "Sex Differences in Tempero-limbic and frontal brain Volumes of healthy adults." Cerebral Cortex. 12(9) pp. 998-1003.

6. · Cahill, "Sex-related hemispheric Lateralization of Amygdala Function in emotionally Influenced Memory: An fMRI investigation."

   · Cahill, "His Brain Her Brain."

   · Cahill, "Why sex matters for neuroscience."

   · Xia-Nian, Z., Kelly, C. et al. 2010. "Growing together and growing apart: regional and sex differences in the lifespan developmental trajectories of functional homotopy." The Journal of Neuroscience. 30(45) pp. 15034-15043. doi: 10.1523/ JNEUROSCI.2612-10.2010.

7. · Brizendine, <u>The Male Brain</u>.

　· Brizendine, <u>The Female Brain</u>.

　· Cahill, "Sex-related hemispheric Lateralization of Amygdala Function in emotionally Influenced Memory: An fMRI investigation."

　· Cahill, "His Brain Her Brain."

　· Cahill, "Why sex matters for neuroscience."

　· Kimura, <u>Sex and Cognition</u>.

　· Larrimore & Larrimore, <u>His Brain Her Brain</u>.

　· Moir & Jessel, <u>Brain Sex</u>.

8. · Brizendine, <u>The Male Brain</u>.

　· Brizendine, <u>The Female Brain</u>.

　· Cahill, "Sex-related hemispheric Lateralization of Amygdala Function in emotionally Influenced Memory: An fMRI investigation."

　· Cahill, "His Brain Her Brain."

　· Cahill, "Why sex matters for neuroscience."

　· Kimura, <u>Sex and Cognition</u>.

　· Larrimore & Larrimore, <u>His Brain Her Brain</u>.

　· Moir & Jessel, <u>Brain Sex</u>.

9. · Bateup, H.S. et al. 2002. "Testosterone, cortisol and Women's competition." <u>Journal of Evolution and Human Behavior</u>. 23(3) pp. 387-394.

　· Hyyppa, M.T., Alaranta, M.D. 2006. "Gender Differences in psychological and cortisol responses to distress: A five year follow-up of patients with back pain." <u>Stress Medicine</u>. 4(2) pp. 117-121.

　· Pert, "Opiate Agonists and Antagonists Discriminated by Receptor Binding in the Brain."

　· Pert, <u>Molecules of Emotion</u>.

　· Taylor & Klein, "Biobehavioral responses to stress in females."

10. · Andreano & Cahill, "Sex influences on the neurobiology of learning and memory."

　· Brizendine, <u>The Male Brain</u>.

　· Brizendine, <u>The Female Brain</u>.

　· Cahill, "Sex-related hemispheric Lateralization of Amygdala Function in emotionally Influenced Memory: An fMRI investigation."

　· Cahill, "His Brain Her Brain."

　· Cahill, "Why sex matters for neuroscience."

　· Halpern, <u>Sex Differences in Cognitive Abilities</u>.

　· Moir & Jessel, <u>Brain Sex</u>.

　· Pinker, <u>The Sexual Paradox</u>.

　· Shaywitz, "Sex Differences in the Functional Organization of the Brain for Language."

　· Springer & Deutsch, <u>Left Brain, Right Brain</u>.

· Witelson, "Deep, Dark Secrets of His and Her Brains."

· Witelson, "Sandra Witelson."

· Witelson, "It's Partly in Your Head."

11. · Brizendine, The Male Brain.

· Brizendine, The Female Brain.

· Pert, "Opiate Agonists and Antagonists Discriminated by Receptor Binding in the Brain."

· Pert, Molecules of Emotion.

12. · Church, The Genie in Your Genes.

· Dingfelder, S.F. 2008. "An insidious enemy." American Psychological Association. http://www.apa.org/monitor/2008/10/stress-immune.aspx.

· Holland, E. 1999. "Researchers learn how stress slows wound healing." Ohio State University. http://researchnews.osu.edu/archive/ilwound.htm.

· Kiecolt-Glaser, J., Loving, T. et al. 2005. "Hostile Interactions, Proinflammatory cytokine Production and Wound Healing." Archives of General Psychiatry. 62(12) pp. 1377-1384.

· USA Today. 2005. "Study: A Happy Marriage Can Help Mend Physical Wounds."

Chapter 22: Empathy: Discovering the Power of Mirror Neurons

1. · Church, The Genie in Your Genes.

· Lipton, The Biology of Belief.

· Lipton, Differentiation.

· Newberg & Waldman, How God Changes Your Brain.

2. · Cahill, "His Brain Her Brain."

· Cheng, Y., Tzeng, O. et al. 2006. "Gender differences in the human mirror system: a magnetoencephalography study." Cognitive Neuroscience and Neuropsychology. 17(11) pp. 1115-1119.

· Cheng, Y., Chou, K. et al. 2009. "Sex differences in the neuroanatomy of human mirror-neuron system: a voxel-based imorphometric nvestigation." Neuroscience. 158 pp. 713-720.

· Hojat, M. 2011. "Development of Prosocial Behavior and Empathy in the Hand that Rocks the Cradle." World Congress of Families III. http://www.worldcongress.org/wcf3_spkrs/wcf3_hojat.htm.

· Iacoboni, M., Molnar-Szakacs I. et al. 2005. "Grasping the intentions of others with one's own mirror neuron system." PLoS Biology. 3 pp. e79.

· Larrimore & Larrimore, His Brain Her Brain.

· Pinker, The Sexual Paradox.

· Rizzolatti, G., Fogassi, L. et al. 2001. "Neurophysiological mechanisms underlying the understanding and imitation of action." Nature Reviews Neuroscience. 2:661–670.

· Rizzolatti, G., Craighero, L. 2004. "The mirror-neuron system." Annual Review Neuroscience. 27 pp. 169–192.

· Schulte-Rüther, M., Markowitsch, H.J. et al. 2008. "Gender differences in brain networks supporting empathy." Neuroimage. 42(1) pp. 393–403.

· Yamasue, H., Abe, O. et al. 2008. "Sex-linked neuroanatomical basis of human altruistic cooperativeness." Cereb Cortex. 18 pp. 2331–2340.

3. · Blakeslee, S. 2006. "Cells That Read Minds." The New York Times. http://www.nytimes.com/2006/01/10/science/10mirr.html?pagewanted=print.

· Rizzolatti & Fogassi, "Neurophysiological mechanisms underlying the understanding and imitation of action."

· Rizzolatti & Craighero, "The mirror-neuron system."

4. · Nova. 2005. "Mirror Neurons." http://www.pbs.org/wgbh/nova/sciencenow/3204/01.html.

· Rizzolatti & Fogassi, "Neurophysiological mechanisms underlying the understanding and imitation of action."

· Rizzolatti & Craighero, "The mirror-neuron system."

5. · Iacoboni, Mirroring People.

· Rizzolatti & Fogassi, "Neurophysiological mechanisms underlying the understanding and imitation of action."

· Rizzolatti & Craighero, "The mirror-neuron system."

6. · Jackson, P.L. et al. 2004. "How Do We Perceive the Pain of Others? A Window into the Neural Processes Involved in Empathy." NeuroImage. 24, pp. 771-779.

· Singer, "Empathy for Pain Involves the Affective but not Sensory Components of Pain."

· Wicker, B. et al. 2003. "Both of Us Disgusted in My Insula: The Common Neural Basis of Seeing and Feeling Disgust." Neuron. 40 pp. 655-664.

7. · Iacoboni, Mirroring People.

· Ramachandran, The Tell-Tale Brain.

· Rizzolatti & Fogassi, "Neurophysiological mechanisms underlying the understanding and imitation of action."

· Rizzolatti & Craighero, "The mirror-neuron system."

8. · Schulte-Rüther, M., Markowitsch, H.J. et al. 2008. "Gender differences in brain networks supporting empathy." Neuroimage. 42(1) pp. 393–403.

· Cheng, Y., Lee, P.L. et al. 2008. "Gender Differences in the Mu Rhythm of the Human Mirror-Neuron System." PLoS ONE. 3(5): e2113. doi:10.1371/journal.pone.0002113.

9. · Cheng & Lee, "Gender Differences in the Mu Rhythm of the Human Mirror-Neuron System."

· Ramachandran, V. 2010. "About Mirror Neurons." http://www.shockmd.com/2010/01/06/about-mirror-neurons/.

· Schulte-Rüther & Markowitsch, "Gender differences in brain networks supporting empathy."

10. · Singer, "Empathy for Pain Involves the Affective but not Sensory Components of Pain."

· Pfeifer, J.H., Iacoboni, M. 2008. "Mirroring others' emotions relates to empathy and interpersonal competence in children." Neuroimage. 39 pp. 2076–2085.

· Cheng & Lee, "Gender Differences in the Mu Rhythm of the Human Mirror-Neuron System."

· Roberts & Pennebaker, "Women's and Men's strategies in perceiving internal state."

Chapter 23: Love & Sex: All You Need is . . . *Oxytocin?*

1.   Fisher, H.E. 2004. Why We Love: The Nature and Chemistry of Romantic Love. Holt. NY.

2.   · Aron, A., Fisher, H. et al. 2005. "Reward, motivation, and emotion systems associated with early-stage intense romantic love." Journal of Neurophysiology. 94 pp. 327–337.

   · Bartels, A. & Zeki, S. 2000. "The neural basis of romantic love." Neuroreport. 11 pp. 3829–3834.

   · Bartels, A. & Zeki, S. 2004. "The neural correlates of maternal and romantic love." Neuroimage. 21 pp. 1155–1166.

   · Fisher, H., Aron, A. et al. 2005. "Romantic love: an fMRI study of a neural mechanism for mate choice." Journal of Comparative Neurolology. 493: 58–62.

   · Mashek, D., Aron, A. et al. 2000. "Identifying, evoking, and measuring intense feelings of romantic love." Represent Res Social Psychology. 24 pp. 48–55.

   · Master, S.L., Eisenberger, N.I. et al. 2009. "A Picture's Worth: Partner Photographs Reduce Experimentally Induced Pain." Psychology Science. 20 pp. 1316–1318.

   · Ortigue, S., Bianchi-Demicheli, F. et al. 2007. "The neural basis of love as a subliminal prime: an event-related functional magnetic resonance imaging study." Journal of Cognitive Neuroscience. 19 pp. 1218–1230.

   · Reynaud, M., Karila, L. et al. 2010. "Is Love Passion an Addictive Disorder?" Am J Drug Alcohol Abuse.

   · Xu, X. & Aron, A. 2010. "Reward and motivation systems: a brain mapping study of early-stage intense romantic love in Chinese participants." Human Brain Mapping.

   · Younger, J., Aron, A. et al. 2010. "Viewing pictures of a Romantic partner Reduces Experimental Pain: Involvement of Neural reward systems." PLoS ONE. 5(10) e13309.

3.   · Doidge, The Brain that Changes Itself.

   · Master & Eisenberger, "A Picture's Worth: Partner Photographs Reduce Experimentally Induced Pain."

   · Reynaud, M., Karila, L. et al. 2010. "Is Love Passion an Addictive Disorder?" Am J Drug Alcohol Abuse.

   · Pert, "Opiate Agonists and Antagonists Discriminated by Receptor Binding in the Brain."

   · Pert, Molecules of Emotion.

4.   · Master & Eisenberger, "A Picture's Worth: Partner Photographs Reduce Experimentally Induced Pain."

   · Younger & Aron, "Viewing pictures of a Romantic partner Reduces Experimental Pain."

5.   · eScience News. 2011 "Acute pain is eased with the touch of a hand."

   · Fisher & Aron, "Romantic love: an fMRI study of a neural mechanism for mate choice."

   · Younger & Aron, "Viewing pictures of a Romantic partner Reduces Experimental Pain."

6.   · Master & Eisenberger, "A Picture's Worth: Partner Photographs Reduce Experimentally Induced Pain."

   · Younger & Aron, "Viewing pictures of a Romantic partner Reduces Experimental Pain."

7.   · "Adolescent Brain." http://www.aea267.k12.ia.us/r4/index.php?page=r4-adolescent-brain.

   · Alvarez, M. 2007. "A Hug A Day Could Save Your Life." Fox News. http://www.foxnews.com/story/0,2933,249138,00.html.

· Berns, G.S., Moore, S. et al. 2009. "Adolescent Engagement In Dangerous Behaviours Is Associated With Increased White Matter Maturity Of Frontal Cortex." PLoS ONE. 4(8) pp. e6773 doi:10.1371/journal. pone.0006773.

·"Brain Briefings: The Adolescent Brain." 2007. Society for Neuroscience. http://www.sfn.org/index. aspx?pagename=brainBriefings_Adolescent_brain.

· Campbell, A. 2010 "Oxytocin and Human behaviour." Personality and Social Psychology Review. 14(3) pp. 281-295.

· Diamond, Enriching Heredity.

· Diamond & Hopson, Magic Trees of the Mind.

· Eshel, N., Nelson, E.E. et al. 2007. "Neural substrates of choice selection in adults and adolescents: development of the ventrolateral prefrontal and anterior cingulate cortices."

· Gied, J.N. 2008. "The teen brain: insights from neuroimaging." Journal of Adolescent Health. 42 pp. 335–343.

· Gied, J. "Jay Gied Interview." Frontline. http://www.pbs.org/wgbh/pages/frontline/shows/teenbrain/ interviews/giedd.html.

· Giorgio, A., Watkins, K.E. et al. 2008. "Changes in white matter microstructure during adolescence." NeuroImage. 39 pp. 52–61. Neuropsychologia. 45 pp. 1270–1279.

· Grewen, K.M., Girdler, S.S. et al. 2005. "Effects of partner support in resting oxytocin, Cortisol, Norepinephrine, and Blood pressure before and after warm partner contact." Psychosomatic Medicine. 67 pp. 531-538.

· Holt-Lunstad, J., Birmingham, W.A. et al. 2008. "Influence of a "warm touch" support enhancement intervention among married couples on ambulatory blood pressure, oxytocin, alpha amylase and cortisol." Psychosomatic Medicine. 70 pp. 976-985.

· Landau, M. "Deciphering the Adolescent Brain." The Harvard University Gazette. http://www.waldorflibrary. org/Articles/Adolesce2.pdf.

· Pert, "Opiate Agonists and Antagonists Discriminated by Receptor Binding in the Brain."

· Pert, Molecules of Emotion.

· Spinks, S. 2000. "Adolescent Brains are Works in Progress." Frontline. http://www.pbs.org/wgbh/pages/ frontline/shows/teenbrain/work/adolescent.html.

8. · "Adolescent Brain." http://www.aea267.k12.ia.us/r4/index.php?page=r4-adolescent-brain.

· Berns & Moore, "Adolescent Engagement In Dangerous Behaviours Is Associated With Increased White Matter Maturity Of Frontal Cortex."

·"Brain Briefings: The Adolescent Brain." http://www.sfn.org/index.aspx?pagename=brainBriefings_ Adolescent_brain.

· Eshel & Nelson, "Neural substrates of choice selection in adults and adolescents."

· Gied, "The teen brain: insights from neuroimaging."

· Gied, "Jay Gied Interview."

· Giorgio & Watkins, "Changes in white matter microstructure during adolescence."

· Landau, "Deciphering the Adolescent Brain."

9. · Keroack, E.J. & Diggs, R.J. Jr. "Bonding Imperative." A Special Report from the Abstinence Medical Council.

· Light, C., Grewen, K.M. et al. 2005. "More frequent partner hugs and higher oxytocin levels are linked to lower blood pressure and heart rate in premenopausal women." Biological Psychology. 69(1) pp. 5-21.

- McDowell, S. 2009. "Why Evolutionary Theory is Wrong about Sex." http://www.conversantlife.com/sex/why-evolutionary-theory-is-wrong-about-sex.

- McIlhaney, J.S. & Mckissie Bush, F. 2008. Hooked: New Science on How Casual Sex is Affecting Our Children. Northfield Publishing. Chicago.

- Rector, R., Johnson, K. et al. 2003. Harmful Effects of Early Sexual Activity and Multiple Sexual Partners Among Women: Charts." The Heritage Foundation. http://www.heritage.org/research/reports/2003/06/harmful-effects-of-early-sexual-activity-and-multiple-sexual-partners-among-women-charts.

- "Women who have multiple sexual partners damage their ability to bond with a future partner due to low oxytocin levels." http://secularheretic-st.blogspot.com/2009/01/woman-who-have-multiple-sexual-partners.html.

10. · Baumeister, R, F., Wotman, S.R. et al. 1993. "Unrequited love: On heartbreak, anger, guilt, scriptlessness, and humiliation." Journal of Personality and Social Psychology. 64(3) pp. 377-394.

- Fisher, H.E. & Brown, L.L. et al. 2009. "Reward, Addiction, and Emotion Regulation Systems associated With Rejection in Love." Journal Physiology. 104(1) pp. 51-60.

- Pert, "Opiate Agonists and Antagonists Discriminated by Receptor Binding in the Brain."

- Pert, Molecules of Emotion.

11. · Acevedo, B.P., Aron, A. et al. 2011. "Neural correlates of long-term intense romantic love." Social Cognitive and Affective Neuroscience. doi: 10.1093/scan/nsq092.

- Fisher & Aron, "Romantic love: an fMRI study of a neural mechanism for mate choice."

12. · Cahill, L., Uncapher, M. et al. 2004. "Sex-Related Hemispheric Lateralization of Amygdala Function in Emotionally Influenced Memory: An fMRI Investigation." Learning and Memory. 11(3) pp. 261–266.

- Campbell, A. 2010. "Oxytocin and Human behaviour." Personality and Social Psychology Review. 14(3) pp. 281-295.

- Francis, D., Young, L et al. 2002. "Naturally Occurring Differences in Maternal Care are Associated with the Expression of Oxytocin and Vasopressin (V1a) Receptors: Gender Differences." Journal of Neuroendocrinology. 14 pp. 349–353. http://www.dafml.unito.it/anatomy/panzica/neuroendo/articolipdf/2002FrancisJNeuroEndo.pdf.

- Holt-Lunstad & Birmingham, "Influence of a "warm touch" support enhancement intervention among married couples on ambulatory blood pressure, oxytocin, alpha amylase and cortisol."

- Pert, "Opiate Agonists and Antagonists Discriminated by Receptor Binding in the Brain."

- Pert, Molecules of Emotion.

13. Slatcher, R.B. & Pennebaker, J.W. 2006. "How do I love thee? Let me count the words: The social effects of expressive writing." Psychological Science. 17 pp. 660-664.

14. · Brizendine, The Female Brain.

- Brizendine, The Male Brain.

- Darlington, The Female Brain.

- Kimura, Sex and Cognition.

- Larrimore & Larrimore, His Brain Her Brain.

- Moir & Jessel, Brain Sex.

- Pert, "Opiate Agonists and Antagonists Discriminated by Receptor Binding in the Brain."

- Pert, <u>Molecules of Emotion</u>.
- Pinker, <u>The Sexual Paradox</u>.

15.
- Brizendine, <u>The Female Brain</u>.
- Brizendine, <u>The Male Brain</u>.
- Darlington, <u>The Female Brain</u>.
- Kimura, <u>Sex and Cognition</u>.
- Larrimore & Larrimore, <u>His Brain Her Brain</u>.
- Moir & Jessel, <u>Brain Sex</u>.
- Pert, "Opiate Agonists and Antagonists Discriminated by Receptor Binding in the Brain."
- Pert, <u>Molecules of Emotion</u>.
- Pinker, <u>The Sexual Paradox</u>.

16.
- Brizendine, <u>The Female Brain</u>.
- Brizendine, <u>The Male Brain</u>.
- Darlington, <u>The Female Brain</u>.
- Kimura, <u>Sex and Cognition</u>.
- Larrimore & Larrimore, <u>His Brain Her Brain</u>.
- Moir & Jessel, <u>Brain Sex</u>.
- Pert, "Opiate Agonists and Antagonists Discriminated by Receptor Binding in the Brain."
- Pert, <u>Molecules of Emotion</u>.
- Pinker, <u>The Sexual Paradox</u>.

17.
- Brizendine, <u>The Female Brain</u>.
- Brizendine, <u>The Male Brain</u>.
- Pert, "Opiate Agonists and Antagonists Discriminated by Receptor Binding in the Brain."
- Pert, <u>Molecules of Emotion</u>.
- Uvnas-Moberg, "Oxytocin: World's expert talks about this calming hormone."

Chapter 24: Gray and White Matter: He's Like a Supercomputer, She's Like the Internet

1.
- Brizendine, <u>The Female Brain</u>.
- Brizendine, <u>The Male Brain</u>.
- Darlington, <u>The Female Brain</u>.
- Fields, R.D. 2004. "The Other Half of the Brain." <u>Scientific American</u>. 290(4) pp. 54-61.
- Haier & Jung, "The neuroanatomy of general intelligence."
- Jausovec, N. & Jausovec, K. 2005. "Sex differences in brain activity related to general and emotional intelligence." <u>Brain and Cognition</u>. 59(3) pp. 277-286.

· Jung & Haier, "The Parieto-Frontal-Integration Theory (P-FIT) Of Intelligence."

· Kimura, Sex and Cognition.

· Luders, E., Narr, K. et al. 2007. "Positive correlations between corpus callosum thickness and intelligence." Neuroimage. 37(4) pp. 1457-1464.

· Moir & Jessel, Brain Sex.

· Neubauer, A., Fink, A. et al. 2002. "Intelligence and neural efficiency: The influence of task content and sex on the brain-IQ relationship." Intelligence. 30(6) pp. 515-536.

· Pinker, The Sexual Paradox.

· Tang, C.Y., Eaves, E.L. et al. 2010. "Brain Networks for working memory and factors of intelligence assessed in males and females with fMRI and DTI." Intelligence. 38(3) pp. 293-303.

· Witelson, "Deep, Dark Secrets of His and Her Brains."

· Witelson, "Sandra Witelson."

· Witelson, "It's Partly in Your Head."

2. · Coyle, "The Talent Code."

· Fields, "The Other Half of the Brain."

· Fields, R.D. 2005. "Myelination: An Overlooked Mechanism of Synaptic Plasticity?" Neuroscientist. 11(6) pp. 528-531.

· Fields, "White matter matters."

· Pujol, J. 2006. "Myelination of Language-Related Areas in the Developing Brain." Neurology. 66 pp. 339-343.

3. · Coyle, "The Talent Code."

· Fields, "The Other Half of the Brain."

· Fields, "Myelination: An Overlooked Mechanism of Synaptic Plasticity?"

· Fields, "White matter matters."

· Pujol, "Myelination of Language-Related Areas in the Developing Brain."

4. · Coyle, "The Talent Code."

· Diamond, Scheibel, Murphy & Harvey, "On the Brain of a Scientist: Albert Einstein."

· Diamond, Enriching Heredity.

· Diamond & Hopson, Magic Trees of the Mind.

· Ericsson, "The Role of Deliberate Practice in the Acquisition of Expert Performance."

· Fields, "White matter matters."

· Haier & Jung, "The neuroanatomy of general intelligence."

5. Leaf, The Gift in You.

6. · Fusion, J. "Difference Between Boys and Girls Memory." eHow. http://www.ehow.co.uk/about_5244222_difference-between-boys-girls-memory.html.

· Haier & Jung, "The neuroanatomy of general intelligence."

· Jung, R.E., Haier, R.J. et al. 2005. "Sex differences in N-Acetylaspartate correlates of general intelligence: an H-MRS study of normal human brain." Neuroimage. 26 pp. 965-972.

· Jung, R.E. & Haier, R.J. "The Parieto-Frontal Integration Theory (P-FIT) of intelligence: Converging neuroimaging evidence." Behavioral and Brain Sciences. 30 pp. 135-187. DOI: 10.1017/S0140525X07001185.

· University of California, Irvine. 2005. "Intelligence in Men and Women is A Gray and White Matter." Science Daily. http://www.sciencedaily.com/releases/2005/01/050121100142.htm.

7.   · Witelson, Sex differences in the neurology of cognition.

· Witelson, "Deep, Dark Secrets of His and Her Brains."

· Witelson, "Sandra Witelson."

· Witelson, "It's Partly in Your Head."

8.   · Cahill, "Why sex matters for neuroscience."

· Cahill, "His Brain Her Brain."

· Gur, R.C. & Gur, R.E. et al. 1987. "Age and regional cerebral blood flow at rest and during cognitive activity." Arch Gen Psychiatry. 44 pp. 617-621.

· Gur, "Sex differences in regional cerebral glucose metabolism during a resting state."

· Gur, R.C., Ragland, J.D. 2009. "Regional Differences in the coupling between resting cerebral blood flow and metabolism may indicate action preparedness as a default state." Cerebral Cortex. 19(2) pp. 375-382.

· Gurian, M. & Annis, B. 2008. Leadership and the Sexes. Jossey-Bass. San Francisco, CA.

· Hamilton, A. 2010. "Studies: An Idle Brain May be Ripe for Learning." TIME. http://www.time.com/time/health/article/0,8599,1957114,00.html.

· Mintun, M.A. & Lundstrom, B.N. et al. 2001. "Blood flow and oxygen delivery to human brain during functional activity: theoretical modeling and experimental data." Proc Natl Acad Sci USA. 98 pp. 6859-6864.

· Pease & Pease, Why Men Don't Listen and Women Can't Read Maps.

· Pinker, The Sexual Paradox.

· Raichle & Gusnard, "Intrinsic brain activity sets the stage for expression of motivated behavior."

· Raichle, M.E. & Snyder, A.Z. 2007. "A default mode of brain function: a brief history of an evolving idea." Neuroimage. 37 pp. 1083-1090.

· Richard, J. 2006. "The Vast Arctic Tundra of the Male Brain." http://itre.cis.upenn.edu/~myl/languagelog/archives/003551.html.

· Sax, Why Gender Matters.

9.   · Brizendine, The Female Brain.

· Darlington, The Female Brain.

· Fusion, "Difference Between Boys and Girls Memory."

· Haier & Jung, "The neuroanatomy of general intelligence."

· Jung & Haier, "Sex differences in N-Acetylaspartate correlates of general intelligence."

· Jung & Haier, "The Parieto-Frontal-Integration Theory (P-FIT) Of Intelligence."

· Kimura, Sex and Cognition.

· Moir & Jessel, Brain Sex.

· Pinker, The Sexual Paradox.

· University of California, Irvine, "Intelligence in Men and Women is A Gray and White Matter."

10. · Cahill & Uncapher, "Sex-Related Hemispheric Lateralization of Amygdala Function in Emotionally Influenced Memory."

· Cahill, "His Brain, Her Brain."

· Canli & Desmond, "Sex differences in the neural basis of emotional memories."

· Douglas, K. 1996. "Cherchez la différence." New Scientist.

· Geary, D.C. 1998. "Male, female: The evolution of human sex differences." American Psychological Association. ISBN 1557985278.

· Gouchie, C. & Kimura, D. 1991. "The relationship between testosterone levels and cognitive ability patterns." Psychoneuroendocrinology. 16 (4) pp. 323–324. doi:10.1016/0306-4530(91)90018-O. PMID 1745699.

· Nyborg, H. 1984. Performance and intelligence in hormonally different groups. Prog. Brain Res. 61 pp. 491–508. doi:10.1016/S0079-6123(08)64456-8. PMID 6396713.

· Resnick, S.M. & Berenbaum, S.A. et al.1986. "Early hormonal influences on cognitive functioning in congenital adrenal hyperplasia." Developmental Psychology. 22 (2) pp. 191–8. doi:10.1037/0012-1649.22.2.191.

·"Sexes handle emotions differently." 2002. BBC News—Health. http://news.bbc.co.uk/2/hi/health/2146003.stm.

· University of California, Las Angelas. 2003. "Gender Differences In Brain Response To Pain." Science Daily.

11. Baron-Cohen, S. 2003. The Essential Difference: The Truth about the Male and Female Brain. Basic Books. NY.

Chapter 25: Spatial Perception: He Uses a Compass, She Paints a Picture

1. · Brizendine, The Female Brain.

· Brizendine, The Male Brain.

· Darlington, The Female Brain.

· Diamond & Hopson, Magic Trees of the Mind.

· Gron, G. & Wunderlich, A.P. 2000. "Brain activation during human navigation: gender-different neural networks as sunstrate of performance." Nature Neuroscience. 3 pp. 404-408.

· Gurian, What Could He Be Thinking?

· Kimura, Sex and Cognition.

· Mozley, L.H., Gur, R. et al. 2001. "Striatal dopamine transporters and cognitive functioning in healthy men and women." Am J of Psychiatry. 158 pp. 1492-1499.

· Pinker, The Sexual Paradox.

· Sax, Why Gender Matters.

· Springer & Deutsch, Left Brain, Right Brain.

· Witelson, Sex differences in the neurology of cognition.

· Witelson, "Deep, Dark Secrets of His and Her Brains."

· Witelson, "Sandra Witelson."

· Witelson, "It's Partly in Your Head."

2. · Brizendine, The Female Brain.

· Brizendine, The Male Brain.

- Darlington, The Female Brain.
- Kimura, Sex and Cognition.
- Newcombe, N.S. 2007. "Taking Science Seriously: Straight thinking about spatial sex differences." in Ceci, S. & Williams, W. (Eds.): "Why aren't more women in science? Top researchers debate the evidence." American Psychological Association. pp. 69-77.

3. · Brizendine, The Female Brain.
   · Brizendine, The Male Brain.
   · Darlington, The Female Brain.
   · Eals, M. & Silverman, I. 1992. "Sex differences in spatial abilities: evolutionary theory and data." The Adapted Mind: Evolutionary Psychology and the Generation of Culture. edited by J. H. Barkow. Oxford University Press. NY.
   · Geary, "Male, female: The evolution of human sex differences."
   · Jones, C. & Healy, S.D. 2006. "Differences in cue use and spatial memory in men and women." Proceedings of the Royal Society of London Series B. 273 pp. 2241-2247.
   · Kimura, Sex and Cognition.

4. · Brizendine, The Female Brain.
   · Brizendine, The Male Brain.
   · Darlington, The Female Brain.
   · Kimura, D. 2002. "Sex Differences in the brain: Men and Women Display Patterns of Behavioral and Cognitive Differences That reflect Varying Hormonal Influences on Brain Development." Scientific American.
   · Marano, "The New Sex Scorecard: Men and women's minds really do work differently—but not on everything."
   · Schaie, K.W. 2005. Developmental Influences on Adult Intelligence: the Seattle longitudinal study. Oxford University Press. NY.

5. · Gron & Wunderlich, "Brain activation during human navigation."
   · Schaie, Developmental Influences on Adult Intelligence.

6. · Gurian, What Could He Be Thinking?
   · Pearlson, G.D. 1995."Structure differences in the cerebral cortex of normal male and female subjects." Psychiatry Research—Neuroimaging. 61 pp. 129-135.
   · Pinker, The Sexual Paradox.
   · Sax, Why Gender Matters.
   · Witelson, "Deep, Dark Secrets of His and Her Brains."
   · Witelson, "Sandra Witelson."
   · Witelson, "It's Partly in Your Head."

7. · Gurian, What Could He Be Thinking?
   · Pinker, The Sexual Paradox.
   · Witelson, "Deep, Dark Secrets of His and Her Brains."
   · Witelson, "Sandra Witelson."

- Witelson, "It's Partly in Your Head."
- Sax, Why Gender Matters.

8.
- Hausmann, M. & Schoofs, D. et al. 2009. "Interactive effects of sex hormones and gender stereotypes on cognitive sex differences—A psychobiological approach." Psychoneuroendocrinology. 34 (3) pp. 389–401 doi:10.1016/j.psyneuen.2008.09.019. PMID 18992993.
- McGlone, M. S. & Aranson, J. 2006. Stereotype threat. identity salience, and spatial reasoning. Journal of Applied Developmental Psychology. 27 (5) pp. 486-493. doi:10.1016/j.appdev.2006.06.003.
- Newcombe, "Taking Science Seriously."
- Pease, A. & Pease, B. 2003. Why Men Don't Listen and Women Can't Read Maps. Pease International. Great Britain.
- Pease, A. & Pease, B. 2004. Why Men Don't Have a Clue and Women Always Need More Shoes. Broadway Books.
- Sharps, M.J. & Price, J. L. 1994. "Spatial cognition and gender: Instructional and stimulus influences on mental image rotation performance." Psychology of Women Quarterly. 18 (3) pp. 413–425. doi:10.1111/j.1471-6402.1994.tb00464.x.

9.
- Darlington, The Female Brain.
- Pease & Pease, Why Men Don't Listen and Women Can't Read Maps.
- Pease & Pease, Why Men Don't Have a Clue and Women Always Need More Shoes.
- Sinclair, B. 2007. "University of Toronto study finds lasting benefits from just 10 hours of game play." http://www.gamespot.com/news/6180510.html.

10.
- Baron-Cohen, The Essential Difference.
- Brizendine, The Female Brain.
- Brizendine, The Male Brain.
- Chrisler, J.C. & McCreary, D.R. 2010. Handbook of Gender Research in psychology Volume 1. Springer. NY.
- Diamond & Hopson, Magic Trees of the Mind.
- Darlington, The Female Brain.
- Gron & Wunderlich, "Brain activation during human navigation."
- Gur, R. et al. 2001. "Striatal dopamine transporters and cognitive functioning in healthy men and women." Am J of Psychiatry. 158 pp. 1492-1499.
- Gurian, What Could He Be Thinking?
- Kimura, Sex and Cognition.
- Moir & Jessel, Brain Sex.
- Pinker, The Sexual Paradox.
- Sax, Why Gender Matters.
- Springer & Deutsch, Left Brain, Right Brain.
- Witelson, Sex differences in the neurology of cognition.
- Witelson, "Deep, Dark Secrets of His and Her Brains."
- Witelson, "Sandra Witelson."

· Witelson, "It's Partly in Your Head."

11. · Chrisler & McCreary, <u>Handbook of Gender Research in psychology Volume 1</u>.

   · Baron-Cohen, <u>The Essential Difference</u>.

   · Diamond & Hopson, <u>Magic Trees of the Mind</u>.

12. · Pease & Pease, <u>Why Men Don't Listen and Women Can't Read Maps</u>.

   · Wolf, C.C. & Ocklenburg, S. et al. 2009. "Sex differences in real life spatial cognition." <u>Poster, 16th annual meeting of the Cognitive Neuroscience Society</u>. San Francisco, USA.

   · Wolf, C.C., Ocklenburg, S. et al. 2009. "Sex differences in parking. Nature or nurture? Poster, 5th annual meeting of the Young Neuroscientist Congress. <u>Neuo-Visionen</u>.

   · Wolf, C.C., Ocklenburg, S. et al. 2010. "Sex-differences in parking are affected by biological and social factors." <u>Psychological Research</u>. 74 (4) pp. 429-435.

13. · Pease & Pease, <u>Why Men Don't Listen and Women Can't Read Maps</u>.

   · Wolf & Ocklenburg, "Sex differences in real life spatial cognition."

   · Wolf & Ocklenburg, "Sex differences in parking. Nature or nurture?"

   · Wolf & Ocklenburg, "Sex-differences in parking are affected by biological and social factors."

14. · Gurian, <u>What Could He Be Thinking?</u>

   · Larrimore & Larrimore, <u>His Brain Her Brain</u>.

   · Moir & Jessel, <u>Brain Sex</u>.

15. · Gurian, <u>What Could He Be Thinking?</u>

   · Larrimore & Larrimore, <u>His Brain Her Brain</u>.

   · Moir & Jessel, <u>Brain Sex</u>.

16. Cahill & Uncapher, "Sex-Related Hemispheric Lateralization of Amygdala Function in Emotionally Influenced Memory."

17. Gur & Ragland, "Regional Differences in the coupling between resting cerebral blood flow and metabolism may indicate action preparedness as a default state."

RECOMMENDED READING

The concepts I teach in this book cover a very wide spectrum and years of reading, researching and working with clients, in private practice, schools and business corporations. If I had to provide all the citations to document the origin of each fact for complete scientific scholarship that I have used, there would be almost as many citations as words. So I have used a little flexibility to write this book in a more popular style, helping me to communicate my message as effectively as I can. There are only a few citations in the actual text that are more general, and the book list that follows is less of a bibliography (which would be too long) and more of a recommended reading list of some of the great books and scientific articles I have used in my research.

Disclaimer: This body of work was created from years of doing clinical and practical research, researching thousand's of scientific journals, books, articles and papers. While Dr. Leaf agrees with the science, research and findings in these materials, she does not necessarily agree with all the interpretations of the findings. For a better understanding of Dr. Leaf's perspective on brain research and findings please also reference *Who Switched off My Brain? Controlling toxic thoughts and emotions,* as well as, *The Gift in You: Discover new life through gifts hidden in your mind.*

1. Acevedo, B.P., Aron, A. et al. 2011. "Neural correlates of long-term intense romantic love." Social Cognitive and Affective Neuroscience. doi: 10.1093/scan/nsq092.

2. Achiron, R. & Shlomo Lipitz, S. et al. 2001. "Sex-related differences in the development of the human fetal corpus callosum: In utero ultrasonographic study." Prenatal Diagnosis. pp. 116–120.

3. Ackermann, H. & Riecker, A. 2010. "The contribution(s) of the insula to speech communication: a review of the clinical and functional imaging literature." Brain Structure and Function. 214 pp. 5–6. doi:10.1007/ s00429-010-0257-x.

4. "Adolescent Brain." http://www.aea267.k12.ia.us/r4/index.php?page=r4-adolescent-brain.

5. "Affairs of the lips." 2008. Scientific American Mind. www.sciAmMind.com.

6. Ali, M.S. & Suliman, M.I. et al. 2009. "Comparison of gender performance on an intelligence test among medical students." Journal of Ayub Medical College, Abbottabad JAMC. 21 (3) pp. 163–5.

7. Allen, L.S. & Hines, M. et al. 1989. "Two sexually dimorphic cell groups in the human brain." J Neurosci. 9(2)pp. 497–506.

8. Allen, L.S. & Gorski, R.A. 1990. "Sex difference in the bed nucleus of the stria terminalis of the human brain." J Comp Neurol. 302(4) pp. 697–706.

9. Allen, L.S. & Gorski, R.A. 1991. "Sexual dimorphism of the anterior commissure and massa intermedia of the human brain." J Comp Neurol. 312(1) pp. 97–104.

10. Allen, L.S. & Richey, M.F. et al. "Sex differences in the corpus callosum of the living human being." J Neurosci. 11(4) pp. 933–942.

11. Allman, J. 2007. "A Small Part of the Brain and Its Profound Effects." http://www.biopsychiatry.com/tobacco/insula.htm.

12. Allman, J. & Woodward, J. 2008. "What are Moral Intuitions and Why should we care about them? A Neurobiological Perspective." Philosophical Issues. 18(1) pp. 164-185.

13. Allman, J.M. & Tetreault, N.A. et al. 2010. "The von Economo neurons in frontoinsular and anterior cingulate cortex in great apes and humans." Brain Struc Func. 214 pp. 5–6 doi:10.1007/ s00429-010-0254-0.

14. Allman, J. 2011. "Mechanisms of Economic and Social Decision-Making." http://www.allmanlab.caltech.edu/research.html.

15. Alvarez, M. 2007. "A Hug A Day Could Save Your Life." Fox News. http://www.foxnews.com/story/0,2933,249138,00.html.

16. Amen, D.G. 1998. Change Your Brain Change Your Life. Three Rivers Press. NY.

17. Amen, D.G. 2008. Magnificent Mind at Any Age. Harmony Books. USA.

18. Amend, A.E. 1989. "Defining and Demystifying Baroque, Classic and Romantic Music." Journal of the Society. for Accelerative Learning and Teaching. 14 (2), pp. 91-112.

19. Andreason, P.J. & Zametkin et al. 1994. "Gender-related differences in regional cerebral glucose metabolism in normal volunteers." Psychiatry Research. 51(2) pp. 175–183.

20. Andreano, J. & Cahill, L. 2009. "Sex influences on the neurobiology of learning and memory." Learning Memory. 16 pp. 248-266. http://www.learnmem.org/cgi/doi/10.1101/lm.918309.

21. Annis, B. 2000. Same Words, Different Language. Piatkus, UK.

22. Anokhin, A.P. et al. 2000. "Complexity of electrocortical dynamics in children: developmental aspects." Developmental Psychobiology. 36 pp. 9-22.

23. Arnold, A.P. 2004. "Sex chromosomes and brain gender." Nature Reviews Neuroscience. 5(9) pp. 701-708.

24. Aron, A., Fisher, H. et al. 2005. "Reward, motivation, and emotion systems associated with early-stage intense romantic love." Journal of Neurophysiology. 94 pp. 327–337.

25. "Autism Linked to Mirror Neuron Dysfunction." 2005. RxPG News.

26. Azari, N.P. & Pettigrew, K.D. et al.1992. "Sex differences in patterns of hemispheric cerebral metabolism: a multiple regression/discriminate analysis of positron emission tomographic data." Int J Neurosci. 1992a;8 pp. 1–20.

27. Baillargeon, R.H. et al. 2007. "Gender differences in physical aggression: A prospective population-based survey of children before and after 2 years of age." Developmental Psychology. 43(1) pp. 13-26. doi:10.1037/0012-1649.43.1.13.

28. Baron-Cohen, S. 2002. "The extreme male brain theory of autism." Trends Cogn Sci. 6 pp. 248–254.

29. Baron-Cohen, S. 2003. The Essential Difference: The Truth about the Male and Female Brain. Basic Books. NY.

30. Baron-Cohen, S. & Knickmeyer, R.C. et al. 2005. "Sex differences in the brain: implications for explaining autism." Science. 4 pp. 819–823.

31. Bartels, A. & Zeki, S. 2000. "The neural basis of romantic love." Neuroreport. 11 pp. 3829–3834.

32. Bartels, A. & Zeki, S. 2004. "The neural correlates of maternal and romantic love." Neuroimage. 21 pp. 1155–1166.

33. Bateup, H.S. et al. 2002. "Testosterone, cortisol and Women's competition." Journal of Evolution and Human Behavior. 23(3) pp. 387-394.

34. Bauer, P. J. 1993. "Memory for Gender-Consistent and Gender-Inconsistent Event Sequences by Twenty-Five-Month-Old Children." Child Development. 64 pp. 285–297. doi: 10.1111/j.1467-8624.1993.tb02910.x.

35. Baumeister, R. F., Wotman, S.R. et al. 1993. "Unrequited love: On heartbreak, anger, guilt, scriptlessness, and humiliation." Journal of Personality and Social Psychology. 64(3) pp. 377-394.

36. Baxter, M.G. & Murray, E.A. 2002. "The amygdala and reward." Nat Rev Neurosci. 3 pp. 563–573.

37. Baxter, R., Cohen, S.B. & Ylvisaker, M. 1985. "Comprehensive Cognitive Assessment." in Ylvisaker, M. Head Injury Rehabilitation: Children and adolescents. pp. 247-275. College-Hill Press. CA.

38. Beaton, D. 2003. "Effects of Stress and Psychological Disorders on the Immune System." Rochester Institute of Technology. http://www.personalityresearch.org/papers/beaton.html.

39. Begley, S. 2010. "The Hidden Brain: What scientist can learn from 'nothing'." Newsweek. www.newsweek.com/2010/05/31/the-hidden-brain.html.

40. Belsky, J. 2002. "Quantity Counts." Developmental and Behavioral Pediatrics. pp. 167-170.

41. Benbow, C. 2000. "Sex Differences in Mathematical Reasoning Abilities at Age 13: Their Status 20 Years Later." Psychological Science. 11(6).

42. Benson, H. 2010. Relaxation Revolution. Simon & Schuster. NY.

43. Berger, E. 2007. "Men talk as much as women, study says." Houston Chronicle. http://www.chron.com/disp/story.mpl/chronicle/4947103.html.

44. Berns, G.S., Moore, S. et al. 2009. "Adolescent Engagement In Dangerous Behaviours Is Associated With Increased White Matter Maturity Of Frontal Cortex." PLoS ONE. 4(8) pp. e6773 doi:10.1371/journal.pone.0006773.

45. Blakeslee, S. 2007. "A Small Part of the Brain, and Its Profound Effects." The New York Times. http://www.nytimes.com/2007/02/06/health/psychology/06brain.html.

46. Blakeslee, S. 2006. "Cells That Read Minds." The New York Times. http://www.nytimes.com/2006/01/10/science/10mirr.html?pagewanted=print.

47. Blakeslee, S. 2007. "The Insula - body in the brain." http://www.ithou.org/node/1595.

48. Blair, J. 2000. Who gets sick? Peak. Houston, TX.

49. Blanton, R.E., et al. 2004. "Gender Differences in the left Inferior Frontal Gyrus in Normal Children." NeuroImage. 22.

50. Blinkhorn, S. 2005. "Intelligence: A gender bender." Nature. 438 7064 pp. 31.

51. Bremner, J.D. et al. 2001. "Gender differences in cognitive and neural correlates of remembrance of emotional words." Pscyhopharmacology Bulletin. 35, 2001.

52. Boyle, P. 2009. http://esciencenews.com/articles/2009/06/15/having.a.higher.purpose.life.reduces.risk.death.among.older.adults.

53. Bradshaw, J.L. & Mattingley, J.B. 2001. "Allodynia: a sensory analogue of motor mirror neurons in a hyperaesthetic patient reporting instantaneous discomfort to another's perceived sudden minor injury?" J Neurol Neurosurg Psychiatry.

54. "Brain may hardwire Sexuality before birth." 2003. Science Daily. www.sciencedaily.com/releases/2003/10/031022062408.htm.

55. Brain and Mind Symposium. Columbia University. 2004. http://c250.columbia.edu/c250_events/symposia/brain_mind/brain_mind_vid_archive.html.

56. "Brain Briefings: The Adolescent Brain." 2007. Society for Neuroscience. http://www.sfn.org/index.aspx?pagename=brainBriefings_Adolescent_brain.

57. Brass, M. & Haggard, P. 2010. "The hidden side of intentional action: the role of the anterior insular cortex." Brain Structure and Function. 214 pp. 5–6. doi:10.1007/s00429-010-0269-6.

58. Braten, I. 1991. "Vygotsky as Precursor to Metacognitive Theory, II: Vygotsky as metacognitivist." Scandinavian Journal of Educational Research. 35 (4), pp. 305-320.

59. Braun, A. 1999. The New Neuropsychology of Sleep Commentary. Neuro-Psychoanalysis. (1) 196-201.

60. Brener N.D., Simon TR, Krug E.G., Lowry R. 1999. "Recent trends in violence- related behaviors among high school students in the United States." JAMA. 282:440 – 446.

61. Breslau, N. et al. 1997. "Sex differences in post-traumatic stress disorder." Arch Gen Psychiatr. 54:1044.

62. Brizendine, L. 2007. The Female Brain. Transworld Publishers. UK.

63. Brizendine, L. 2010. The Male Brain. Three Rivers. NY.

64. Bryner, J. 2007. "The Last Word: Men Talk as Much as Women." Live Science. http://www.livescience.com/7330-word-men-talk-women.html.

65. Buckley, H. M. & Roach, M. E. 1974. "Clothing as a nonverbal communicator of social and political attitudes." Home Economics Research Journal. 3, 94-102.

66. Bultman, S. J., Michaud, E. J. & Woychik, R. P. 1992. Molecular characterization of the mouse agoutilocus. Cell 71:1195-1204.

67. Burton, L., Hafetz. et al. 2008. "Aggression, gender-typical childhood play, and a prenatal hormonal index." Social Behavior and Personality.

68. Burton, L., Hafetz, J. & Henninger, D. 2007. "Gender Differences in Relational and Physical Aggression." Soical Behavior and Personality. 35(1), 41-50.

69. Cahill, L. et al. 2001. "Sex-related difference in amygdala activity during emotionally influenced memory storage." Neurobiol Learn Mem. 75 pp. 1.

70. Cahill, L., Uncapher, M. et al. 2004. "Sex-Related Hemispheric Lateralization of Amygdala Function in Emotionally Influenced Memory: An fMRI Investigation." Learning and Memory. 11(3) pp. 261–266. http://www.learnmem.org/cgi/doi/10.1101/lm.70504.

71. Cahill, L. 2005. "His Brain Her Brain." Scientific American. 292 (5) pp. 40-47.

72. Cahill, L. 2006. "Why sex matters for neuroscience." Nature Reviews. 7 pp. 477-484.

73. Cahill, L. 2007. "Human Brain Imaging studies of Emotional Memory: Uncovering Influences of sex and hemisphere." in Neural Plasticity nd Memory: from Genes to Brain Imaging. Bermudez-Rattoni, F. (ed.). Boca Raton, FL.

74. Calvin, C.M. Fernandes, C. 2010. "Sex, Intelligence and educational achievement in a national cohort of over 175000 11-year-old school children in England." Intelligence. 38(4) pp. 424-432.

75. Cameron, D. 1998. "Gender, Language and discourse: A review essay." Signs. 23(4) pp. 945-973.

76. Cameron, D. 2005. "Language, gender and Sexuality: Current issues and new directions." Applied Linguistics. 26(4) pp 482-502.

77. Campbell, A. 2008. "Attachment, aggression and affiliation: The role of oxytocin in female social behavior." Biological Psychology. 77 pp. 1–10.

78. Campbell, A. 2010. "Oxytocin and Human behaviour." Personality and Social Psychology Review. 14(3) pp. 281-295.

79. Cancian, F.M. 1985. "Gender Politics: love and power in the public and private spheres." Gender and the life Course. Rossi, A. (ed.). Aldine, NY.

80. Canli, T. & Desmond, J.E. et al. 2002. "Sex differences in the neural basis of emotional memories." Proceedings of the National Academy of Sciences of the United States of America. 99 (16) pp. 10789-10794.

81. Carr, Laurie. et al. 2003. "Neural Mechanisms of Empathy in Humans: A Relay from Neural Systems for Imitation to Limbic Areas." PNAS.

82. Carrel, L. & Huntington, F.W. 2005. "X-inactivation profile reveals extensive variability in X-linked gene expression in females." Nature. 434(7031) pp. 279-80.

83. Carson, R.C., Butcher, J.N. & Mineka, S. 2002. "Fundamentals of abnormal psychology and modern life." Allyn and Bacon. Boston.

84. Casey, K.L. & Minoshima, S. et al. 1996. "A comparison of human cerebral activation patterns during cutaneous warmth, heat pain and deep cold pain." J Neurophys. 76 pp. 571–581.

85. Casiere, D. A. & Ashton, N. L. 1996. "Eyewitness accuracy and gender." Perceptual and Motor Skills. 83, 914-914.

86. Cassidy, J. & Ditty, K. 2001. "Gender Differences Among Newborns on a Transient Otoacoustic Emissions Test for Hearing." Journal of Music Therapy. 38 pp. 28-35.

87. Castro-Schilo, L., Kee, D.W. 2010. "Gender Differences in the relationship between emotional intlligence and right hemisphere lateralization for facial expression." Brain and Cognition. 73(1) pp. 62-67.

88. Chaogan, Y. & Gong, G. et al. "Sex- and Brain Size-Related Small-World Structural Cortical Networks in Young Adults: A DTI Tractography Study." Cerebral Cortex. 21(2) pp. 449-458.

89. Cheng, Y., Tzeng, O. et al. 2006. "Gender differences in the human mirror system: a magnetoencephalography study." Cognitive Neuroscience and Neuropsychology. 17(11) pp. 1115-1119.

90. Cheng, Y., Lee, P.L. et al. 2008. "Gender Differences in the Mu Rhythm of the Human Mirror-Neuron System." PLoS ONE. 3(5): e2113. doi:10.1371/journal.pone.0002113.

91. Cheng, Y., Chou, K. et al. 2009. "Sex differences in the neuroanatomy of human mirror-neuron system: a voxel-based imorphometric nvestigation." Neuroscience. 158 pp. 713-720.

92. Childre, D. & Martin, H. 1999. The Heartmath Solution. Harper-Collins. San Francisco, CA.

93. Chrisler, J.C. & McCreary, D.R. 2010. Handbook of Gender Research in psychology Volume 1. Springer. NY.

94. Christiansen, K. 2001. "Behavioral effects of androgen in men and women." Journal of Endocrinology. 170(1).

95. Church, D. 2009. The Genie in Your Genes. 2nd Ed. Energy Psychology Press. Santa Rosa, CA.

96. Clancey, W. 1990. "Why Today's Computers Don't Learn the Way People Do." Paper presented at the Annual Meeting of the American Educational Research Association. Boston, MA.

97. Clark, A.J. 2005. "Forgiveness: A neurological model." Medical Hypotheses. (65):649-54.

98. Clinical research doesn't do enough to study sex and gender differences, analysis finds. 2010. http://www.sciencedaily.com/releases/2010/11/101108190137.htm.

99. Cohen, D. 2004. "Men, Empathy, and Autism." The Chronicle of Higher Education.

100. Cone-Wesson, B. & Ramirez, G. "Hearing Sensitivity in Newborns Estimated from ABR's to Bone-Conducted Sounds." Journal of the American Academy of Audiology. 8 pp. 299-307.

101. Connellan, J. & Baron-Cohen, S. et al. 2000. "Sex Differences in Human Neonatal Social Perception." Infant Behavior and Development. (23) pp. 113-18.

102. Cook, N.D. 1984. "Colossal Inhibition: The key to the brain code." Behavioral Science. 29, pp. 98-110

103. Corothers, A. & Deary, I.J. 2008. "Sex Differeneces In Vaiability In General Intelligence: A New Look At The Old Question." Perspectives on Psychological Science. 3(6) pp. 518-531.

104. Cousins, N. 1981. Anatomy of an Illness as Perceived by the Patient. Bantam, NY.

105. Cousins, N. 1979. "Anatomy of an Illness as Perceived by the Patient." New England Journal of Medicine. 295(1976) 1458-63.

106. Cowan, R.L. et al. 2000. "Sex differences in response to red and blue light in human primary visual cortex: a bold fMRI study." Psychiatry Res. 100 pp. 129.

107. Coyle, D. 2009. "The Talent Code." Bantam Books. USA.

108. Craig, A.D. 2002. "How do you feel? Interoception: the sense of the physiological condition of the body." Nat Rev Neurosci. 3 pp. 655–666.

109. Craig, A.D. 2006. "Interoception and Emotion: A Neuroanatomical Perspective." Lewis et al. (eds) The Handbook of Emotion. 3rd Ed. Ch. 16. http://brainimaging.waisman.wisc.edu/-perlman/papers/EmotionTheory08/InteroceptionandEmotion.pdf.

110. Craig, A.D. 2009. "How do you feel—now? The anterior insula and human awareness." Nat Rev Neurosci. 10 pp. 59–70.

111. Craig, A.D. 2010. "Barrow scientist leads insula research." eScience News. http://esciencenews.com/articles/2010/07/07/barrow.scientist.leads.insula.research.

112. Craig, A.D. 2010. "Once an island, now the focus of attention." Brain Structure and Function. 214 pp. 395-396.

113. Crick, F. The Astonishing Hypothesis: The scientific search for the soul. Charles Scribner & Sons. NY.

114. Crick, F.H.C. 1981. "Thinking about the Brain." Scientific American. 241 (3), p. 228.

115. Cross, S. E. & Madson, L. 1997. "Models of the self: Self-construals and gender." Psychological Bulletin. 122, 5-37.

116. Damasio, A. R. 1999. The Feeling of What Happens: Body and motion in the making of consciousness. Harcourt, Brace & Company. NY.

117. Damasio, A. & Damasio, H. 2006. "Minding the Body." Daedalus. 135 pp. 15–22.

118. Darlington, C. 2009, <u>The Female Brain</u>. 2nd Ed. CRC. FL.

119. Darnall, B.D. & Suarez, E.C. 2009. "Sex and gender in psychoneuroimmunology research: Past, present and future." <u>Brain, Behavior, and Immunity</u>. 23(5) pp. 55-604.

120. Dartigues, J. F. 1994. "Use It or Lose It." <u>Omni</u>. Feb. 1994, p. 34.

121. Davis, L. L. 1984. "Clothing and human behavior: A review." <u>Home Economics Research Journal</u>. 12, 325-339.

122. Davis, M. & Wheelen, P.J. 2001. "The amygdala, vigilance and emotion." <u>Molecular Psychiatry</u>. 6 pp. 13-34.

123. Davis, P. J. 1999. "Gender differences in autobiographical memory for childhood emotional experiences." <u>Journal of Personality and Social Psychology</u>. 76, 498-510.

124. Deborah Blum, D. 1998. <u>Sex On The Brain: The Biological Differences Between Men and Women</u>. Penguin Books.

125. Decety, J. & Grezes, J. 2006. "The Power of Simulation: Imagining one's own and other's behavior." <u>Brain Research</u>. 1079, 4-14.

126. Decety, J. & Jackson, P.L. 2006. "A Social Neuroscience Perspective of Empathy." <u>Current Directions in Psychological Science</u>. 15, 54-58.

127. Deloris, 2009. "Gender Differences and Aggression:Males and females are different when it comes to expressing aggressive behaviors." http://socyberty.com/psychology/gender-differences-and-aggression//.

128. De Vries, J. et al. 2002. "A model system for study of sex chromosome effects on sexually dimorphic neural and behavioral traits." <u>Journal of Neuroscience</u>. 22(20) pp. 9005-14.

129. Dewing, P. & Vilain. E. et al. 2003. "Sexually dimorphic gene expression in mouse brain precedes gonadal differentiation." 118 (1-2) pp 82-90.

130. Diamond, M. 1984. "Cortical change in response to environmental enrichment and impoverishment." Brown, C. (Ed.) <u>The Many Facets of Touch</u>. Skillman, Johnson & Johnson. N.J.

131. Diamond, M., Scheibel, A., Murphy, G. & Harvey, T. 1985. "On the Brain of a Scientist: Albert Einstein." <u>Experimental Neurology</u>. 88(1):198-204.

132. Diamond, M. 1988. <u>Enriching Heredity: The impact of the environment on the brain</u>. Free Press. NY.

133. Diamond, M. & Hopson, J. 1999. "How to Nurture Your Child's Intelligence, Creativity and Healthy Emotions from Birth through Adolescence." <u>Magic Trees of the Mind</u>. Penguin. USA.

134. Diamond, M. 2003. "Male and Female Brains: Summary of Lecture for Women's Forum West Annual Meeting." New Horizons for Learning. San Francisco, California. http://www.newhorizons.org.

135. Diamond, S. & Beaumont, J. (Eds.) <u>Hemisphere Function of the Human Brain</u>. pp. 264-278.

136. Dienstbier, R. 1989. "Periodic Adrenalin Arousal Boosts Health Coping." <u>Brain-Mind Bulletin</u>. 14(9a).

137. Dingfelder, S.F. 2008. "An insidious enemy." <u>American Psychological Association</u>. http://www.apa.org/monitor/2008/10/stress-immune.aspx.

138. Dispenza, J. 2007. "Evolve Your Brain: The science of changing your brain." Health Communications, Inc. FL.

139. Doherty, R. W. 1997. "The Emotional Contagion Scale: A measure of individual differences." <u>Journal of Nonverbal Behavior</u>. 21, 131-154.

140. Doidge, N. 2007. <u>The Brain that Changes Itself: Stories of personal triumph for the frontiers of brain science</u>. Penguin Books. USA.

141. Dossey, L. 2006. "The Extraordiany Healing Power of Ordinary Things." Harmony, NY.

142. Douglas, K. 1996. "Cherchez la différence." <u>New Scientist</u>.

143. Douty, H. 1963. "Influence of clothing on perception of persons." <u>Journal of Home Economics</u>. 55, 197-202.

144. Dowd, M. 2005. "X-celling over men." <u>New York Times</u>. 434(7031) pp 279-280. http://www.nytimes.com/2005/03/20/opinion/20dowd.html?scp=1&sq=march%2020,%202005%20x-celling%20over%20men&st=cse. http://www.marioninstitute.org/node/241.

145. Drakich, D. & Drakich, J. 1993. "Understanding Gender Differences In Amount of talk: A Critical Review of Research." Gender and Conversational Interaction. Tannen, D. (ed.). Oxford University Press. NY.

146. Driscoll, D. M., Kelly, J. R. & Henderson, W. L. 1998. "Can perceivers identify likelihood to sexually harass?" Sex Roles. 38, 557-588.

147. Duke Medicines News and Communications. "'Reset Switch' for Brain Cells Discovered." http://www.dukehealth.org/health_library/news/7136.

148. Duncan, J., Seitz, R. & Kolodny, J. et al. 2000. "A Neural Basis for General Intelligence." Science. 289:457-460.

149. Eals, M. & Silverman, I. 1992. "Sex differences in spatial abilities: evolutionary theory and data." The Adapted Mind: Evolutionary Psychology and the Generation of Culture. edited by J. H. Barkow. Oxford University Press. NY.

150. Eals, M. & Silverman, I. 1994. "The hunter-gatherer theory of spatial sex differences: Proximate factors mediating the female advantage in recall of object arrays." Ethology and Sociobiology. 15, 95-105.

151. Edmonds, M. "How Albert Einstein's Brain Worked." http://health.howstuffworks.com/einsteins-brain1.htm.

152. Economist. 2004. "I get a kick out of you: Scientists are finding that, after all, love really is down to a chemical addiction between people." http://www.oxytocin.org/oxytoc/love-science.html.

153. The Economist. 2006. Learning without learning. (23) pp. 89.

154. Einstein, A. 1999. "Albert Einstein: Person of the century." TIME. Dec. 31, 1999.

155. Einstein, A. 1979. The Human Side: New glimpses from his archives. Princeton University Press. Princeton, NJ.

156. Eisenberger, N. & Lieberman, M.D. 2003. "Does rejection hurt? An fMRI study of Social Exclusion." Science. 10 pp. 290-292.

157. Eisenburger, N. 2008. "Understanding the Moderators of Physical and Emotional Pain: A neural systems-based approach." Psychological Inquiry (19) 189-195.

158. Else-Quest, N. M., Hyde, J. S., Goldsmith, H. H. & Van Hulle, C. 2006. Gender differences in temperament: A meta-analysis. Psychological Bulletin. 132, 33-72.

159. "Endorphin and enkephalim." http://www.discoveriesinmedicine.com/Com-En/Endorphin-and-Enkephalin.html.

160. eScience News. 2011. "Acute pain is eased with the touch of a hand." http://esciencenews.com/articles/2010/09/23/acute.pain.eased.with.touch.a.hand.

161. eScience News. 2011. "Mindfulness meditation training changes brain structure in 8 weeks." http://esciencenews.com/articles/2011/01/21/mindfulness.meditation.training.changes.brain.structure.8.weeks.

162. Epigenetics. 2004. http://www.sciencemag.org/feature/plus/sfg/resources/res_epigenetics.dtl.

163. Epigenetics. 2006. http://discovermagazine.com/2006/nov/cover.

164. Epigenetics. 2006. http://www.ehponline.org/members/2006/114-3/focus.html.

165. Epstein, R. 2010. "How Science Can Help You Fall in Love." in Scientific American Mind. Jan/Feb 2010. 26-33.

166. Ericsson, A. et al. 1993. "The Role of Deliberate Practice in the Acquisition of Expert Performance." American Psychological Association. 100(3) pp. 363-406.

167. Ericsson, K. & Lehmann, A. 1996. "Expert and Exceptional Performance: Evidence of Maximal Adaption to Task Constraints." Annual Review of Psychology. 47. http://www.questia.com/googleScholar.qst?docId=5000321924.

168. Eriksen, C.W. & Botella, J. 1992. "Filtering Versus Parallel Processing in RSVP Tasks." Perception and Psychophysics. 51 (4), pp. 334-343.

169. Eshel, N., Nelson, E.E. et al. 2007. "Neural substrates of choice selection in adults and adolescents: development of the ventrolateral prefrontal and anterior cingulate cortices."

170. Esposito, G., Van Horn, J.D. et al. 1996. "Gender differences in cerebral blood flow as a function of cognitive state with PET." J Nucl Med. 37(4) pp. 559–564.

171. "Even at rest, Men's and Women's brains behave differently." http://medicineworld.org/cancer/lead/4-2006/mens-and-womens-brains-behave-differently.html.

172. Feinberg, R. A., Mataro, L. & Burroughs, W. J. 1992. "Clothing and social identity." Clothing and Textiles Research Journal. 11, 18-23.

173. Feine, J.S., Bushnell, M.C. et al. 1991. "Sex differences in the perception of noxious heat stimuli." Pain. 44 pp. 255–262.

174. Feingols, A. 1994. "Gender Differences in Personality: A Meta-Analysis." Psychological Bulletin. 116(3) pp. 429-456.

175. Feinstein, J.S. & Stein, M.B. et al. 2006. "Anterior insula reactivity during certain decisions is associated with neuroticism." Soc Cogn Affect Neurosci. 1(2) pp. 136-142.

176. Felliti, V.J. et al. 1998. "Relationship of childhood abuse and household dysfunction to many of the leading causes of death in adults. The adverse child experiences study (ACE)." American Journal of Preventative Medicine. (4) 245.

177. Frewen, P.A. & Dozois, D.J.A. et al. 2010. "Neuroimaging social emotional processing in women: fMRI study of script-driven imagery." Social Cognitive and Affective Neuroscience. doi: 10.1093/scan/nsq047.

178. Fields, R.D. 2004. "The Other Half of the Brain." Scientific American. 290(4), pp. 54-61.

179. Fields, R.D. 2005. "Myelination: An Overlooked Mechanism of Synaptic Plasticity?" Neuroscientist. 11(6) pp. 528-531.

180. Fields, R.D. 2008. "White matter matters." Scientific American. pp. 54-61.

181. Fisher, H.E. 2004. Why We Love: The Nature and Chemistry of Romantic Love. Holt. NY.

182. Fisher, H., Aron, A. et al. 2005. "Romantic love: an fMRI study of a neural mechanism for mate choice." Journal of Comparative Neurololgy. 493: 58–62.

183. Fisher, H.E. & Brown, L.L. et al. 2009. "Reward, Addiction, and Emotion Regulation Systems associated With Rejection in Love." Journal Physiology. 104(1) pp. 51-60.

184. Fine, C. 2010. Delusions of Gender. W.W. Norton & Company. NY.

185. Fisher, H., Aron, A. et al. 2005. "Romantic love: an fMRI study of a neural mechanism for mate choice." Journal of Comparative Neurololgy. 493: 58–62.

186. Flitzpatrick, L. 2010. "The Male Brain: More Complex Than You Think." http://www.time.com/time/health/article/0,8599,1976274,00.html#ixzz0yzEH6M7E.

187. Fodor, J. 1983. The Modularity of Mind. MIT/Bradford. Cambridge.

188. Forgiveness. 2004. https://www.health.harvard.edu/press_releases/power_of_forgiveness.

189. Forgiveness. 2005. http://www.aolhealth.com/conditions/five-for-2005-five-reasons-to-forgive.

190. Francis, D., Young, L. et al. 2002. "Naturally Occurring Differences in Maternal Care are Associated with the Expression of Oxytocin and Vasopressin (V1a) Receptors: Gender Differences." Journal of Neuroendocrinology. 14 pp. 349–353. http://www.dafml.unito.it/anatomy/panzica/neuroendo/articolipdf/2002FrancisJNeuroEndo.pdf.

191. Frederikse, M. & Angela Lu, A. et al. 1999. "Sex differences in the inferior parietal lobule." Cerebral Cortex. 9 pp. 896-901.

192. Freeman, W.J. 1995. Societies of Brains: A study in the neuroscience of love and hate. Lawrence Eribaun Associates. Hillside, NJ.

193. Fusion, J. "Difference Between Boys and Girls Memory." eHow. http://www.ehow.co.uk/about_5244222_difference-between-boys-girls-memory.html.

194. Fuster, J.M. 2008. The Prefrontal Cortex. 4th Ed. Academic Press, London. http://www.elsevierdirect.com/product.jsp?isbn=9780123736444.

195. Gabriel, S. & Gardner, W. L. 1999. "Are there "his" and "hers" types of interdependence? The implications of gender differences in collective versus relational interdependence for affect, behavior, and cognition." Journal of Personality and Social Psychology. 77, 642-655.

196. Galaburda, A. "Albert Einstein's Brain." Lancet. 1999; 354: 182.

197. Galton, F. 1907. Inquiries into Human Faculty and Its Development. L. M. Dent. London.

198. Gardner, H. & Wolfe, D.P. 1983. "Waves and Streams of Symbolization." in Rogers, D. & Slabada, J.A. (Eds.) The Acquisition of Symbolic Skills. Plenum Press. London.

199. Gazzaniga, M.S. 1977. Handbook of Neuropsychology. Plenum. NY.

200. Gazzaniga, M.S. 2004. (Ed.) The New Cognitive Neurosciences. Bradford Books. The MIT Press.

201. Gazzaniga, M. 2008. "Human: The Science behind What Makes Us Unique." Harper Collins. NY.

202. Geary, D.C. 1998. "Male, female: The evolution of human sex differences." American Psychological Association. ISBN 1557985278.

203. Gefen, D. 1997. Gender differences in the perception and use of email: An extension to the technology acceptance model. MIS quarterly. 21(4).

204. Gender Differences In Brain Response To Pain. 2003. Science Daily.

205. George Gryn, G. & Wunderlich, A. et al. 2000. "Brain activation during human navigation: gender-different neural networks as substrate of performance." Nature neuroscience. 3(4) pp. 404-408.

206. George, M.S. & Ketter, T.A. et al. 1996. "Gender differences in regional cerebral blood flow during transient self-induced sadness or happiness." Biol Psychiatry. 40 pp. 859.

207. Gied, J.N. 2008. "The teen brain: insights from neuroimaging." Journal of Adolescent Health. 42 pp. 335–343.

208. Gied, J. "Jay Gied Interview." Frontline. http://www.pbs.org/wgbh/pages/frontline/shows/teenbrain/interviews/giedd.html.

209. Giorgio, A., Watkins, K.E. et al. 2008. "Changes in white matter microstructure during adolescence." NeuroImage. 39 pp. 52–61. Neuropsychologia. 45 pp. 1270–1279.

210. Girdler, S.S., Jamner, L.D. et al. 1997. "Hostility, testosterone, and vascular reactivity to stress: Effects of sex." International Journal of Behavioral Medicine. 4 pp. 242–263.

211. Gong, G. & Rosa-Neto, P. et al. 2009. "Age- and Gender-Related Differences in the Cortical Anatomical Network." Journal of Neuroscience. 29(50) pp. 15684-15693.

212. Goolkasian, P. 1985. "Phase and sex effects in pain perception: a critical review." Psychol Women Q. 9 pp. 15–28.

213. Greenfield, S. 2000. The private life of the brain: Emotions, consciousness, and the secret of the self. John Wiley & Sons, Inc. NY.

214. Grewen, K.M., Girdler, S.S. et al. 2005. "Effects of partner support in resting oxytocin, Cortisol, Norepinephrine, and Blood pressure before and after warm partner contact." Psychosomatic Medicine. 67 pp. 531-538.

215. Gron, G. & Wunderlich, A.P. 2000. "Brain activation during human navigation: gender-different neural networks as sunstrate of performance." Nature Neuroscience. 3 pp. 404-408.

216. Gouchie, C. & Kimura, D. 1991. "The relationship between testosterone levels and cognitive ability patterns." Psychoneuroendocrinology. 16 (4) pp. 323–324. doi:10.1016/0306-4530(91)90018-0. PMID 1745699.

217. Guiffre, G.L. et al. 2007. "Changes in color discrimination during the menstrual cycle." Opthalmologica. (221) pp. 47-50.

218. Gur, R.C. & Gur, R.E. et al. 1982. "Sex and handedness differences in cerebral blood flow during rest and cognitive activity." Science. 17 pp. 659–660.

219. Gur, R.C. & Gur, R.E. et al. 1987. "Age and regional cerebral blood flow at rest and during cognitive activity." Arch Gen Psychiatry. 44 pp. 617-621.

220. Gur, R.E. & Gur, R. 1990. "Gender differences in regional cerebral blood flow." Schizophrenia bulletin." 16(2).

221. Gur, R. et al. 1995. "Sex differences in regional cerebral glucose metabolism during a resting state." Science. 267(5197) pp. 528-531.

222. Gur, R.C., Turetsky, B.I. et al. 1999. "Sex differences in brain gray and white matter in healthy young adults." Journal of Neuroscience. 19 pp. 4065-4072.

223. Gur, R.C., Alsop, D. et al. 2000. "An fMRI study of sex differences in regional activation to a verbal and a spatial task." Brain and Language. 74 pp. 157-170.

224. Gur, R. et al. 2001. "Striatal dopamine transporters and cognitive functioning in healthy men and women." Am J of Psychiatry. 158 pp. 1492-1499.

225. Gur, R.C., Gunning-Dixon, F. et al. 2002. "Sex Differences in Tempero-limbic and frontal brain Volumes of healthy adults." Cerebral Cortex. 12(9) pp. 998-1003.

226. Gur, R.C., Ragland, J.D. 2009. "Regional Differences in the coupling between resting cerebral blood flow and metabolism may indicate action preparedness as a default state." Cerebral Cortex. 19(2) pp. 375-382.

227. Gur, R.C. & Mozley, L.H. et al. "Sex differences in regional cerebral glucose metabolism during a resting state." Science. 267 pp. 528–531.

228. Gurian, M. 1997. "The Wonder of Boys." Tarcher/Putnam. NY.

229. Gurian, M. et al. 2001. "Boys and GirlsLearn Differently!" Jossey-Bass/John Wiley. San Francisco.

230. Gurian, M. 2002. "The Wonder of Girls." Atria, NY.

231. Gurian, M. 2003. What Could He Be Thinking? St. Martin's Press. NY.

232. Gurian, M. & Stevens, K. 2004. "With Boys and Girls in Mind." Educational Leadership. Vol 62, #3.

233. Gurian, M. & Stevens, K. 2005. "The Minds of Boys." Jossey-Bass/John Wiley. San Francisco.

234. Gurian, M. & Annis, B. 2008. Leadership and the Sexes. Jossey-Bass. San Francisco, CA.

235. Haber, R.N. 1981. "The Power of Visual Perceiving." Journal of Mental Imagery. 5, pp. 1-40.

236. Hall, J. 1978. "Gender effects in decoding nonverbal cues." Psychological Bulletin. 85(4) pp. 845-857.

237. Haier, R.J., Jung, R.E. et al. 2005. "The neuroanatomy of general intelligence: sex matters." Neuroimage. 25(1) pp. 320-327.

238. Hall, J. 1984. Nonverbal Sex Differences. John Hopkins. Baltimore.

239. Hall, J.A. & Veccia, E.M. 1990. More "Touching" Observations: New Insights on Men, Women and Interpersonal Touch. Journal of Personality and Social Psychology. 59, 1155-1162.

240. Hall, J & Carter. et al. 2000. "Gender differences in nonverbal communication of emotion." Gender and Emotion: social psychological issues. Fischer, A. (ed) pp. 97. Cambridge University Press. UK.

241. Hall J. A., Carter J. D. & Horgan, T. G. 2001. "Status roles and recall of nonverbal cues." Journal of Nonverbal Behavior. 25, 79-100.

242. Hall, J.A. & Matsumoto, D. 2004. "Gender Differences in judgments of multiple emotions from facial expressions." Emotion. Vol. 4.

243. Hall, G.B. & Witelson, S.F. et al. 2004. "Sex differences in functional activation patterns revealed by increased emotion processing demands." Neuroreport. 15 pp. 219-223.

244. Halpern, D. 1993. "Sex, Brains and Hands – Gender Differences in Cognitive Abilities." Skeptic. Vol. 2. No. 3. pp. 96-103. http://www.skeptic.com/eskeptic/05-03-15/.

245. Halpern, D. 2000. Sex Differences in Cognitive Abilities. Lawrence Erlbaum Associates. New Jersey.

246. Halpern, D. F. & Tan, U. 2001. "Stereotypes and steroids: Using a psychobiosocial model to understand cognitive sex differences." Brain and Cognition. 45(3), pp. 392-414.

247. Halpern, D.F., Benbow, C. P., Geary, D.C., Gur, R.C., Shibley Hyde, J. & Gernsbacher, M.A. 2007. "The Science of Sex Differences in Science and Mathematics." Psychological Science in the Public Interest. Volume 8, No. 1.

248. Hamann, S. et.al. 2004. "Men and women differ in amygdala response to visual sexual stimuli." Nature Neuroscience. Vol. 4.

249. Hamann, S. 2005. "Sex Differences in the Responses of the Human Amygdala." Neuroscientist. 11 (4) pp. 288-293.

250. Hamilton, A. 2010. "Studies: An Idle Brain May be Ripe for Learning." TIME. http://www.time.com/time/health/article/0,8599,1957114,00.html.

251. Hanlon, H., Thatcher, R. & Cline, M. 1999. "Gender Differences in the Development of EEG Coherence in normal children." Developmental Neuropsychology. 16(3) pp. 479-506.

252. Harley, W.J. 2001. His needs Her needs. Revell. MI.

253. Harrell, K.D. 1995. Attitude is Everything: A tune-up to enhance your life. Kendall/Hunt Publishing Company. USA.

254. Harris, M. B., Harris, R. J. & Bochner, S. 1982. "Fat, four-eyed, and female: Stereotypes of obesity, glasses, and gender." Journal of Applied Social Psychology. 12, 503-516.

255. Harrison, C.J. 1993. "Metacognition and Motivation." Reading Improvement. 28 (1), pp. 35-39.

256. Harvard. https://www.health.harvard.edu/topic/stress.

257. Harvard University Gazette. 1996. "Aging Brains Lose Less Than Thought." http://www.hno.harvard.edu/gazette/1996/10.03/AgingBrainsLose.html.

258. Harvard University Gazette. 2003. "Childhood Abuse Hurts the Brain." http:/www.hno.harvard.edu/gazette/2003/05.22/01-brain.html.

259. Harvard University Gazette. 1998. "Sleep, Dreams and Learning." http://www.news.harvard.edu/gazette/1996/02.08/ResearchLinksSl.html.

260. Harvard Health Publications. 2009. "Positive Psychology: Harnessing the power of happiness, personal strength and mindfulness." https://www.health.harvard.edu/special_health_reports/Positive-Psychology.

261. Harvard Health Publications. 2009. https://www.health.harvard.edu/newsweek/Prevalence-and-treatment-of-mental-illness-today.htm.

262. Hatfield, E. & Sprecher, S. 1986. "Measuring passionate love in intimate relationships." J Adolesc. 9 pp. 383–410.

263. Hatfield, R. 1994. "Touch and Human Sexuality." in V. Bullough, B. Bullough, & A. Stein (Eds.). Human Sexuality: An Encyclopedia. Garland Publishing. NY. http://faculty.plts.edu/gpence/PS2010/html/Touch%20and%20Human%20Sexuality.htm.

264. Hatton, G.I. 1997. "Function-related Plasticity in the Hypothalamus." Annual Review of Neuroscience. 20:375-97.

265. Hausmann, M. & Schoofs, D. et al. 2009. "Interactive effects of sex hormones and gender stereotypes on cognitive sex differences - A psychobiological approach." Psychoneuroendocrinology. 34 (3) pp. 389–401 doi:10.1016/j.psyneuen.2008.09.019. PMID 18992993.

266. Heart Science. http://www.heartmath.org/research/science-of-the-heart.html.

267. Healy, J. "Why Kids Can't Think: Bottom Line." Personal. 13 (8), pp. 1-3.

268. Hendrich, B, D., Plenge, R.M. & Willard, H.F. 1997. "Identification and characterization of the human xist gene promoter: implications for models of X chromosome inactivation." Nucleic Acids Research. 25(13) pp. 2661-2671.

269. Herbert, C. & Thomas Ethofer, T. et al. 2009. "Amygdala activation during reading of emotional adjectives—an advantage for pleasant content." Soc Cogn Affect Neurosci. 4(1) pp. 35-39.

270. Herlitz, A., Nilsson, L. G. & Backman, L. 1997. "Gender differences in episodic memory." Memory and Cognition. 25, 801-811.

271. Herlitz, A. 2008. "Psychologists Explore Possibility Of Gender Differences In Memory, Findings Favor Females." http://www.medicalnewstoday.com/articles/98144.php.

272. Herrmann, D. J., Crawford, M. & Holdsworth, M. 1992. "Genderlinked differences in everyday memory performance." British Journal of Psychology. 83, 221-231.

273. Hinton, G.E. & Anderson, J.A. 1981. Parallel Models of Associate Memory. Erlsbaum. Hillsdale, NJ.

274. Hite, S. 1987. The Hite Report: Women and Love. Alfred A Knopf. NY.

275. Hobson, A. 2002. Dreaming: An introduction to the science of sleep.

276. Hoff Somers, C. 1994. Who Stole Feminism? Simon & Schuster. NY.

277. Hojat, M. 2011. "Development of Prosocial Behavior and Empathy in the Hand that Rocks the Cradle." World Congress of Families III. http://www.worldcongress.org/wcf3_spkrs/wcf3_hojat.htm.

278. Holland, E. 1999. "Researchers learn how stress slows wound healing." Ohio State University. http://researchnews.osu.edu/archive/ilwound.htm.

279. Holleran, S. & Whitehead, J. et al. 2010. Social Psychology and Personality Science. 2(1) pp. 65-71.

280. Holt-Lunstad, J., Birmingham, W.A. et al. 2008. "Influence of a "warm touch" support enhancement intervention among married couples on ambulatory blood pressure, oxytocin, alpha amylase and cortisol." Psychosomatic Medicine. 70 pp. 976-985.

281. Horgan, T. G. 2001. "Thinking more versus less about interpreting nonverbal behavior: A gender difference in decoding style." Unpublished doctoral dissertation. Northeastern University.

282. Horgan. et al. 2004. "Gender Differences in Memory for the appearance of others." Personality and Social Psychology Bulletin. Vol. 30, no. 2, 185-196.

283. Horstman, J. 2009. The Scientific American Day in the Life of Your Brain. Jossey-Bass. San Francisco, CA.

284. Howard, P. 2006. The Owner's Manual For The Brain. Bard Press. Austin, TX.

285. Hubel, D.H. 1979. "The Brain." Scientific American. 24 (13), pp. 45-53.

286. "The Humor Gap." 2010. Scientific American Mind. www.scientificAmerican.com/mind.

287. Hunter, C. & Hunter F. 2008. Laugh Yourself Healthy. Christain Life. FL.

288. Hurlbert, A.C. & Ling, Y. 2007. "Biological components of sex differences in color preference." Current Biology. (170) pp. 623-25.

289. Hyde, J. S. 2005. "The gender similarities hypothesis." American Psychologist. 60, 581-592.

290. Hyden, H. 1977. "The Differentiation of Brain Cell Protein, Learning and Memory." Biosystems. 8(4), pp. 22-30.

291. Hyman, S.E. 2005. "Addiction: A disease of learning and memory." Am J Psychiatry. 162:1414-22.

292. Hyyppa, M.T., Alaranta, M.D. 2006. "Gender Differences in psychological and cortisol responses to distress: A five year follow-up of patients with back pain." Stress Medicine. 4(2) pp. 117-121.

293. Iaccino, J. 1993. Left Brain-Right Brain Differences: Inquiries, evidence and new approaches. Lawrence Erlbaum & Associates. Hillsdale, NJ.

294. Iacoboni, M., Molnar-Szakacs I. et al. 2005. "Grasping the intentions of others with one's own mirror neuron system." PLoS Biology. 3 pp. e79.

295. Iacoboni, M. 2009. Mirroring People. Picador. NY.

296. Insel, T. & Huilhan, T. 1995. "A gender-specific mechanism for pair bonding: Oxytocin and partner preference formation in monogamous voles." Behavioral Neuroscience. 109(4) pp. 782-789 doi: 10.1037/0735-7044.109.4.782. http://psycnet.apa.org/psycinfo/1995-43085-001.

297. "It's the Truth - Pain Hurts Women More than Men." 2005. News Medical. www.news-medical.net/?id=11498.

298. Jackson, L. A., Sullivan, L. A. & Hymes, J. S. 1987. "Gender, gender role, and physical appearance." Journal of Psychology. 121, 51-56.

299. Jackson, P.L. et al. 2004. "How Do We Perceive the Pain of Others? A Window into the Neural Processes Involved in Empathy." NeuroImage. 24, pp. 771-779.

300. Jacobs, B.L., Van Praag, H. et al. 2000. "Depression and the Birth and Death of Brain Cells." American Scientist. 88 (4):340-46.

301. Janowsky, J.S. & Oviatt, S.K. et al. 1994. "Testosterone influences spatial cognition in older men." Behav Neurosci. 108 (2) pp. 325–32. doi:10.1037/0735-7044.108.2.325.

302. Jausovec, N. & Jausovec, K. 2005. "Sex differences in brain activity related to general and emotional intelligence." Brain and Cognition. 59(3) pp. 277-286.

303. Jobson, S. & Watson, J. S. 1984. "Sex and age differences in choice behavior: The object-person dimension." Perception. 13, 719-724.

304. Johnson, S.C., Farnworth, T. et al. 1994. "Corpus callosum surface area across the human adult life span: Effect of age and gender." Brain Research Bulletin. 4 pp. 373-377.

305. Johnson, D., McDermott, R. et al. 2006. "Overconfidence in wargames: experimental evidence on expectations, aggression, gender and testosterone." Proc Biol Sci. 273(1600) pp. 2513-2520 doi: 10.1098?rspb.2006.3606.

306. Johnson, W. & Corothers, A. et al. 2009. " A Role For the X Chromosome in Sex Differences in Variabiluty in general Intelligence?" Perspectives on Psychological Science. 4(6) pp. 598-611.

307. Jones, C. & Healy, S.D. 2006. "Differences in cue use and spatial memory in men and women." Proceedings of the Royal Society of London Series B. 273 pp. 2241-2247.

308. Jones, J. 2003. Stress responses, pressure ulcer development and adaptation. British Journal of Nursing. 12, 17-23.

309. Jouvet, M. 2009. "Working on a Dream." Nature Neuroscience. (12) 811.

310. Jung, R.E., Haier, R.J. et al. 2005. "Sex differences in N-Acetylaspartate correlates of general intelligence: an H-MRS study of normal human brain." Neuroimage. 26 pp. 965-972.

311. Jung, R.E. & Haier, R.J. 2007. "The Parieto-Frontal-Integration Theory (P-FIT) Of Intelligence: Converging Neuroimaging Evidence." Behavioural and Brain Sciences. 30 pp. 135-154.

312. Jung, R.E. & Haier, R.J. "The Parieto-Frontal Integration Theory (P-FIT) of intelligence: Converging neuroimaging evidence." Behavioral and Brain Sciences. 30 pp. 135-187. DOI: 10.1017/S0140525X07001185.

313. Kaiser, S. 1990. The social psychology of clothing. New York: Macmillan.

314. Kaiser, A., Haller, S., Schmitz, S. & Nitsch, C. 2009. On sex/gender related similarities and differences in fMRI language research. In Brain Research Reviews. 61(2): 49-59.

315. Kalin, N.H. 2001. "The primate amygdala mediates acute fear but not the behavioral and physiological component of anxious temperament." The Journal of Neuroscience. 21:2067-74. www.biopsychiatry.com/amygdala.htm.

316. Kalivas, P.W. & Volkow N.D. 2005. "The Neural Basis of Addiction: A pathology of motivation and choice." Am J Psychiatry. 162: 1403-1413.

317. Kandel, E.R. 1998. "A New Intellectual Framework for Psychiatry." American Journal of Psychiatry. 155(4): 457-69.

318. Kandel, E.R. 2006. In Search of Memory: The emergence of a new science of mind. W.W. Norton & Company. NY.

319. Kandel, E.R., Schwartz, J.H., Jessell, T.M. (Eds.) 1995. Essentials of Neural Science and Behavior. Appleton & Lange. USA.

320. Kandel, E.R., Schwartz, J.H., Jessell, T.M. (Eds.) 2000. Principles of Neural Science. 4th Ed. McGraw-Hill. NY.

321. Kandel. 2000. http://nobelprize.org/nobel_prizes/medicine/laureates/2000/kandel-lecture.pdf.

322. Kansaku, K. & Kitazawa, S. 2001. "Imaging Studies on Sex Differences in the Lateralization of Language." Journal of Neuroscience Research. (41) 4. pp. 333-337.

323. Kaplan, E. & Benardete, E. 2001. "The Dynamics Of Primate Retinal Ganglion Cells." Progress in Brain Research. (134) pp 17-34.

324. Karten, N. 2002. Communication Gaps and How to Close them. Dorset House Publishing. NY.

325. Kelley, A.E. & Berridge, K.C. 2002. "The neuroscience of natural rewards: relevance to addictive drugs." J Neurosci. 22 pp. 3306–3311.

326. Kempermann, G. & Gage, F. 1999. "New nerve cells for the adult brain." Scientific American. 280, pp 48.

327. Keroack, E.J. & Diggs, R.J. Jr., "Bonding Imperative." A Special Report from the Abstinence Medical Council.

328. Kiecolt-Glaser, J., Loving, T. et al. 2005. "Hostile Interactions, Proinflammatory cytokine Production and Wound Healing." Archives of General Psychiatry. 62(12) pp. 1377-1384.

329. Killgore, W., Oki, M. & Yurgelun-Todd, D. 2001. "Sex-specific developmental changes in amygdala responses to affective faces." NeuroReport. 12:427-433.

330. Killgore, W.D. & Yurgelun-Todd, D.A. 2001. "Sex differences in amygdala activation during the perception of facial affect." Neuroreport. 12 pp. 2543.

331. Killgore, W.D. & Yurgelun-Todd, D.A. 2004. "Sex-related developmental differences in the lateralized activation of the prefrontalcortex and amygdala during perception of facial effect." Perceptual and Motor Skills Journal. Vol: 99.

332. Kilpatrick, L.A. & Zald, D.H. 2006. "Sex-related differences in amygdala functional connectivity during resting conditions." Neuroimage. 30 pp. 452.

333. Kimara, D. 1973. "The Assymmetry of the Human Brain." Scientific American. 228 (3), pp. 70-80.

334. Kimara, D. September, 1992. "Sex Differences in the Brain." Scientific American. pp. 119-125.

335. Kimura, D. 1987. "Are men's and women's brains really different?" Can Psychol. 28 pp. 133–147.

336. Kimura, D. 1992. "Sex differences in the brain." Sci Am. 267(3) pp. 118–125.

337. Kimura, D. 1993. "Neuromotor mechanisms in human communication." Oxford University Press. NY.

338. Kimura, D. 1996. "Sex, sexual orientation and sex hormones influence human cognitive function." Curr Opin Neurobiol. 6(2) pp. 259–263.

339. Kimura, D. 2000. Sex and Cognition. MIT. USA.

340. Kimura, D. 2002. "Sex Differences in the brain: Men and Women Display Patterns of Behavioral and Cognitive Differences That reflect Varying Hormonal Influences on Brain Development." Scientific American.

341. Kimura, D. 2002. "Women's advantage on verbal memory is not restricted to concrete words." Psychological Reports. (91) pp. 1137-1142.

342. Kimura, D. 2008. "An Alternative to the Broca/ Wernicke Hypothesis Of Speech Representation In The Brain." http://www.sfu.ca/-dkimura/ Publications/An%20Alternative%20to%20the%20 BrocaWernicke%20Hypothesis%20of%20Speech%20 Representation%20in%20the%20Brain.pdf.

343. Kirschbaum, C. & Kudielka, B. et al. 1999. "Impact of Gender, Menstrual Cycle Phase, and Oral Contraceptives on the Activity of the Hypothalamus-Pituitary-Adrenal Axis." Psychosomatic Medicine. 61 pp. 154–162.

344. Kline, P. 1990. Everyday Genius. Great Ocean Publishers. Arlington, VA.

345. Knapp, M. L. & Hall, J. A. 2002. Nonverbal communication in human interaction. Belmont, CA: Thomson Learning.

346. Knowles, M. 1990. The Adult Learner: A neglected species. Gulf Publishing Company. Houston.

347. Kolb, B. & Cioe, J. 1996. "Sex-related differences in cortical function after medial frontal lesions in rats." Behavioral Neuroscience. 110:1271-1281.

348. Kontos, D., Megalooikonomou, Gee, V. & James, C. "Morphometric analysis of brain images with reduced number of statistical tests: a study on the gender-related differentiation of the corpus callosum." Artificial Intelligence in Medicine. 47(1) pp. 75-86.

349. Kopp, M.S. & Rethelyi, J. 2004. "Where Psychology Meets Physiology: Chronic stress and premature mortality – the Central-Eastern European health paradox." Brain Research Bulletin. 62: 351-367.

350. Kosslyn, S.M. & Koenig, O. 1995. Wet Mind: The new cognitive neuroscience. Free. NY.

351. Kramer, J. H. & Delis, D. C. et al.1997. "Developmental sex differences in verbal learning." Neuropsychology. 11(4) pp. 577-84.

352. Kramer, J. H. & Yaffe, K. et al. 2003. "Age and gender interactions on verbal memory performance." Journal of the International Neuropsychological Society. 9(1) pp. 97-102.

353. Kross, E. & Berman, M. et al. 2011. "Social rejection shares somatosensory representations with physical pain." PNAS. 108(15) pp. 6270-6275.

354. Kruger, D.J. & Nesse, R.M. 2004. "Sexual selection and the male-female mortality ratio." Evolutionary Psychology. Vol. 2.

355. Kruszelnicki, 2004. Karl S. "Einstein Failed School." http://www.abc.net.au/science/ articles/2004/06/23/1115185.htm.

356. Kubzansky, L.D., Kawachi, A. et al. 1997. "Is Worrying Bad for Your Heart? A prospective study of worry and coronary heart disease in the normative aging study." Circulation. (94):818-24.

357. Kudielka, B.M. & Kirschbaum, C. 2005. "Sex differences in HPA axis responses to stress: a review." Biological Psychology. 69 pp. 113–132.

358. Kulynych, J., Vladar, K. et al. 1994. "Gender differences in the normal lateralization of the supratemporal cortex: MRI surface-rendering morphology of Heschl's gyrus and planum temporal." Cerebral Cortex. 4 pp. 107–118.

359. Kurth, F. & Zilles, K. et al. 2010. "A link between the systems: functional differentiation and integration within the human insula revealed by meta-analysis." Brain Struc Func. 214 pp. 5–6 doi:10.1007/ s00429-010-0255-z.

360. Kwon, Y. 1997. Sex, sex-role, facial attractiveness, social self-esteem and interest in clothing. Perceptual & Motor Skills. 84, 899-907.

361. Lacoste M., Holloway, R. & Woodward, D. 1986. "Sex differences in the fetal human corpus callosum." Human Neurobiology. 5(2):93-6.

362. Lahaye, T. & Noebel, D. 2000. "Mind Siege." The Battle for Truth in the New Millennium. Word Publishing. TN.

363. Landau, M. "Deciphering the Adolescent Brain." The Harvard University Gazette. http://www.waldorflibrary.org/Articles/Adolesce2.pdf.

364. Larrimore, W. & Larrimore, B. 2008. His Brain Her Brain. Zondervan .USA.

365. Larsson, G. & Starrin, B. 1988. "Effect of Relaxation Training on Verbal Ability, Sequential Thinking and Spatial Ability." Journal of the Society of Accelerative Learning and Teaching. 13 (2), pp. 147-159.

366. Larsson, M. & Nilsson, L. G. et al. 2003. "Sex differences in recollective experience for olfactory and verbal information." Acta Psychologica. 112(1) pp. 89-103.

367. Laughter. 2007. http://thehealingpoweroflaughter.blogspot.com/2007/07/how-marx-brothers-brought-norman.html.

368. Laughter. 2006. http://heyugly.org/LaughterOneSheet2.php.

369. Lautenbacher, S. & Rollman, G.B. 1993. "Sex differences in responsiveness to painful and non-painful stimuli are dependent upon the method of stimulation." Pain. 53 pp. 255–264.

370. Lautenbacher, S. & Strian, F. 1991. "Sex differences in responsiveness to painful and thermal sensitivity: the role of body size." Percept Psychophys. 50 pp. 179–183.

371. Lazar, S.W. & Kerr, C.E. 2005. "Meditation Experience is Associated with Increased Cortical Thickness." NeuroReport. 16(17): 189-97.

372. Lea, L. 1980. Wisdom: Don't live life without it. Highland Books. Guilford, Surrey.

373. Leaf, C.M. 1985. "Mind Mapping as a Therapeutic Intervention Technique." Unpublished workshop manual.

374. Leaf, C.M. 1989. "Mind Mapping as a Therapeutic Technique." Communiphon. 296, pp. 11-15. South African Speech-Language-Hearing Association.

375. Leaf, C.M. 1990. "Teaching Children to Make the Most of Their Minds: Mind Mapping." Journal for Technical and Vocational Education in South Africa. 121, pp. 11-13.

376. Leaf, C.M. 1990. "Mind Mapping: A therapeutic technique for closed head injury." Masters Dissertation, University of Pretoria. Pretoria, SA.

377. Leaf, C.M. 1992. "Evaluation and Remediation of High School Children's Problems Using the Mind Mapping Therapeutic Approach." Remedial Teaching. Unisa, 7/8, September 1992.

378. Leaf, C.M., Uys, I.C. & Louw, B. 1992. "The Mind Mapping Approach (MMA): A culture and language-free technique." The South African Journal of Communication Disorders. Vol. 40. pp. 35-43.

379. Leaf, C.M. 1993. "The Mind Mapping Approach (MMA): Open the door to your brain power: Learn how to learn." Transvaal Association of Educators Journal (TAT).

380. Leaf , C.M. 1997. "The Mind Mapping Approach: A model and framework for Geodesic Learning." Unpublished D. Phil Dissertation, University of Pretoria. Pretoria, SA.

381. Leaf, C.M. 1997. "The Development of a Model for Geodesic Learning: The Geodesic Information Processing Model." The South African Journal of Communication Disorders. Vol. 44. pp. 53-70.

382. Leaf, C.M. 1997. "The Move from Institution Based Rehabilitation (IBR) to Community Based Rehabilitation (CBR): A paradigm shift." Therapy Africa. 1 (1) August 1997, p. 4.

383. Leaf, C.M. 1997. "An Altered Perception of Learning: Geodesic Learning." Therapy Africa. 1 (2), October 1997, p. 7.

384. Leaf, C.M., Uys, I. & Louw, B. 1997. "The Development of a Model for Geodesic Learning: The Geodesic Information Processing Model." The South African Journal of Communication Disorders. 44.

385. Leaf, C.M. 1998. "An Altered Perception of Learning: Geodesic Learning: Part 2." Therapy Africa. 2 (1), January/February 1998, p. 4.

386. Leaf, C.M., Uys, I.C. & Louw, B. 1998. "An Alternative Non-Traditional Approach to Learning: The Metacognitive-Mapping Approach." The South African Journal of Communication Disorders. 45, pp. 87-102.

387. Leaf. C.M. 2002. Switch on Your Brain with the Metacognitive-Mapping Approach. Truth Publishing.

388. Leaf, C.M. 2005. Switch on Your Brain: Understand your unique intelligence profile and maximize your potential. Tafelberg. Cape Town, SA.

389. Leaf, C.M. 2007. Who Switched Off My Brain? Controlling Toxic Thoughts and Emotions. Switch on Your Brain. USA. Dallas, TX.

390. Leaf, C.M. 2007. "Who Switched Off My Brain? Controlling Toxic Thoughts and Emotions." DVD series. Switch on Your Brain. Johannesburg, SA.

391. Leaf, C.M., Copeland M. & Maccaro, J. 2007. "Your Body His Temple: God's plan for achieving emotional wholeness." DVD series. Life Outreach International. Dallas, TX.

392. Leaf, C.M. 2008. Switch on Your Brain 5 Step Learning Process. Switch on Your Brain USA. Dallas, TX.

393. Leaf, C.M. 2009 Who Switched Off My Brain? Controlling Toxic Thoughts and Emotions. Revised Edition. Inprov. Dallas, TX.

394. Leaf, C.M. 2009. The Gift in You: Discover new life through gifts hidden in your mind. Inprov. Dallas, TX.

395. Leaper, C. & Ayres, M. 2007. "A Meta-Analytic Review of Gender Variations in Adults' Language use: Talkativeness, Affiliative Speech, and Assertive speech." Personality and Psychology Review. 11(4) pp. 328-363.

396. LeDoux, J. 2002. Synaptic Self: How our brains become who we are. NY.

397. Lee, DJ., Chen, Y. et al. 2002. "Corpus callosum: musician and gender effects." Neuroreport. 14(2) pp. 205-209.

398. Lehrer, J. August 17,2008. Of course I love you, and I have the brain scan to prove it – We're looking for too much in brain scans. In Boston Globe. K1.

399. Lenroot, R.K. & Schmitt, J.E. et al. 2009. "Differences in genetic and environmental influences on the human cerebral cortex associated with development during childhood and adolescence." Human Brain Mapping. 30(1) pp. 163-174.

400. Lepore, F.E. 2001. "Dissecting Genius: Einstein's brain and the search for the neural basis of intellect." Cerebrum. http://www.dana.org/news/cerebrum/detail.aspx?id=3032.

401. Leuchter, A.F., Cook, I.A. et al. 2002. "Changes in Brain Function of Depressed Subject During Treatment with Placebo." American Journal of Psychiatry. 159(1): 122-129.

402. Levy, J. 1985. "Interview." Omni. 7 (4).

403. Levy, J. 1983. "Research Synthesis on Right and Left Hemispheres: We think with both sides of the brain." Educational Leadership. 40 (4), pp. 66-71.

404. Lewin, C. & Wolgers, G. et al. 2001. "Sex differences favoring women in verbal but not in visuospatial episodic memory." Neuropsychology. 15(2) pp. 165-73.

405. Lewin, C. & Herlitz, A. 2002. "Sex differences in face recognition–women's faces make the difference." Brain and Cognition. 50(1) pp. 121-8.

406. Li, H. et al. 2005. "Sex differences in cell death." Ann Neurol. 58 pp. 317.

407. Lieberman, M. 2006. "Sex Differences in "Communication Events" Per Day?" http://itre.cis.upenn.edu/~myl/languagelog/archives/003894.html.

408. Lieberman. M.D. et al. 2007. "Putting feelings into words: Affect labeling disrupts amygdala activity in response to affective stimuli." Psychol Sci. 18 pp. 421–428.

409. Lieberman, M. 2007. "Sex-linked lexical Budgets." http://itre.cis.upenn.edu/~myl/languagelog/archives/003420.html. http://www.google.com/search?hl=en&client=safari&rls=en&sa=X&ei=1R3ITYO CD5S5tgeq1eW0BA&ved=0CBUQBSgA&q=http%3A//.cis.upenn.edu-my/language+log/archives/003420.html.&spell=1.

410. Liederman, J. & Gilbert, K. "Are Women More Influenced By Top-down Semantic Information When Listening to Disrupted Speech?" Language and Speech. 54(1) pp. 33-48.

411. Light, C., Grewen, K.M. et al. 2005. "More frequent partner hugs and higher oxytocin levels are linked to lower blood pressure and heart rate in premenopausal women." Biological Psychology. 69(1) pp. 5-21.

412. Lighthall, N.R., Mather, M. et al. "Acute stress Increases sex differences in risk seeking in the balloon analogue risk task" PLoS. 14(70) pp. e6002 doi1371/journal.pone.0006002.

413. Lim, K. & Basser, P. "Development of higher-resolution diffusion tensor imaging techniques." http://www.technologyreview.com/biomedicine/16473/page1/.

414. Lindholm, T. & Christianson, S. A. 1998. Gender effects in eyewitness accounts of a violent crime. Psychology, Crime and Law. 4, 323-339.

415. Lipton, B. 2008. The Biology of Belief: Unleashing the power of consciousness, matter and miracles. Mountain of Love Productions. USA.

416. Lipton, B.H., Bensch, K.G. et al. 1991. "Microvessel Endothelial Cell Transdifferentiation: Phenotypic Characterization." Differentiation. 46:117-133.

417. Lledo, P. M. & Alonso, M. et al. 2006. "Adult neurogenesis and functional plasticity in neuronal circuits." Nature Reviews Neuroscience. 7(3) pp. 179-93.

418. LoPresti, M.L., Schon, K. et al. 2008 " Working memory for social cues recruits orbitofrontal cortex and amygdala: A functional magnetic resonance imaging study of delayed matching to sample for emotional expressions." The Journal of Neuroscience. 28(14) pp. 3718-3728.

419. "Love and Neuroscience." 2009. http://www.nature.com/nature/journal/v457/n7226/full/457148a.html.

420. Lowe, P. A. & Mayfield, J. W. et al. 2003. "Gender differences in memory test perfor- mance among children and adolescents." Archives of Clinical Neuropsychology. 18(8) pp. 865-78.

421. Lowry R., Powell K.E., Kann L., Collins J.L., Kolbe L.J. "Weapon-carrying, physical fighting, and fight-related injury among U.S. adolescents." Am J.

422. Luders, E., Narr, K. et al. 2007. "Positive correlations between corpus callosum thickness and intelligence." Neuroimage. 37(4) pp. 1457-1464.

423. Luders, E. & Gaser, C. et al. 2009. "Why Sex Matters: Brain Size Independent Differences in Gray Matter Distributions between Men and Women." Journal of Neuroscience. 29(45) pp. 4265-14270.

424. Lundberg, J. K. & Sheehan, E. P. 1994. The effects of glasses and weight on perceptions of attractiveness and intelligence. Journal of Social Behavior and Personality. 9, 753-760.

425. Luria, A.R. 1980. Higher Cortical Functions in Man, 2nd Ed. Basic Books. NY.

426. Lutchmaya, S., Baron-Cohen, S. & Raggat, P. 2002. "Fetal Testosterone and Eye Contact in 12 -Month-Old Infants." Infant Behavior and Development. (25) pp. 327-35.

427. Lutz, K.A. & Rigney, J.W. 1977. The Memory Book. Skin & Day. NY.

428. Lynn, R. & Irwing, P. 2004. "Sex differences on the Progressive Matrices: A meta-analysis." Intelligence. 32 (5) pp. 481–498. doi:10.1016/j.intell.2004.06.0.

429. Mack, C. McGivern, R., Hyde, L. & Denenberg, V. 1996. "Absence of postnatal testosterone fails to demasculinize the male rat's corpus callosum." Developmental Brain Research. 95:252-254.

430. Maitland, S. B. & Herlitz, A. et al. 2004. "Selective sex differences in declarative memory." Memory & Cognition. 32(7) pp. 1160-1169.

431. Mantini, D., Perucci, M.G. et al. 2007. "Electrophysiological signatures of resting state networks in the human brain." Proceedings of the National Academy of Sciences USA. 104(320 pp. 13170-13175.

432. Martin, K. 2009. www.biolchem.ucla.edu/labs/martinlab/links.htm.

433. Martin, K. 2009. http://www.foxnews.com/story/0,2933,529187,00.html.

434. Marano, H.E. 2003. "The New Sex Scorecard: Men and women's minds really do work differently – but not on everything." July/August 2003. Psychology Today. psychologytoday.com/articles/pto-20030624-000003.html.

435. Marano, H.E. 2003. "The Opposite Sex: The New Sex Scorecard." Psychology Today. pp. 38-44.

436. Mashek, D., Aron, A. et al. 2000. "Identifying, evoking, and measuring intense feelings of romantic love." Represent Res Social Psychology. 24 pp. 48–55.

437. Master, S.L., Eisenberger, N.I. et al. 2009. "A Picture's Worth: Partner Photographs Reduce Experimentally Induced Pain." Psychology Science. 20 pp. 1316–1318.

438. Matheny, K.B. & McCarthy, J. 2000. Prescription for Stress. Harbinger Publications. USA.

439. Mather, M., Lighthall, N.R. et al. 2010. "Sex differences in how stress affects brain activity during face viewing." NeuroReport. 21 (14) 933 DOI: 10.1097/WNR.0b013e32833ddd92.

440. Mathes, E.W. & Kempher, S.B. 1976. Clothing as a nonverbal communicator of sexual attitudes and behavior. Perceptual and Motor Skills. 43, 495-498.

441. Mazanec, N. & McCall, G. J. 1975. Sex, cognitive categories, and observational accuracy. Psychological Reports. 37, 987-990.

442. McAdams, D. P. & Constantian, C. A. 1983. Intimacy and affiliation motives in daily living: An experience sampling analysis. Journal of Personality and Social Psychology. 45, 851-861.

443. McClure, E. 2000. "A Meta-Analytic Review of Sex Differences in Facial Expression Processing and Their Development in Infants, Children and Adolescents." Psychological Review. 126 pp. 424-53.

444. McClure, E.B. et al. 2004. "A developmental examination of gender differences in brain engagement during evaluation of threat." Biological Psychiatry. Vol. 55.

445. McDowell, S. 2009. "Why Evolutionary Theory is Wrong about Sex." http://www.conversantlife.com/sex/why-evolutionary-theory-is-wrong-about-sex.

446. McEwan, B.S. 1999. "Stress and Hippocampal Plasticity." Annual Review of Neuroscience. 22:105-22.

447. McEwan, B.S. & Lasley, E.N. 2002. The End of Stress as We Know It. National Academies Press. WA.

448. McEwan, B.S. & Seeman, T. 1999. "Protective & Damaging Effects of Mediators of Stress: Elaborating and testing the concepts of allostasis and allostatic load." Annals of the New York Academy of Sciences. 896:30-47.

449. McGaugh, J.L. & Intrioni-Collision, I.B. 1990. "Involvement of the Amygdaloidal Complex in Neuromodulatory Influences on Memory Storage." Neuroscience and Behavioral Reviews. 14 (4), pp. 425-431.

450. McGivern, R.F., Mutter, K.L., Anderson, J., Wideman, G., Bodnar, M. & Huston, P.J. 1998. Gender differences in incidental learning and visual recognition memory: Support for a sex difference in unconscious environmental awareness. Personality and Individual Differences. 25, 223-232.

451. McGlone, M. S. & Aranson, J. 2006. "Stereotype threat. identity salience, and spatial reasoning." Journal of Applied Developmental Psychology. 27 (5) pp. 486-493. doi:10.1016/j.appdev.2006.06.003.

452. McGuinness, D. 1972. "Hearing: individual differences in perceiving." Perception. 1 pp. 465-473.

453. McGuinness, D. & Symonds, J. 1977. Sex differences in choice behavior: The object-person dimension. Perception. 6, 691-694.

454. McGuiness, D. 1976. "Sex Differences in Organisation, Perception and cognition." Exploring Sex Differences. Lloyd, B & Archer, J. (eds). Academic Press. London. pp. 123-55.

455. McIlhaney, J.S. & Mckissie Bush, F. 2008. Hooked: New Science on How Casual Sex is Affecting Our Children. Northfield Publishing. Chicago.

456. McKelvie, S. J. 1981. Sex differences in memory for faces. Journal of Psychology. 107, 109-125.

457. McKelvie, S. J., Standing, L., St. Jean, D. & Law, J. 1993. Gender differences in recognition memory for faces and cars: Evidence for the interest hypothesis. Bulletin of the Psychonomic Society. 31, 447-448.

458. McKenna, E. et al. "Competitive vs. Collaborative: Game Theory and Communication Games." UPenn. edu.

459. McRae, K. & Ochsner, K. et al. 2008. "Gender Differences in Emotion Regulation: An fMRI Study of Cognitive Reappraisal." Group Processes Intergroup Relations. 11 pp. 143-162.

460. Meaney, M.J. & Szyf, M. 2005. "Environmental programming of stress responses through DNA methylation: Life at the interface between a dynamic environment and a fixed genome." Dialogues Clin Neurosci. 7 pp. 103–123.

461. Mehl, M.R. & Pennebaker, J.W. et al. 2001. "The Electronically Activated Recorder (EAR): A Device for Sampling naturalistic daily activities and conversations." Behavior Research Methods, Instruments and Computers. 33 pp. 517-523.

462. Mehl, M.R. & Pennebaker, J.W. 2003. "The sounds of social life: A psychometric analysis of students daily social environments and natural conversations." Journal of Personality and Social Psychology. 84 pp. 857-870.

463. Mehl, M.R. & Vazine, S. 2007. "Are Women Really More Talkative Than Men?" Science. 317(5834) pp. 82.

464. Meissirel, C. et al. 1997. "Early Divergence of Magnocellular and Parvocellular Functional Subsystems in the embryonic Primate Visual System." Proceedings of the National Academy of Sciences. (94) pp. 5900-5905.

465. Men's and Women's Immune Systems Respond Differently to PTSD. 2011. http://www.sciencedaily.com/releases/2011/04/110426161535.htm.

466. Men tend to leap to judgement where omen seeks more shades of gray, research shows. 2011. http://www.sciencedaily.com/releases/2011/04/110418083345.htm.

467. Merkle, R.C. 1989. "Energy Limits to the Computational Power of the Human Brain in Foresight Update (6)."

468. Merzenich, M.M. 2001. "Cortical Plasticity Contributing to Chilhood Development." in McClelland, J.L. & Siegler R.S. (Eds.) Mechanisms of Cognitive Deleopment: Behavioural and neural perspectives. Lawrence Eribaum Associates. Mahwah, NJ.

469. Merzenich, M. 2009. http://merzenich.positscience.com/.

470. Meyer, J. 1995. The Battlefield of the Mind. Faith Words. USA.

471. Meyer, J. 2000. Life without Strife: How God can heal and restore troubled relationships. Charisma House. FL.

472. Miller, G.A. 1956. "The Magical Number Seven, Plus or Minus Two: Some limits on our capacity for processing information." Psychological Review. 63, pp. 81-97.

473. "Mind/Body Connection: How emotions affect your health." 2009. http://family doctor.org/online/famdocen/home/healthy/mental/782.html.

474. Mintun, M.A. & Lundstrom, B.N. et al. 2001. "Blood flow and oxygen delivery to human brain during functional activity: theoretical modeling and experimental data." Proc Natl Acad Sci USA. 98 pp. 6859-6864.

475. Mrsic-Flogel, T. 2011. "Connectomics: Mapping the Brain's Complexity." http://starson.starsconfidential.com/2011/04/11/connectomics-mapping-the-brains-complexity/.

476. Mogilner, A., Grossman, J.A. et al. 1993. Somatosensory Cortical Plasticity in Adult Humans Revealed by Magneto Encephalography. Proceedings of the National Academy of Sciences. USA 90(8): 3593-97.

477. Moir, J. & Jessel, D. 1991. Brain Sex. Dell Publishing. NY.

478. Motluck, A. 2001. "Read My Mind." New Scientist.

479. Mozley, L.H., Gur, R. et al. 2001. "Striatal dopamine transporters and cognitive functioning in healthy men and women." Am J of Psychiatry. 158 pp. 1492-1499.

480. Nader, K., Schafe, G.E. et al. 2000. "Fear Memories Require Protein Synthesis in the Amygdala for Reconsolidation after Retrieval." Nature. 406(6797): 722-26.

481. Nagy, Z. & Westerberg, H. et al. 2004. "Maturation of white matter is associated with the development of cognitive functions during childhood." Journal of Cognitive Neuroscience. 16 pp. 1227–1233.

482. Nathanielsz, P.W. 1999. Life in the Womb:The Origin of Health and Disease. Promethean Pres. Ithaca, NY.

483. National Institute of Mental Health. 2009. www.nimh.nih.gov/health/topics/statistics/index.shtml.

484. Nelkin, D. 1995. The DNA Mystique. Freeman. NY.

485. Nelson, A. 1988. "Imagery's Physiological Base: The limbic system. A review paper." Journal of the Society for Accelerative Learning and Teaching. 13 (4), pp 363-371.

486. "Neuron Neuron on the Wall." PlayCube.org.

487. Neuroplasticity Research. http://www.uab.edu/uabmagazine/2009/may/plasticbrain2.

488. Neuroscience Review. http://cumc.columbia.edu/dept/cme/neuroscience/neuro/speakers.html.

489. Newberg, A., D'Aquili, E. et al. 2001. "Why God Won't Go Away: Brain science and the biology of belief." Ballantine. NY.

490. Newberg, A. & Waldman, M.R. 2010. How God Changes Your Brain. Ballantine Books Trade Paperbacks. NY.

491. Neubauer, A., Fink, A. et al. 2002. "Intelligence and neural efficiency: The influence of task content and sex on the brain-IQ relationship." Intelligence. 30(6) pp. 515-536.

492. Neumann, I.D. 2008. "Brain oxytocin: A key regulator of emotional and social behaviours in both females and males." Journal of Neuroendocrinology. 20 pp. 858–865.

493. Newcombe, N.S. 2007. "Taking Science Seriously: Straight thinking about spatial sex differences." in Ceci, S. & Williams, W. (Eds.) "Why aren't more women in science? Top researchers debate the evidence." American Psychological Association. pp. 69-77.

494. Newman, M.L. & Groom, C.J. et al. (in press) "Gender Differences in language use: An analysisi of 14000 text samples." Discourse Processes.

495. Nicoli, R. & Siggins, G. et al. 1977. "Neuronal actions of endorphins and enkephalins among brain regons: a comparative microiontopho retic study." PNAS. 74(6) pp. 2584-2588.

496. Nishizawa, S. & Benkelfat, S. et al. 1997. "Differences between males and females in rates of serotonin synthesis in human brain." PNAS. 94(10) pp. 5308-5313. USA. http://www.ncbi.nlm.nih.gov/pmc/articles/PMC24674/.

497. Norretranders, T. 1998. The User Illusion: Cutting Consciousness Down to Size. Penguin Books. NY.

498. Nova. 2005. "Mirror Neurons." http://www.pbs.org/wgbh/nova/sciencenow/3204/01.html.

499. Nowicki, S. Jr. & Duke, M. P. 2001. Nonverbal receptivity: The Diagnostic Analysis of Nonverbal Accuracy (DANVA). in J. A. Hall & F. J. Bernieri (Eds.), Interpersonal sensitivity: Theory and measurement. pp. 183-198. Mahwah, NJ: Lawrence Erlbaum.

500. Nyborg, H. 1984. "Performance and intelligence in hormonally different groups." Prog. Brain Res. 61 pp. 491–508. doi:10.1016/S0079-6123(08)64456-8. PMID 6396713.

501. O'keefe, J. & Nadel, L. 1978. The Hippocampus as a Cognitive Map. Oxford University Press. NY.

502. Onion, A. 2004. "Sex in the brain: Research showing men and women differ in more than one area." ABC News.

503. Ornstein, R.E. 1975. The Psychology of Consciousness. Penguin Books. NY.

504. Ornstein, R. 1997. The Right Mind. Harcourt, Brace and Company. Orlando, FL.

505. Ortigue, S., Bianchi-Demicheli, F. et al. 2007. "The neural basis of love as a subliminal prime: an event-related functional magnetic resonance imaging study." Journal of Cognitive Neuroscience. 19 pp. 1218-1230.

506. Otto, M.W. & Dougher, M.J. 1985. "Sex differences and personality factors in responsivity to pain." Percept Motor. Skills. 61 pp. 383-390.

507. Packard, M.G. & Cahill, L. 2001. "Affective modulation of multiple memory systems" Current Opinion in Neurobiology." 11 pp. 752-756. http://bobhall.tamu.edu/epsy602/Topics/Articles/PackardandCahill.pdf.

508. Panksepp, J. 2003. "Feeling the Pain of Social Loss." Neuroscience. 302(5643) pp. 237-239.

509. Parker, S. 2007. The Human Body. Dorling Kindersley Limited. London.

510. Pascuale-Leone, A. & Hamilton, R. 2001. "The Metamodal Organization of the Brain." in Casanova, C. & Ptito. (Eds.) Progress in Brain Research. Volume 134. Elsevier Science. San Diego, CA.

511. Paterniti, M. 2000. "Driving Mr. Albert: A trip across America with Einstein's Brain." The Dial Press. New York.

512. Paul-Brown, D. 1992. "Professional Practices Perspective on Alternative Service Delivery Models." ASHA Bulletin. 12.

513. Paulson, P. & Minoshima, S. et al. 1998. "Gender differences in pain perception and patterns of cerebral activation during noxious heat stimulation in humans." Pain. 76(2) pp. 223-229.

514. Pearlson, G.D. 1995."Structure differences in the cerebral cortex of normal male and female subjects." Psychiatry Research – Neuroimaging. 61 pp. 129-135.

515. Pease, A. & Pease, B. 2003. Why Men Don't Listen and Women Can't Read Maps. Pease International. Great Britain.

516. Pease, A. & Pease, B. 2004. Why Men Don't Have a Clue and Women Always Need More Shoes. Broadway Books.

517. Penaloza, C.B. & Estevez, B. 2009. "Sex of the cell dictates its response: differential gene expression and sensitivity to cell death inducing stress in male and female cells." FASEB J. 23 pp. 1869-1879.

518. Pennebaker, J.W. & King, L.A. 1999. "Linguistic styles: Language use as an individual difference." Journal of Personality and Social Psycholog. 77, 1296-1312. A series of studies that reveal how language use reflects personality, health, and social behaviors.

519. Perlemutter, D. & Coleman, C. 2004. The Better Brain Book. Penguin Group. USA.

520. Persinger, M. A. & Richards, P. M. 1995. "Women reconstruct more details than men for a complex five-minute narrative: Implications for right-hemispheric factors in the serial memory effect." Perceptual and Motor Skills. 80(2) pp. 403-410.

521. Pert, C. et al. 1973. "Opiate Agonists and Antagonists Discriminated by Receptor Binding in the Brain." Science. (182): 1359-61.

522. Pert, C.B. 1997. Molecules of Emotion: Why you feel the way you feel. Simon and Schuster. UK.

523. Peter, K. & Horn, L. 2006. "Gender differences in participation and completion of undergraduate education and how they have changed over time." Education Statistics Quarterly. 7(1 & 2).

524. Peters, T. 2003. Playing God? Genetic Determinism and Human Freedom, 2nd Ed. Routledge. NY.

525. Petrie, K.J., Booth, R.J. & Pennebaker, J.W. 1998. "The immunological effect of thought suppression." Journal of Personality and Social Psychology. 75 pp. 1264-1272.

526. Pfeifer, J.H., Iacoboni, M. 2008. "Mirroring others' emotions relates to empathy and interpersonal competence in children." Neuroimage. 39 pp. 2076–2085.

527. Phillips, M., Lowe, M., Lurito, J.T., Dzemidzic, M. & Matthews, V. 2001. "Temporal lobe activation demonstrates sex-based differences during passive listening." Radiology. 220:202-207.

528. Pinker, S. 2008. The Sexual Paradox. Scribner. NY.

529. Pickett, W. & Craig, W. et al. 2005. "Cross-national Study of Fighting and Weapon Carrying as Determinants of Adolescent Injury." http://www.pediatrics.org/cgi/content/full/116/6/e855.

530. "The Pleasure Centers Affected by Drugs." http://thebrain.mcgill.ca/flash/i/i_03/i_03_cr/i_03_cr_par/i_03_cr_par.html.

531. Pliner, P., Chaiken, S. & Flett, G. L. 1990. Gender differences in concern with body weight and physical appearance over the life span. Personality and Social Psychology Bulletin. 16, 263-273.

532. Plomin, R. et al. 1998. "Genetic Influence on Language Delay in Two-Year old Children." Nature Neuroscience. 1(4) pp. 324-328.

533. Plotsky, P.M. & Meaney, M.J. 1993. "Early Postnatal Experience Alters Hypothalamic Corticotrophin-releasing Factor (CRF) mRNA, Median Eminence CRF Content and Stress-induced Release in Adult Rats." Molecular Brain Research. 18:195-200.

534. Powers, P. A., Andriks, J. L. & Loftus, E. F. 1979. Eyewitness accounts of females and males. Journal of Applied Psychology. 64, 339-347.

535. Praag, A.F., Schinder, B.R. et al. 2002. "Functional Neurogenesis in the Adult Hippocampus." Nature. 415(6875): 1030-34.

536. Price, M.A. et al. 2001. "The role of psychosocial factors in the development of breast carcinoma: Part I. The cancer prone personality." Cancer. 91 pp. 679–685.

537. Proverbio, A.M. & Brignone, V. et al. 2006. "Gender differences in hemispheric asymmetry for face processing." BMC Neuroscience. 7:44.

538. Proverbio, A.M. & Adorni, R. 2009. "Sex Differences in the Brain response to affective scenes with or without humans." Neuropsychologia. 47(12) pp. 2374-2388.

539. Pujol, J. 2006. "Myelination of Language-Related Areas in the Developing Brain." Neurology. 66 pp. 339-343.

540. Pulvermuller, F. 2002. The Neuroscience of Language. Cambridge University Press.

541. Raichle, M.E. & MacLeod, A.M. et al. 2001. "A default mode of brain function." Proc Natl Acad Sci USA. 98 pp. 676-682.

542. Raichle, M. E. & Gusnard, D.A. 2005. "Intrinsic brain activity sets the stage for expression of motivated behavior." The Journal of Comparative Neurolology. 493 pp. 167-176.

543. Raichle, M.E. & Snyder, A.Z. 2007. "A default mode of brain function: a brief history of an evolving idea." Neuroimage. 37 pp. 1083-1090.

544. Ramachandran, V.S. & Blakeslee, S. 1998. Phantoms in the Brain. William Morrow. NY.

545. Ramachandran, V. 2011. The Tell-Tale Brain. WW Norton & Company.

546. Ramachandran, V. 2010. "About Mirror Neurons." http://www.shockmd.com/2010/01/06/about-mirror-neurons/.

547. Ratner, C. 2004. "Genes and psychology in the news." New ideas in Psychology.

548. "The real truth about women's brains an the gender gap in science." 2005. TIME. 165 (10) pp. 44-55.

549. Rector, R., Johnson, K. et al. 2003. Harmful Effects of Early Sexual Activity and Multiple Sexual Partners Among Women: Charts." The Heritage Foundation. http://www.heritage.org/research/reports/2003/06/harmful-effects-of-early-sexual-activity-and-multiple-sexual-partners-among-women-charts.

550. Reidy, D.E., Sloan, C. et al. 2008. "Gender role conformity and aggression: influence of perpetrator and victim conformity on direct physical aggression in women Personality and individual differences." 46(2) pp. 231-235.

551. Reinisch, J. 1974. "Fetal Hormones, The Brain, and Human Sex Differences: A heuristic, integrative Review of the recent Literature." Archives of Sexual Behavior. 3(1) 51-90.

552. Reite, M. & Cullum, C.M. et al. 1993. "Neuropsychological test performance and MEG-based brain lateralization: sex differences." Brain Res Bull. 32(2) pp. 325-328.

553. Relax. 2005. http://www.scientificamerican.com/article.cfm?id=want-clear-thinking-relax&page=2.

554. Relaxation. 2005. http://www.scientificamerican.com/article.cfm?id=want-clear-thinking-relax.

555. Religion and Science. 2008. http://www.liebertonline.com/doi/abs/10.1089/acm.2007.0675.

556. Religion and Science. 2009. http://www.time.com/time/health/article\0,8599,1879016,00.html.

557. "Researchers: even at rest, men's and women's brains behave differently." 2006. PHYSorg.com. http://www.physorg.com/news63301200.html.

558. Resnick, S.M. & Berenbaum, S.A. et al.1986. "Early hormonal influences on cognitive functioning in congenital adrenal hyperplasia." Developmental Psychology. 22 (2) pp. 191–8. doi:10.1037/0012-1649.22.2.191.

559. Restak, K. 1979. The Brain: The last frontier. Doubleday. NY.

560. Restak, R. 2000. "Mysteries of the Mind." National Geographic Society. Washington D.C.

561. Restak, R. 2009. Think Smart: A neuroscientists prescription for improving your brain performance. Riverhead Books. NY.

562. Revolver Entertainment. 2005. "What the Bleep Do We Know?"

563. Reynaud, M., Karila, L. et al. 2010. "Is Love Passion an Addictive Disorder?" Am J Drug Alcohol Abuse.

564. Rhoads, S.E. 2004. "Taking Sex Differences Seriously." Encounter Books. San Francisco, CA.

565. Richard, J. 2006. "The Vast Arctic Tundra of the Male Brain." http://itre.cis.upenn.edu/~myl/languagelog/archives/003551.html.

566. Richards, M. H., Crowe, P. A., Larson, R. & Swarr, A. 1998. Developmental patterns and gender differences in the experience of peer companionship during adolescence. Child Development. 69, 154-163.

567. Ridley, M. 2006. Genome. Harper Perennial. NY.

568. Rizzolatti, G & Arbib, M. 1998. "Language within our grasp." Trends in neuroscience. 21 pp. 188-94.

569. Rizzolatti, G., Fogassi, L. et al. 2001. "Neurophysiological mechanisms underlying the understanding and imitation of action." Nature Reviews Neuroscience. 2:661–670.

570. Rizzolatti, G., Craighero, L. 2004. "The mirror-neuron system." Annual Review Neuroscience. 27 pp. 169–192.

571. Rizzolotti, G. 2008. http://www.scholarpedia.org/article/Mirror_neurons.

572. Roberts, T.A. & Pennebaker, J.W. 1995. "Women's and Men's strategies in perceiving internal state." in Zanna, M. (Ed.) Advances in Experimental and Social Psychology. 27 pp. 143-176. Academic Press. New York.

573. Rodrigues, S. M. & Saslow, L. 2009. "Oxytocin receptor genetic variation relates to empathy and stress reactivity in humans." Proc. Natl. Acad. Sci. USA. 106 pp. 21437-21441.

574. Roizen, M. & Mehmet, C. 2008 You: The Owner's Manual. Harper-Collins. NY.

575. Rosenfield, I. 1988. The Invention of Memory. Basic Books. NY.

576. Rosenzweig, M.R. & Bennet, E.L. 1976. Neuronal Mechanisms of Learning and Memory. MIT Press. Cambridge, MA.

577. Rosenzweig, E.S., Barnes, C.A. & McNaughton, B.L. 2002. "Making Room for New Memories." Nature Neuroscience. 5(1): 6-8.

578. Rossi, E. 2002. "The psychobiology of gene expression." Norton, NY.

579. Roter, D. & Hall, J. et al. 2002. "Physician Gender Effects in medical Communication: A Meta-analytic view." JAMA. 288(6) pp. 756-764.

580. Rozin, P. 1975. "The Evolution of Intelligence and Access to the Cognitive Unconscious." Progress in Psychobiology and Physiological Psychology. 6, pp. 245-280.

581. Rubin, M. & Safdieh, J. 2007. Netter's Concise Neuroanatomy. Saunders Elsevier.

582. Salomone, R. 2003. "Same, Different, Equal." Yale University Press. New Haven.

583. Salzano, R. 2003. "Taming Stress." Scientific American. 289, 88-98.

584. Sanders, G., Freilicher, J. et al. 1990. "Psychological stress of exposure to uncontrollable noise increases plasma oxytocin in high emotionality women." Psychoneuroendocrinology. 15 pp. 47–58.

585. Sandstrom, N., Kaufman, J. & Huettel, S. A. 1998. "Males and females use different distal cues in a virtual environment navigation task." Brain Research: Cognitive Brain Research. 6:351-360.

586. Sapolsky, R.M. 1996. "Why Stress is Bad for Your Brain." Science. 273(5276): 749-50.

587. Sarno, J. 1999. The Mind-Body Prescription. Werner Books. NY.

588. Sarter, M., Hasselmo, M.E., Bruno, J.P. and Givens, B. 2005. "Unraveling the Attentional Functions of Cortical Cholinergic Inputs: Interactions between signal-driven and cognitive modulation of signal detection." Brain Res Brain Res Rev. 48(1): 98-111.

589. Saucier D. et al. 2002 "Are sex differences in navigation caused by sexually dimorphic strategies or by differences in the ability to use the strategies?" Behavioral Neuroscience. 116:403-410.

590. Sax, L.M. 2005. Why Gender Matters. Broadway Books. NY.

591. Scamvougeras, A. & Kigar, D.L. et al. 2003. "Size of the human corpus callosum is genetically determined: An MRI study in mono and dizygotic twins." Neuroscience Letters. 338 pp. 91-94.

592. Schaie, K.W. 2005. Developmental Influences on Adult Intelligence: the Seattle longitudinal study. Oxford University Press. NY.

593. Schlaepfer, TE., Harris, G.J., Aylward, E.H., McArthur, H.C., Peng, L.W., Lee, S. & Pearlson, G.D. "Structure differences in the cerebral cortex of normal male and female subjects." Psychiatry Research – Neuroimaging. 61:129-135, 1995.

594. Schmidt, R. 2004. "Understanding Male and Female Brain Differences: The Adult Brain." Family Therapy Magazine. vol. 3 No. 4.

595. Schneider, F., Habel, U. et al. 2000. "Gender differences in regional cerebral activity during sadness." Human Brain Mapping. 9:226-238.

596. Schore, A.N. 2001. "Effects of a secure attachment relationship on right brain development, affect regulation, and infant mental health." Infant Mental Health Journal. Vol. 22, Issue 1-2. Pages: 7-66.

597. Schwartz, J.M. & Begley, S. 2002. The Mind and the Brain: Neuroplasticity and the power of mental force. Regan Books/Harper Collins. NY.

598. Schwarts, T. 2003. "Psychologist and scientist Suzanna Segerstrom '90 studies optimism and the immune system." Chronicle. Lewis & Clark College. Portlan, OR. http://legacy.lclark.edu/dept/chron/positives03.html.

599. Schulte-Rüther, M., Markowitsch, H.J. et al. 2008. "Gender differences in brain networks supporting empathy." Neuroimage. 42(1) pp. 393–403.

600. Schute, N. 2007. "Chatty Cathy, Chatty Charlie: Surprise! A Study finds males talk just as much as females." Us News and World Report. http://www.sciencedaily.com/releases/1999/05/990518072823.htm.

601. ScienceDaily. 2011. "Study Illuminates the 'Pain' of Social Rejection." http://www.sciencedaily.com/releases/2011/03/110328151726.htm.

602. "The Science of Romance." 2008. TIME.171(5) pp. 27–35.

603. Segerstrom, S.C. & Miller, G.E. 2004. "Psychological Stress and the Human Immune System: A meta-analytic study of 30 years of inquiry." Psychological Bulletin. Vol. 130. N04. 601-630.

604. Seidlitz, L. & Diener, E. 1998. Sex differences in the recall of affective experiences. Journal of Personality and Social Psychology. 74, 262-271.

605. "Sex Differenecs found in proportions of Gray and White Matter in the Brain: Links to Differences in Cognitive Performance Seen." 1999. Science Daily. http://www.usnews.com/usnews/news/articles/070708/16talk.htm.

606. "Sex Differences on Spatial Skill Test Linked to Brain Structure." 2008. http://www.sciencedaily.com/releases/2008/12/081217124430.htm.

607. "Sexes handle emotions differently." 2002. BBC News – Health. http://news.bbc.co.uk/2/hi/health/2146003.stm.

608. Shapiro, P. N. & Penrod, S. 1986. Meta-analysis of facial identification studies. Psychological Bulletin, 100, 139-156.

609. Sharps, M.J. & Price, J. L. 1994. "Spatial cognition and gender: Instructional and stimulus influences on mental image rotation performance." Psychology of Women Quarterly. 18 (3) pp. 413–425. doi:10.1111/j.1471-6402.1994.tb00464.x.

610. Shaywitz, B. et al. 1995. "Sex Differences in the Functional Organization of the Brain for Language." Nature. 373 pp. 607-609.

611. Shen, Andrea. 2000. "Seminar: Stereotypes Persist about Women in Academia." Harvard University Gazette.

612. Sheth, B.R. 2006. "Practice Makes Imperfect: Restorative effects of sleep on motor learning." Society for Neuroscience. Program 14-14.

613. Shors, T.J. & Miesegaes, G. 2002. "Testosterone in utero and at birth dictates how stressful experience will affect learning in adulthood." Proceedings of the National Academy of Sciences. 99:13955-13960.

614. Siegal, D.J. 1999. The Developing Mind: How Relationships and the Brain Interact to Shape Who We Are. Guilford. NY.

615. Silverman, I. & Eals, M. 1992. Sex differences in spatial abilities: Evolutionary theory and data. In J. Barkow, L. Cosmides, & J. Tooby (Eds.), The adapted mind: Evolutionary psychology and the generation of culture (pp. 487-503). New York: Oxford University Press.

616. Simmons, R. 2002. Odd Girl Out: The Hidden Culture of Aggression. Harcourt Trade. USA.

617. Sinclair, B. 2007. "University of Toronto study finds lasting benefits from just 10 hours of game play." http://www.gamespot.com/news/6180510.html.

618. Singer, T. 2004. "Empathy for Pain Involves the Affective but not Sensory Components of Pain." Science. 303 pp. 1157-1162.

619. Singer, T. 2004. "How Your Brain Handles Love and Pain." http://www.msnbc.msn.com/id/4313263.

620. Singly, S. 2004. "Touching Behavior." http://www.uhh.hawaii.edu/academics/hohonu/writing.php?id=50.

621. Sizer, T.R. 1984. Horacel's Compromise: The dilemma of the American high school. Houghton Mifflin. Boston, MA.

622. Slatcher, R.B. & Pennebaker, J.W. 2006. "How do I love thee? Let me count the words: The social effects of expressive writing." Psychological Science. 17 pp. 660-664.

623. Sleep. 2003. http://www.applesforhealth.com/lacksleep1.html.

624. Solms, M. 1999. http://www.abc.net.au/rn/talks/8.30/helthrpt/stories/s44369.htm.

625. Solms, M. 2000. "Forebrain Mechanisms of Dreaming are Activated from a Variety of Sources." Behavioral and Brain Sciences. 23 (6): 1035-1040; 1083-1121.

626. Solms, M. 1997. "The Neuropsychology of Dreams: A clinico-anatomical study." Lawrence Erlbaum.

627. Sowell, E. et al. 2002. "Development of cortical and subcortical brain structures in childhood and adolescence: a structural magnetic resonance imaging study." Dev Med Child Neurol. 44: 4-16.

628. Sowell, E., Toga, A. et al. 2003. "Mapping Cortical Change Across the Human Life Span." Nature Neuroscience. 6(3):309-15.

629. Speck, O. & Ernst, T. et al. 2000. "Gender differences in the functional organization of the brain for working memory." Neuroreport. 11 pp. 2581.

630. Spinks, S. 2000. "Adolescent Brains are Works in Progress." Frontline. http://www.pbs.org/wgbh/pages/frontline/shows/teenbrain/work/adolescent.html.

631. Spitz, R. A. 1945-49. The Psychoanalytic Study of the Child. Vols. 1-4. International Universities Press. New York.

632. Spitz, R. A. 1947. "Hospitalism: A follow-up report." In Fenichel, D., Greenacre, P. & Freud, A. (Eds.) The Psychoanalytic Study of the Child. 2 pp. 113-117. International Universities Press. New York.

633. Spitz, R. 1983. http://www.pep-web.org/document.php?id=PPSY.002.0181A.

634. Springer, S.P & Deutsch, G. 1998. Left Brain, Right Brain. W.H. Freeman & Company. NY.

635. Sporer, S. L. 1993. Clothing as a contextual cue in facial recognition. German Journal of Psychology. 17, 183-199.

636. Steinberg, D. 2006. "Determining nature vs. Nurture: molecular evidence is finally emerging to inform the long-standing debate." Scientific American Mind. pp. 12.

637. Stengel, R. 2009. Ed. TIME Your Brain: A User's Guide. TIME Books. Des Moines, IA.

638. Stephan, K.M., Fink, G.R. et al. 1995. "Functional Anatomy of Mental Representation of Upper Extremity Movements in Healthy Subjects." Journal of Neurophysiology. 73(1): 373-86.

639. Stevens, K. 2004. "How Boys and Girls Learn Differently." Primary Leadership. Spring Vol. 7, No. 1.

640. Stickgold, R., Hobson, R. et al. 2001. "Sleep, Learning, and Dreams: Offline memory reprocessing." Science. 294 (554): 1052-57.

641. Stickgold, R. & Wehrwein, P. 2009. "Sleep Now, Remember Later." Newsweek. http://www.newsweek.com/id/194650.

642. Stress in Children. www.cookchildrens.org.

643. Sunderland, J. 2006. Gender and Language: an Advanced Resourcebook. Routledge, London.

644. Swaminathan, N. 2007. "Gender Jabber: Do Women Talk More than Men? In a word: No. But then, how did the rumor get started?" Scientific American. http://www.scientificamerican.com/article.cfm?id=women-talk-more-than-men&SID=mail&sc=emailfriend.

645. Sylwester, R. 1985. "Research on Memory: Major discoveries, major educational challenges." Educational Leadership. pp. 69-75.

646. Sylwester, R. 2002. "Mirror Neurons." BrainConnection.com.

647. Szyf, Moshe. 2009. "Epigenetics." http://www.the-scientist.com/article/display/5583/.

648. Taha, H. 2006. "Females superiority in Phonological and lexical processing." The Reading Matrix. 6(2).

649. Tang, C.Y., Eaves, E.L. et al. 2010. "Brain Networks for working memory and factors of intelligence assessed in males and females with fMRI and DTI." Intelligence. 38(3) pp. 293-303.

650. Tannen, D. 1990. You Just Don't Understand: Men and Women in Conversation. Harper, NY.

651. Taylor, L. C. & Compton, N. H. 1968. Personality correlates of dress conformity. Journal of Home Economics. 60, 653-656.

652. Taylor, S.E., Klein, L.C. et al. 2000. "Biobehavioral responses to stress in females: Tend-and-befriend, not fight-or-flight." Psychological Review. 107 pp. 411–429.

653. Taylor, S.E. & Lerner, J.S. et al. 2004. "Early environment, emotions, responses to stress, and health." J Per. 72 pp. 1365–1393.

654. Taylor, S.E. & Eisenberger, N.I. et al. 2006. "Neural responses to emotional stimuli are associated with childhood family stress." Biol Psychiatry. 60 pp. 296–301.

655. Taylor, S.E. 2006. "Tend and befriend: Biobehavioral Bases of Affiliation Under Stress." Current Directions in Psychological Science. 15(6) pp. 273-277.

656. Taylor, S.E., Gonzaga, G. et al. 2006. "Relation Of Oxytocin To Psychological stress and Hypothalamic-Pituitary-Adrenocortical PA axis Activity in Older women." Psychosomatic Medicine. 68 pp. 238-245.

657. The Teen Brain. 2008. http://harvardmagazine. com/2008/09/the-teen-brain.html.

658. Than, K. 2005. "Scientists Say Everyone Can Read Minds." LiveScience.com.

659. Thayer, J.F. & Johnsen, B.H. 2000. "Sex differences in judgment of facial affect: A multivariate analysis of recognition errors." Scandinavian Journal of Psychology. Vol. 41.

660. Tian, L., Wang, J. et al. 2011. "Hemisphere-and gender reated differences in small world brain networks: a resting-state functional MRI study Neuroimage." 54(1) pp. 191-202.

661. Toga, A.W. & Thompson, P.M. et al. 2006. "Mapping brain maturation." Trends in Neurosciences. 29 pp. 148–159.

662. Touch. Journal of Personality and Social Psychology. 59, 1155-1162.

663. "Touch is Great!" http://www.touchisgreat.com/pb/ wp_0ac8b62c/wp_0ac8b62c.html.

664. Trenerry, M.R. & Jack, C.R. et al. 1995. "Gender differences in post-temporal lobectomy verbal memory and relationships between MRI hippocampal volumes and preoperative verbal memory." Epilepsy Res. 20(1) pp. 69–76.

665. Tunajek, S. 2006. "The Attitude Factor." http:// www.aana.com/uploadedFiles/Resources/ Wellness/nb_milestone_0406.pdf.

666. Turhan Canli, T & Maolin, Q. et al. 2006. "Neural correlates of epigenesist." Proc Natl Acad Sci USA. 103(43) pp. 16033-16038.

667. "Understanding the Different Types of Depression." 2002. www.Depression-Anxiety.com.

668. University of California, Las Angelas. 2003. "Gender Differences In Brain Response To Pain." Science Daily.

669. University of California, Irvine. 2005. "Intelligence in Men and Women is A Gray and White Matter." Science Daily. http://www.sciencedaily.com/ releases/2005/01/050121100142.htm.

670. University of California, Irvine. 2006. "Researchers: even at rest, men's and women's brains behave differently." PHYSorg.com. http://www.physorg. com/news63301200.html. http://www.sciencedaily. com/releases/2006/04/060404090204.htm.

671. University of Montreal. 2010. "Does sex matter? It may when evaluating mental status." Psychology and Sociology. http://www.sciencedaily.com/ releases/2010/11/101118123840.htm.

672. University of Pennsylvania: School of Medicine. 2007. "Brain Imaging Shows How Men And Women Cope Differently Under Stress." Science Daily. http://www.sciencedaily.com/ releases/2007/11/071119170133.htm.

673. University of Southern California. 2010. "Why We Fight: Men Check Out in Stressful Situations, While Women Show Increased Brain Coordination When Looking at Angry Faces." Science Daily.

674. USA Today. 2005. "Study: A Happy Marriage Can Help Mend Physical Wounds."

675. Uvnas-Moberg, K. 2011. "Oxytocin: World's expert talks about this calming hormone." http://www. lifesciencefoundation.org/cmoxtyocin.html.

676. Valla, J. & Ceci, S.J. 2011. "Can Sex Differences in Science Be Tied to the Long Reach of Prenatal Hormones?: Brain Organization Theory, Digit Ratio (2D/4D), and Sex Differences in Preferences and Cognition." Perspectives on Psychological Science. 6(2) pp. 134-146.

677. Van Stegeren, A.H., Wolf, O.T. et al. 2008. "Salivary alpha amylase and cortisol responses to different stress tasks: Impact of sex." International Journal of Psychophysiology. 69 pp. 33–40.

678. Vasdarjanova, A., Cahill, L. & McGaugh, J.I. 2001. "Disrupting basolateral amygdala function impairs unconditional freezing and avoidance." European Journal of Neuroscience. 14 pp. 709-718.

679. Vaynman S. & Gomez-Pinilla. 2005. "License to Run: Exercise impacts functional plasticity in the intact and injured central nervous system by using neurotrophins." Neurorehabilitation and Neural Repair. 19(4): 283-95.

680. Ventral Pallidum: Long-term Relationships, Monogamy, Oxytocin & More. 2010. http://www.neurointerests.com/?p=512.

681. Vilain, E. "Biology in Sex and Gender: Expert Interview Transcript." http://www.learner.org/courses/biology/units/gender/experts/vilain.html.

682. Vythilingam, M. & Heim, C. "Childhood Trauma Associated with Smaller Hippocampal Volume in Women with Major Depression." American Journal of Psychiatry. 159(12): 2072-80.

683. Wagemaker, H. 2006. "Are Girls Better Readers? Gender differences in reading Literacy in 32 countries." International Association for the Evaluation of Educational Achievement. 6(2).

684. Walker, M.P. & Stickgold, R. 2006. "Sleep, Memory and Plasticity." Annual Review of Psychology.

685. Wang J.J., Korczykowski. et al. 2007. "Gender difference in neural response to psychological stress." Social Cognitive and Affective Neuroscience. 2 pp. 227–239.

686. Ward, D. 2001. "Ohio State University Genome Map Reveals Many Additional Probable Genes." http://researchnews.osu.edu/archive/genome.htm.

687. Waterland, R.A. & Jirtle, R.L. 2003. Transposable Elements: Targets for early nutritional Effects on Epigenetic Gene Regulation Molecular and Cellular Biology. (23) pp. 5293-5300.

688. Weaver, I.C. et al. 2004. "Epigenetic programming by maternal behavior." Nat Neurosci. 7 pp. 847–854.

689. Weinhold, R. 2006. "Epigenetics is the science of change." Environmental health perspectives. 114 (3).

690. Weiss, S. 2007. "Psycho physiologic and behavioral effects of tactile stimulation on infants with congenital heart disease." Research in Nursing and Health. (15) 2 pp. 93-101.

691. Wellborn, B.L. & Papademetris, X. et al. 2009. "Variation in orbitofrontal cortex volume: relation to sex, emotion regulation and affect." Social Cognitive and Affective Neuroscience. doi: 10.1093/scan/nsp028.

692. Wellborn, B.L. & Papademetrics, X. et al. 2009. "Variation in orbitofrontal cortex volume: relation to sex, emotion regulation and affect." Social Cognitive and Affective Neuroscience. doi: 10.1093/scan/nsp028.

693. Wells, W. & Siegel, B. 1961. Stereotyped somatypes. Psychological Reports, 8, 77-78.

694. Why evolutionary theory is wrong about sex. 2009. http://www.worldviewweekend.com/worldview-times/article.php?articleid=4853.

695. Wicker, B. et al. 2003. "Both of Us Disgusted in My Insula: The Common Neural Basis of Seeing and Feeling Disgust." Neuron. 40 pp. 655-664.

696. Willis, F. & Briggs. 1992. Journal of Non-verbal Behavior. "Relationship and Touch in Public Settings." 16(1) pp. 55-63.

697. Witelson, S. F. 1978. "Sex differences in the neurology of cognition: psychological, social, educational and clinical implications." In Sullerot, E. (ed). Le Fait Feminin, Paris. Fayard: 287-303.

698. Witelson, S. F. 1989. "Hand and sex differences in the isthmus and genu of the human corpus callosum: A postmortem morphological study." Brain. 112, 799-835.

699. Witelson, S.F. and Kigar, D.L. 1992. "Sylvian fissure morphology and asymmetry in men and women: Bilateral differences in relation to handedness in men." Journal of Comparative Neurology. 323 pp. 326-340.

700. Witelson, S., Glezer, I. & Kigar, D. 1995. "Woman Have Greater Numerical Density of Neurons in the Posterior Temporal Lobe." Journal of Neuroscience. 15 pp. 3418-28.

701. Witelson, S.F., Kigar, D.L. & Harvey, T. 1999. "The Exceptional Brain of Albert Einstein." Lancet. 353:2149-53.

702. Witelson, S.F., Szechtman, H. & Nahmias, C. 2004. "Sex differences in functional activation patterns revealed by increased emotion processing demands." Neuroreport. 15, 219-223.

703. Witelson, S. 2005. "Deep, Dark Secrets of His and Her Brains." http://www.latimes.com/news/printedition/la-sci-brainsex16jun16,0,1790519.story.

704. Witelson, S.F. & Beresh, H. et al. 2006. "Intelligence and brain size in 100 postmortem brains: Sex, lateralization and age factors." Brain: A Journal of Neurology. 129(2) pp. 386-98.

705. Witelson, S. 2007. "Sandra Witelson: Neuroscience, biological basis for cognition in male and female brains." http://www.science.ca/scientists/scientistprofile.php?pID=273.

706. Witelson, S. 2011. "It's Partly in Your Head." http://online.wsj.com/article/SB10001424052748704013604576246612976236624.html.

707. Wolf, C.C., Ocklenburg, S. et al. 2009 "Sex differences in parking. Nature or nurture? Poster, 5th annual meeting of the Young Neuroscientist Congress. Neuo-Visionen.

708. Wolf, C.C. & Ocklenburg, S. et al. 2009. "Sex differences in real life spatial cognition." Poster, 16th annual meeting of the Cognitive Neuroscience Society. San Francisco, USA.

709. Wolf, C.C., Ocklenburg, S. et al. 2010. "Sex-differences in parking are affected by biological and social factors." Psychological Research. 74 (4) pp. 429-435.

710. Wolf, O.T. & Schommer, N.C. et al. "The relationship between stress induced cortisol levels and memory differs between men and women." Psychoneuroendocrinology. 26 pp. 711.

711. Women are best at being buddies. 2007. http://www.sciencedaily.com/releases/2007/03/070308075354.htm.

712. "Women need that healthy touch." Times Online. http://www.timesonline.co.uk/tol/news/uk/article413100.ece.

713. "Women who have multiple sexual partners damage their ability to bond with a future partner due to low oxytocin levels." http://secularheretic-st.blogspot.com/2009/01/woman-who-have-multiple-sexual-partners.html.

714. Wood, G. & Shors, T.J. 1998. "Stress facilitates classical conditioning in males, but impairs classical conditioning in females through activational effects of ovarian hormones." Proceedings of the National Academy of Sciences. 95:4066-4071.

715. Wrase, J., Klein, S. et al. 2003. "Gender differences in the processing of standardized emotional visual stimuli in humans: a functional magnetic resonance imaging study." Neuroscience Letters. 348(1) pp. 41-45.

716. Wright, N.H. 2005. Finding Freedom from Your Fears. Fleming H. Revell. Grand Rapids, MI.

717. Wright, W.1998. Born that way: Genes, Behavior, Personality. Knopf. NY.

718. Xia-Nian, Z., Kelly, C. et al. 2010. "Growing together and growing apart: regional and sex differences in the lifespan developmental trajectories of functional homotopy." The Journal of Neuroscience. 30(45) pp. 15034-15043. doi: 10.1523/JNEUROSCI.2612-10.2010.

719. Xu, X. & Aron, A. 2010. "Reward and motivation systems: a brain mapping study of early-stage intense romantic love in Chinese participants." Human Brain Mapping.

720. Yamasue, H., Abe, O. et al. 2008. "Sex-linked neuroanatomical basis of human altruistic cooperativeness." Cereb Cortex. 18 pp. 2331–2340.

721. Yang, X., Lusis, J. & Drake, T. 2006. "UCLA Study Finds Same Genes Act Differently In Males and Females." Science Daily. University of California. Los Angeles, CA. http://www.sciencedaily.com/releases/2006/07/060707190114.htm.

722. Yarmey, A.D. 1993. Adult age and gender differences in eyewitness recall in field settings. Journal of Applied Social Psychology. 23, 1921-1932.

723. Yarmey, A. D. & Jones, H. P. 1983. Accuracy of memory of male and female eyewitnesses to a criminal assault and rape. Bulletin of the Psychonomic Society. 21, 89-92.

724. Yonker, J. E. & Eriksson, E. et al. 2003. "Sex differences in episodic memory: Minimal influence of estradiol." <u>Brain and Cognition</u>. 52(2) pp. 231.

725. Younger, J., Aron, A. et al. 2010. "Viewing pictures of a Romantic partner Reduces Experimental Pain: Involvement of Neural reward systems". <u>PLoS ONE</u>. 5(10) e13309.

726. Zaborszky, L. 2002. "The Modular Organization of Brain Systems: Basal forebrain; the last frontier. Changing views of Cajal's neuron." <u>Progressing Brain Research</u>. (136) 359-372.

727. Zimmer, C., Basler, H.D. et al. 2003. "Sex differences in cortisol response to noxious stress." <u>Clinical Journal of Pain</u>. 19 pp. 233–239.

Also by Dr. Caroline Leaf

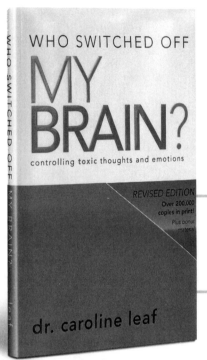

Want to learn more about breaking the cycle of toxic thinking?

In her ground-breaking book, *Who Switched Off My Brain? Controlling Toxic Thoughts and Emotions*, Dr. Caroline Leaf illustrates a step-by-step method for sweeping away areas of toxic thinking.

Who Switched Off My Brain? is now available online, at retailers near you and at drleaf.com.

NOTES

NOTES

NOTES

NOTES